Praise for *The Diary*

'I've watched Steven Bartlett's journey from the start, always knowing he had that raw, fiery spark. Seeing him harness it, seeing him succeed, damn, it fills me with pure, undiluted pride. I'm on the sidelines, cheering him on, because this guy embodies the entrepreneur's spirit.'

Gary Vaynerchuck, author of Twelve and a Half

'Steven Bartlett has overcome seemingly insurmountable odds to become a mega-successful serial entrepreneur. Along the way, he has learned some valuable lessons about the importance of following a different and unconventional path to power, synthesizing his experience into practical laws that will challenge and guide you in the harshly competitive world we live in.'

Robert Greene, bestselling author of Mastery

'Weaving the latest research, his own experiences, and captivating stories, Steven guides readers to redefine success and achieve their potential. This is a must-read for anyone dreaming of doing something audacious.'

Jay Shetty, New York Times *bestselling author and award-winning host of* On Purpose

'Surprising and persuasive in equal measure. Steven's advice will supercharge your chances of achieving your biggest dreams.'

Marie Forleo, author of the #1 New York Times *bestseller* Everything Is Figureoutable

'From "never disagree" to "don't attack beliefs, inspire new ones," this book contains surprising wisdom that will move you forward personally and professionally. I highly recommend.'

Scott Galloway, Professor of Marketing at NYU Stern School of Business and author of Adrift

'It's about time that we read about success in our modern world as seen by one who's navigated the path to success like no other. Intelligent, insightful, and real. I am humbled by how much I learned from Steven's work.'

Mo Gawdat, bestselling author and founder of OneBillionHappy

'There is a new breed of CEO taking over the business world. The blustery, chest beating CEOs who act like they make no mistakes are being replaced by CEOs who talk about their feelings, lead with curiosity and are willing to work on themselves...and Steven Bartlett is leading the revolution! *The Diary Of A CEO* is an essential companion for any leader who wants to take themselves on and lead us into the next generation.'

Simon Sinek, Optimist and New York Times *bestselling author of* Start with Why *and* The Infinite Game

STEVEN BARTLETT

THE DIARY OF A CEO

THE 33 LAWS OF BUSINESS & LIFE

Ebury Edge, an imprint of Ebury Publishing
20 Vauxhall Bridge Road
London SW1V 2SA

Ebury Edge is part of the Penguin Random House group of companies
whose addresses can be found at global.penguinrandomhouse.com

Penguin
Random House
UK

First published by Ebury Edge in 2023

www.penguin.co.uk

A CIP catalogue record for this book is available from the British Library

Hardback ISBN 9781529146509
Trade paperback ISBN 9781529146516

Printed and bound in Great Britain by Clays Ltd, Elcograf S.p.A.

The authorised representative in the EEA is Penguin Random House
Ireland, Morrison Chambers, 32 Nassau Street, Dublin D02 YH68.

Penguin Random House is committed to a sustainable future
for our business, our readers and our planet. This book is
made from Forest Stewardship Council® certified paper.

Dedicated to everyone that listens to and watches
The Diary Of A CEO*!*

Thank you for allowing us to live the greatest dream we never had.

CONTENTS

PILLAR III: THE PHILOSOPHY

PILLAR IV: THE TEAM

INTRODUCTION:
WHO AM I TO WRITE THIS BOOK?

I've been the CEO, founder, co-founder or board member of four industry-leading companies that collectively – at their peaks – reached a cumulative valuation of more than $1 billion.

I'm currently the founder of Flight Story, an innovative marketing agency; thirdweb, a software company; and an investment fund called Flight Fund.

My companies have employed thousands of people in every corner of the world. I've raised almost $100 million of investment for my companies.

I'm an investor in more than 40 companies. I'm on the board of four companies, two of which are currently at the forefront of their respective industries, and I'm 30 years old.

Being the founder of two successful marketing groups that have risen to the top of their industry, within their market, has meant that I spend much of my professional life in boardrooms working with and advising the CEOs, CMOs and leaders of the biggest brands in the world on how to do marketing and how to tell their story online; Uber, Apple, Coca-Cola, Nike, Amazon, TikTok, Logitech, you name it – they have been my clients.

Additionally, I've spent the last four years interviewing the world's most successful individuals from business, sports, entertainment and academia. I have 700 hours of recordings where I've interviewed your favourite authors, actors and CMOs; the world's leading neuroscientists; the captain of your favourite sports team; the manager of your favourite sports team; the CEOs of the billion-dollar companies you use every day; and more of the world's leading psychologists than I could possibly name.

I published these conversations in the form of a podcast called *The Diary Of A CEO*, and that podcast quickly became the most downloaded podcast here in Europe and one of the top business podcasts in the USA, Ireland, Australia and the Middle East. It is arguably one of the fastest-growing podcasts in the world right now, increasing its listenership by 825 per cent last year alone.

I've been lucky enough to be exposed to some unique experiences, and a few years ago it dawned on me how much valuable and powerful information I've gained – and only a handful of people on earth have access to that information. I also realised that at the very heart of all the success and failure I've seen, both in my own entrepreneurial journey and the hundreds of interviews I've conducted, were a set of laws that could stand the test of time, transfer to any industry, and be used by anyone who is trying to build something great or become someone great.

This is not a book about business strategy. Strategy changes like the seasons. This is a book about something much more permanent. This is a book about the fundamental, enduring laws of building great things and becoming great yourself.

These laws can be used by anyone, regardless of your industry or occupation.

These laws will work now or 100 years from now.

These laws are rooted in psychology, science and centuries of research, and to further validate these laws I surveyed tens of thousands of people across every continent, every age group and every profession.

☆ ☆ ☆

The design of this book is based on five core beliefs:

1. I believe most books are longer than they need to be.
2. I believe most books are more complicated than they need to be.
3. I believe pictures paint a thousand words.
4. I believe stories are more powerful than data, but both are important.
5. I believe in nuance and that the truth is often somewhere in the middle.

In short, it aims to embody a quote often attributed to Einstein:

'Everything should be as simple as possible, but not simpler.'

To me, this means giving you the fundamental truth and understanding of each law, in the exact number of words necessary to do so – no less, no more – and using powerful imagery and incredible real stories to bring the key points to life.

★ THE FOUR PILLARS OF GREATNESS

Becoming great, and building great things, requires mastery within four pillars. I call these the four pillars of greatness.

PILLAR I: THE SELF

As Leonardo da Vinci asserted, 'One can have no smaller or greater mastery than mastery of oneself; you will never have a greater or lesser dominion than that over yourself; the height of your success is gauged by your self-mastery, the depth of your failure by your self-abandonment. Those who cannot establish dominion over themselves will have no dominion over others.'

This pillar is about you. Your self-awareness, self-control, self-care, self-conduct, self-esteem and self-story. The self is the only thing we have direct control over; to master it, which is no easy task, is to master your entire world.

PILLAR II: THE STORY

Everything that stands in your way is a human. Science, psychology and history have shown that there is no graph, data or information that stands a greater chance of positively influencing those humans than a truly great story.

Stories are the single most powerful weapon any leader can arm themselves with – they are the currency of humanity. Those who tell captivating, inspiring, emotional stories rule the world.

This pillar is about storytelling and how to harness the laws of storytelling to persuade the humans that stand in your way to follow you, to buy from you, to believe you, to trust you, to click, to act, to hear you and to understand you.

PILLAR III: THE PHILOSOPHY

In business, sports and academia, an individual's personal philosophies are the single biggest predictors of how they'll behave, now and in the future – if you know someone's philosophy or beliefs, you can accurately forecast how they'll behave in any situation.

This pillar is about the personal and professional philosophies that great people believe and live by and how those philosophies result in behaviour that leads to greatness. Your philosophy is the set of beliefs, values or principles that guide your behaviour – they are the fundamental beliefs that underpin your actions.

PILLAR IV: THE TEAM

The definition of the word 'company' is 'group of people'; at its essence, every company, project or organisation is just a group of people. Everything the organisation produces, good or bad, originates from the minds of the members of your group of people. The most important success factor in your work is who you choose to work with.

I've never seen anyone build a great company, project or organisation without a group of people, and I've never seen anyone reach personal greatness without the support of a group of people.

This pillar is about how to assemble and get the best out of your group of people. Assembling any group of people is not enough; for your group of people to become a truly great team, you need the right people, bound together by the right culture. When you have great people bound by a great culture, the whole team becomes greater than the sum of its parts. When $1 + 1 = 3$, great things happen.

PILLAR 1
THE SELF

LAW 1

FILL YOUR FIVE BUCKETS IN THE RIGHT ORDER

This law explains the five buckets that determine your human potential, how to fill them and, crucially, in which order you should fill them.

My friend David was in the front garden of his home, enjoying his morning espresso, as a sweaty, confused-looking, panting man in tired gym attire jogged towards him slowly.

The jogging man paused in his stride and greeted my friend David as he struggled to catch his breath. He cracked an unintelligible joke, appeared to laugh frantically at it, then began erratically talking about the spaceship he was building, the microchips he was going to put in monkeys' brains, and the AI-powered house robots he was going to create.

Moments later, the jogging man said goodbye to David, and continued his slow, sweaty trudge down the street.

That sweaty jogging man was Elon Musk. Billionaire founder of Tesla, SpaceX, Neuralink, OpenAI, Paypal, Zip2 and The Boring Company.

Before I revealed the identity of the sweaty jogging man, you may have understandably assumed he was an escapee of the local psychiatric facility, or suffering from some psychotic break. But once you heard his name, all those extraordinary aforementioned ambitions suddenly became believable.

So believable, in fact, that when Elon tells the world of his ambitions, people will blindly give billions of dollars of their children's inheritance to back him, they'll quit their jobs and relocate to work for him, and they'll pre-order his products before he's even created them.

This is because Elon has filled his five buckets – in fact all of the people I've met that possess the power to build truly great things have five brimming buckets.

The sum of these five buckets is the sum of your professional potential. The fullness of these buckets will determine how big, believable and achievable your dreams are to you, and to those that hear them.

Those that achieve great things have spent years, often decades, pouring into these five buckets. Someone fortunate enough to have five full buckets has all the potential needed to change the world.

When you're seeking employment, selecting the next book you want to read or deciding what dream to pursue, you must be aware of how full your buckets are.

★ THE FIVE BUCKETS

1. What you know (your knowledge)

2. What you can do (your skills)

3. Who you know (your network)

4. What you have (your resources)

5. What the world thinks of you (your reputation)

At the start of my career, as an 18-year-old start-up founder, I was haunted by a moral question that I couldn't seem to shake: is focusing my time and energy on building a company (which would ultimately enrich me) a more noble pursuit than going back to where I was born in Africa and investing my time and energy in saving even one life?

This question remained at the front of my mind for several years until one chance encounter in New York granted me some much-needed clarity. I attended an event hosted by Radhanath Swami, a world-renowned guru, monk and spiritual leader, at an event he was holding in New York.

As I squeezed in among a sea of Swami's mesmerised followers, who were starry-eyed and hanging on to his every word in a perfectly still, appreciative silence, the guru asked if anyone in the crowd had a question for him.

I raised my hand. The guru gestured at me to deliver my question. I asked, 'Is building a business, and enriching myself, a more noble pursuit than going back to Africa to try and save lives?'

The guru stared at me as if he could see into the depths of my soul, and after a long, blinkless pause he proclaimed: 'You cannot pour from empty buckets.'

Almost a decade on from that moment, it's never been clearer what the guru meant. He was telling me to focus on filling my own buckets, because someone with full buckets can positively bend the world in any way he or she desires.

Having now built several large companies, worked with the biggest organisations in the world, become a multimillionaire, managed thousands of people, read hundreds of books and spent 700 hours interviewing the world's most successful people, my buckets are sufficiently full. Because of this, I now possess the **knowledge, skills, network, resources and reputation** to help millions of people all over the world, which is exactly what I intend to spend the rest of my life doing, through my philanthropic work, the donations I make, the organisations I create, the media companies I build and the school I'm working to launch.

These five buckets are interconnected – filling one helps to fill another – and they are generally filled in order from left to right.

We usually start our professional life acquiring **knowledge** (school, university, etc.), and when this knowledge is applied, we call it a **skill**. When you have knowledge and skills you become professionally valuable to others and your **network** grows. Consequently, when you have knowledge, skills and a network, your access to **resources** expands, and once you have knowledge, skills, a valuable network and resources, you will undoubtedly earn a **reputation**.

With these five buckets and their interconnected relationship in mind, it's clear that an investment in the first bucket (knowledge) is the highest-yielding investment you can make. Because when that knowledge is applied (skill), it inevitably cascades to fill your remaining buckets.

If you truly understand this, you'll understand that a job that pays you slightly more cash (resources), but gives you far less knowledge and fewer skills, is a lower-paying job.

The force that clouds our ability to act upon this logic is usually ego. Our ego has an incredible ability to persuade us to skip the first two buckets – convincing us to take a job simply for more money (bucket 4) or a job title, status or reputation (bucket 5), without the knowledge (bucket 1) or skills (bucket 2) to succeed in that role.

When we succumb to this temptation, we're building our career on weak foundations. These short-term decisions – your inability to delay your gratification, be patient and invest in your first two buckets – will ultimately catch up with you.

In 2017, a very talented 21-year-old employee called Richard walked into my office and told me he had some news to share with me. He told me that he had been offered a job as CEO of a new marketing company halfway across the world, and that he wanted to leave my company – where he had been flourishing – to take it. He told me the role offered him an enormous pay rise (almost double what we paid him), an equity package and a chance to live in New York City – a far cry from the dreary village he was raised in and an apparent step up from Manchester, England, where he worked for my company.

To be totally frank, I didn't believe him. I couldn't fathom that a legitimate business would offer a junior employee, with no management experience, such a prominent role.

Nonetheless, I accepted his claims and told him that we would support him in his transition out of our company.

It turns out I was wrong – Richard was telling the truth. The job offer did exist and a month later he became CEO of the company, moved to New York and started his new life as a C-suite executive in the Big Apple, leading a team of more than 20 people, in a rapidly growing marketing start-up.

Unfortunately, that is not where the story ends; as life would come to teach both me and Richard, there is no skipping the first two buckets of knowledge and skills if you're playing for long-term, sustainable results. Any attempt to do so is equivalent to building your house on sand.

Within 18 months, the once-promising company Richard had joined had gone under, lost its key employees, run out of money and become shrouded in controversy relating to management practices. After the company closed, Richard was unemployed, far from home, and searching for a new, more junior role, in the same industry that we had employed him in.

When deciding which path to take in life, which job to accept or where to invest your spare time, remember that knowledge, when applied (skill), is power. Prioritise filling those first two buckets and your foundations will have the long-term sustainability you need to prevail, regardless of how life's tectonic plates move and shake beneath you.

I define a professional earthquake as an unpredictable career event that adversely impacts you. This could be anything: a technological innovation that disrupts your whole industry, being fired by your employer, or if you're a founder, your company going under.

> There are only two buckets that any such professional earthquake can never empty — it can take away your network, it can take your resources, it can even impact your reputation, but it can never remove your knowledge and it can never unlearn your skills.

These first two buckets are your longevity, your foundation and the clearest predictor of your future.

★ THE LAW: FILL YOUR FIVE BUCKETS IN THE RIGHT ORDER

Applied knowledge is skill, and the more you can expand and apply your knowledge, the more value you'll create in the world. This value will be repaid in a growing network, abundant resources and a robust reputation. Make sure you fill your buckets in the right order.

Those who hoard gold have riches for a moment.

Those who hoard knowledge and skills have riches for a lifetime.

True prosperity is what you know and what you can do.

LAW 2

TO MASTER IT, YOU MUST CREATE AN OBLIGATION TO TEACH IT

This law explains the simple technique that the world's most renowned intellectuals, authors and philosophers use to become the masters of their craft and how you can use it to develop any skill, master any topic and build an audience.

★ THE STORY

It felt like the entire population of planet Earth had gathered to watch me melt on stage that evening, but in reality, it was just a handful of my fellow secondary school pupils, their parents and a few teachers.

I was 14 years old and had been tasked with saying a few closing remarks at my school's exam awards evening. As I walked out onto the stage, the auditorium fell into an anticipatory silence.

And there I stood, frozen, terrified and mute, for one of the longest minutes anyone has ever endured, staring down at the trembling piece of paper clasped between my clammy, nervous hands, on the verge of urinating into my own underwear, experiencing what people refer to as 'stage fright'.

The script I had planned to deliver was shaking with such ferocity that I couldn't see the words. Eventually I blurted out some improvised, clichéd, nonsensical remarks before darting off stage and out of the door as if I were being followed by a firing squad.

Fast-forward ten years from that traumatic day and I'm speaking on stage 50 weeks a year in every corner of the globe – I'm headlining alongside Barack Obama in front of tens of thousands in São Paulo, I'm speaking in sold-out arenas in Barcelona, I'm touring the UK and speaking at festivals from Kyiv to Texas to Milan.

★ THE EXPLANATION

I went from being a train wreck of a public speaker, to rubbing shoulders with some of the very best to ever do it, and there is one simple law that I credit with this transformation.

This law is not just responsible for my on-stage composure, performance and delivery (my skills), it's also the reason why I have something interesting to share while I'm on stage (my knowledge):

I created an obligation to teach.

> The late spiritual leader Yogi Bhajan once said, 'If you want to learn something, read about it. If you want to understand something, write about it. If you want to master something, teach it.'

At 21 years old, I made a promise to myself that every day at 7pm, I would write a tweet or make a video delivering a single idea, and then post it online at 8pm.

Of all the things I've done in my life to advance my knowledge and skills – to fill my first two buckets – this is the thing that made the most difference. It's no exaggeration to say that it has completely changed the trajectory of my life, and consequently it's the piece of advice I urge most strongly upon anyone looking to become a better thinker, speaker, writer or content creator.

The key factor here is that I made learning, then writing/recording and sharing it online, a daily obligation, not just an interest.

✸ SKIN IN THE GAME

Soon after creating this obligation, I got feedback in the form of comments from my audience and analytics from the social platforms; this helped me to improve, and in turn, created a community of people that were following me purely for this daily idea. This started as tens of people and almost ten years later that community has grown to almost 10 million followers across all channels.

From the first idea I shared, I created a 'social contract' with my audience – essentially a social obligation to the people who were following me specifically for this daily idea – which motivated me to continue posting and gave me something to lose – their attention and my reputation – if I stopped.

Having something to lose is fundamentally what an obligation is, and having something to lose is sometimes referred to as having 'skin in the game'.

'Skin in the game' is an important psychological tool to harness if you want to accelerate your learning curve in any area of your life. Having skin in the game raises the stakes of your learning by building deeper psychological incentives to perform a behaviour. The 'skin' can be anything from money to a personal public commitment.

You want to learn more about a specific company? Buy a few shares of the stock. You want to learn about Web 3.0? Buy an NFT. If you want to be consistent in the gym, make a WhatsApp group with your friends where you share your workouts every day. In these three examples, either monetary or social currency is at stake.

'Skin in the game' works because across several global studies it's been demonstrated that human behaviour is more strongly driven by the motivation to avoid losses than to pursue gains, which is what scientists call 'loss aversion'.

Give yourself something to lose.

★ THE FEYNMAN TECHNIQUE REVISED

So, **if you want to master something, do it publicly and do it consistently**. Publishing your written ideas forces you to learn more often and to write more clearly. Publishing a video forces you to improve your speaking skills and to articulate your thoughts. Sharing your ideas on stage teaches you how to hold an audience and tell captivating stories. In any area of your life, doing it in public, and creating an obligation that forces you to do it consistently, will lead you to mastery.

One of the most valuable elements of this obligation was having to distil any idea I wanted to share down to its 140-character essence, so that it could fit within the constraints of a tweet.

Being able to simplify an idea and successfully share it with others is both the path to understanding it and the proof that you do. One of the ways we mask our lack of understanding of any idea is by using more words, bigger words and less necessary words.

This challenge of simplifying an idea to its essence is often referred to as the Feynman technique, named after the renowned American scientist Richard Feynman. Feynman won a Nobel Prize in 1965 for his groundbreaking work in quantum electrodynamics. He had a gift for explaining the most complex, baffling ideas in simple language that even a child could understand.

'I couldn't reduce it to the freshman level. That means we really don't understand it.'

Richard Feynman

The Feynman technique is a powerful mental model for self-development. It forces you to strip away unnecessary complexity, distil a concept to its purest essence, and develop a rich, in-depth understanding of whatever discipline you seek to master.

The Feynman technique follows a few key steps, which I've simplified and updated based on my own learning experience:

STEP 1: LEARN
First you must identify the topic you want to understand, research it thoroughly and grasp it from every direction.

STEP 2: TEACH IT TO A CHILD

Secondly, you should write the idea down as if you were teaching it to a child; use simple words, fewer words and simple concepts.

STEP 3: SHARE IT

Convey your idea to others; post it online, post it on your blog, share it on stage or even at the dinner table. Choose any medium where you'll get clear feedback.

STEP 4: REVIEW

Review the feedback; did people understand the concept from your explanation? Can they explain it to you after you've explained it to them? If not, go back to step 1; if they did, move on.

★ ★ ★

As we look over history, this is the one thing that every great speaker, renowned author and prominent intellectual I've ever encountered or interviewed has in common.

When *Prospect* magazine released their list of the top 100 modern intellectuals, every name on the list followed this law.

When I researched the pre-eminent philosophers from history, every single one of them embodied and were often staunch advocates of this law.

At some point in their life, through intention or accident, they had created an obligation to think, write and share their ideas, consistently.

Whether it's leading modern authors like James Clear, Malcolm Gladwell or Simon Sinek who write tweets, online blogs and create social media videos, or ancient philosophers like Aristotle, Plato and Confucius, who wrote on papyrus scrolls and spoke on stages, they all abide by this crucial law; all of them have created an obligation to teach, and in turn they've become masters of both knowledge and delivery.

> 'The person who learns the most in any classroom is the teacher.'
>
> **James Clear**

★ THE LAW: TO MASTER IT, YOU MUST CREATE AN OBLIGATION TO TEACH IT

Learn more, simplify more and share more. Your consistency will further your progress, the feedback will refine your skill and following this law will lead to mastery.

You don't become a master because you're able to retain knowledge.

You become a master when you're able to release it.

LAW 3
YOU MUST NEVER DISAGREE

This law will make you a master of communication, negotiation, conflict resolution, winning arguments, being heard and changing people's minds. It also explains why most of your arguments are never productive.

★ THE STORY

For most of my childhood I witnessed my mother shouting heatedly at my father as he sat watching TV, apparently completely oblivious to her presence. These ear-piercing screaming marathons were like nothing I'd ever witnessed before and nothing I've witnessed since.

She could shout at him for five or six hours – about the same thing – using the same words, without any apparent reduction in volume or enthusiasm. On occasion, my father might try and argue back for a brief moment, and when he inevitably failed to land his rebuttal, he would either continue to ignore her or flee to another part of the house, lock himself in his bedroom, or jump in the car and drive off.

It took me 20 years to realise that I'd learned this exact conflict-resolution strategy from him, while I was lying in bed at 2am as my angry girlfriend badgered me, on repeat, about something she was unhappy about. I rebutted her with

'I disagree' and attempted to make a convincing counter-argument. Needless to say, I failed. Like throwing petrol onto a bonfire, she carried on shouting at me with increased volume, making the same point, using the exact same words.

Eventually, I got up and tried to leave, and she followed me, so I locked myself inside my walk-in wardrobe, where I remained until almost 5am, being shouted at through the door – about the same thing, using the same words, like a broken record player – without any apparent reduction in volume or enthusiasm.

She's now my ex-girlfriend; unsurprisingly, that relationship didn't last.

✶ THE EXPLANATION

The truth is, in every interpersonal conflict in your life – business, romantic or platonic – communication is both the problem and the solution.

You can predict the long-term health of any relationship by whether each conflict makes the relationship stronger or weaker.

> Healthy conflict strengthens relationships because those involved are working against a problem; unhealthy conflict weakens a relationship because those involved are working against each other.

I sat down with Tali Sharot, professor of cognitive neuroscience at University College London and MIT, to understand what the science of the brain can teach us about the laws of effective communication, and what she shared with me changed my personal life, romantic relationships and business negotiations for ever.

Sharot and her team's study, published in *Nature Neuroscience*, recorded the brain activity of volunteers during disagreements to find out what was happening inside their minds.

The experiment was based on asking 42 people, grouped into pairs, to make a financial evaluation. Each pair lay, separated by a glass wall, in a brain-imaging scanner. Their reactions to the experiment were recorded. They were shown pictures of real estate and asked, individually within their pairs, to guess its value and to place a bet on the accuracy of their valuation. Each volunteer was able to see the valuation of their partner on a screen.

When the couple agreed on a valuation, they each placed higher bets on its accuracy and the researchers monitoring their brain activity saw their brains light up, indicating that they were more cognitively receptive and open. However, if they disagreed about a valuation, their brains seemed to freeze and shut down, causing them to turn off to the other's opinion and value that opinion less.

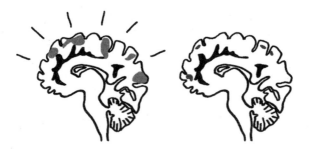

Sharot's findings shed light on some recent trends around contentious areas of political discourse. An example being climate change: despite scientists presenting more and more irrefutable evidence over the last ten years showing that climate change is man-made, a survey conducted by the Pew Research Centre indicates that the number of US Republicans who believe the scientific evidence *has decreased* in the same ten-year period. Furious arguing, regardless of evidence, is clearly not working.

So, here's what needs to be done if we want to increase our chances of being heard by someone on an opposing side. According to Sharot, **if you want to keep someone's brain lit up and receptive to your point of view, you must not start your response with a statement of disagreement**.

When you find yourself disagreeing with someone, avoid the emotional temptation, at all costs, to start your response with 'I disagree' or 'You're wrong', and instead introduce your rebuttal with what you have in common, what you agree on, and the parts of their argument that you can understand.

The strength of any carefully reasoned, logical argument isn't likely to be recognised when you open with disagreement – regardless of how much evidence you have or how objectively correct you are.

Instead, if we start from a place of agreement, of common ground, we increase the chance that the strength of our arguments, the accuracy of our logic and the weight of the evidence will be received at all.

This third law – to never disagree – is the critical skill that will allow you to become an effective negotiator, speaker, salesperson, business leader, writer – and partner.

When I interviewed Julian Treasure, the speaking and communication coach whose TED talk has been viewed 100 million times, and Paul Brunson, the matchmaking and relationship expert known as 'the love doctor', they both explained that the art of becoming a great communicator, conversationalist or partner is first listening so that the other person feels 'heard', and then making sure you reply in a way that makes them feel 'understood'.

Tali Sharot's studies in neuroscience now provide clear scientific evidence that shows why this approach of making someone feel 'heard and understood' is so crucial in changing someone's mind. It's no surprise that the people who are most likely to change our minds are the ones we agree with on 98 per cent of topics – we feel that they fundamentally understand us, so we're more open to listening to them.

THE LAW: YOU MUST NEVER DISAGREE

In the midst of a negotiation, debate or heated argument, try and remember that the key to changing someone's mind is finding a shared belief or motive that will keep their brain open to your point of view.

Our words should be bridges to comprehension, not barriers to connection.

Disagree less, understand more.

LAW 4

YOU DO NOT GET TO CHOOSE WHAT YOU BELIEVE

This law will teach you how to change any belief that you have – whether that's your self-belief, beliefs about others or beliefs about the world – while also showing you how to change the stubborn beliefs of others.

Think of someone that you absolutely love: your mother, your father, your partner, your dog – the most important person (or animal) in your life.

Now visualise them tied to a chair, being held at gunpoint by an aggressive terrorist.

Now imagine that the terrorist says to you, 'If you don't believe that I'm Jesus Christ right now, I will pull the trigger and kill them!'

What do you do?

The truth is, the most you could do is lie – the most you could do is tell them that you believe they're Jesus Christ, in the hope that your loved one would be spared. But you couldn't, genuinely, make yourself believe it.

This thought experiment illuminates a profound and controversial point about the true nature of our beliefs. In my hypothetical scenario, when everything was on the line, you still couldn't choose to believe something that you don't. So, what makes you think you can 'choose' any of your beliefs?

To investigate this concept further, I surveyed 1,000 people and asked them all the following question: 'Do you think you choose your beliefs?' Incredibly, 857 (85.7 per cent) of them said that they did.

On the next page of the survey, when I asked people if they could genuinely believe a terrorist holding their loved one at gunpoint was Jesus Christ if it meant it would save their loved one's life, 98 per cent of people admitted that they couldn't choose that belief – the most they could do was lie.

The fundamental beliefs you hold about yourself, the fundamental beliefs you hold about others, the fundamental beliefs you hold about the world – you've 'chosen' none of them.

When people hear this, they tend to have a visceral negative reaction, because it sounds disempowering and attacks our sense of 'free will', control and independence. If I can't choose a belief, how can I ever *change* a belief? Does that condemn me to the current beliefs I have about the world, others and myself?

Thankfully, it doesn't.

Your life is a testament to the fact that your beliefs do continually change and evolve – I'm assuming you don't still believe in Santa Claus?

Society too, continues to change its beliefs at an increasing speed; in the 1700s, people thought tobacco was healthy and doctors would blow tobacco smoke up the arse of a drowned person in an attempt to revive them; in the 1800s we believed clitoral orgasms were a sign of insanity and doctors would medically treat people who had them; as recently as the 1970s, people believed space aliens were sending us coded messages by flattening our crops on farms in middle America; and medieval doctors pulled their cures out of their arses, literally – poop was believed to be a cure for everything from headaches to epilepsy.

Thankfully, **beliefs change**.

Our brains consume a huge amount of energy and have therefore evolved strategies to preserve energy in order to survive. Because one of the brain's main purposes is to predict by spotting patterns and making assumptions based on those patterns, it must do so as efficiently and in as little time as possible. Beliefs allow the brain to make such forecasts quickly.

Having stubborn beliefs is a useful survival tool for humans because beliefs drive behaviour – your ancestors, who stubbornly held the belief that lions are dangerous, fire is hot and deep water is to be avoided, survived long enough because of these beliefs to have babies who possessed the same stubbornness.

Going back to the example of the terrorist holding your loved one hostage under threat of execution; now imagine the terrorist grabbed a glass of water and turned it into wine (an act Jesus is known for). Would this change your beliefs about the terrorist? Would you now believe that the terrorist is in fact Jesus Christ?

In my survey, 77 per cent said that this would be enough to convince them that the terrorist was in fact Jesus Christ, and in total 82 per cent said their beliefs about the terrorist would change – the act of witnessing someone turn water into wine was strong enough evidence to cause them to change their belief.

This thought experiment and the corresponding survey reveal a fundamental truth about the nature of all of our beliefs: the things you believe are fundamentally based on some form of primary evidence. However, scientific studies have repeatedly proved that whether that evidence is objectively true or false doesn't actually matter – we subjectively accept evidence to be true based on our experiences and biases.

There are still 300,000 Americans who believe the earth is flat; in a recent Ipsos survey, 21 per cent of adult Americans said they believed Santa Claus is real; a disturbing number of people believe King Charles is a vampire; one in three Americans believe Bigfoot exists; and one in four Scottish people believe there is a giant monster living in a lake near Inverness.

To change their beliefs, simply telling them they're wrong, as we've seen in Law 3, won't work. Showing a flat-earther a legitimate picture of a round Planet Earth also doesn't work, and despite what motivational coaches might say, telling someone who had their confidence destroyed at seven years old by vicious playground bullies (very strong evidence) to simply believe in themselves or to repeat affirmations in a mirror, won't do anything to change their underlying beliefs about themselves either.

SEEING IS BELIEVING

Just showing a flat-earther a picture of the spherical Earth taken from space by NASA doesn't work because in order to believe what they're seeing, they have to trust not only the picture, but the credibility of the source from which the picture came – NASA. Flat-earthers trust neither; they believe NASA is fraudulent, astronauts are actors and the scientific community is in on it.

In Dr Robert Cialdini's renowned book *Influence*, he explains that if we trust someone's authority on a matter – if Lionel Messi tells us that Adidas football boots are better than Nike, if a personal trainer tells us we're lifting a weight incorrectly or if a doctor tells us we need to take a pill – we're very likely to defer to their authority, adopt their belief and do what they say.

'For some of our most important beliefs we have no evidence at all, except that people we love and trust hold these beliefs. Considering how little we know, the confidence we have in our beliefs is preposterous – and it is also essential.'

2002 Nobel Prize laureate Daniel Kahneman

Authority figures are powerful forces for belief change, but the most powerful force of all is **first-party evidence from our own five physical senses**. As the phrase goes, seeing is believing. Because the flat-earth community is so distrustful of science, astronomy and really anyone qualified, the only conceivable way that you could upend their stubborn beliefs is to send them to space to have a look for themselves.

This need to see evidence with our own eyes explains why so many crazy conspiracy theories withstand the test of time – why people dismiss climate change, believe the earth is flat and question the efficacy of vaccines – these things are impossible for most of us to see for ourselves.

Likewise, someone lacking confidence in their speaking abilities is unlikely to become confident just because their mum tells them they're a good speaker – they will need to acquire first-party evidence themselves, by speaking on stage and getting positive feedback from bias-free sources they trust.

We believe ourselves and our own eyes to be trusted sources, making it important for scientists to involve our five senses to make their insights accessible to us. With this principle in mind, climate-change educators are now trying to translate scientific insights about the occurrence and speed of climate change into 'local lessons', for example showing the impact of climate change on things in our local area so that we can go and see it for ourselves.

✭ CONFIDENCE IN EXISTING BELIEFS

I asked Tali Sharot, who we met in the previous law, 'How do we change our or someone else's belief?' She has spent years researching and conducting multiple studies on why beliefs exist, why they're hard to change and how to change them.

She told me that the brain considers any new evidence alongside the current evidence it has stored. So, if I told you I had seen a pink elephant flying in the sky, your brain will compare this new evidence to your existing evidence that elephants aren't pink and they can't fly, and likely reject it.

However, if I told a three-year-old that I had seen a pink elephant flying in the sky, they would likely believe me because they have yet to form strong opposing beliefs about elephants, aviation and the laws of physics.

Sharot asserts that there are four factors that determine whether a new piece of evidence will change an existing belief:

1. A person's current evidence.

2. Their confidence in their current evidence.

3. The new evidence.

4. Their confidence in that new evidence.

And as we learn from the widely discussed phenomenon called 'confirmation bias', whereby humans tend to search for, favour and recall information in a way that confirms or supports their existing beliefs or values – the further the new evidence is from their current beliefs, the less likely it is to change their thinking.

☆ WE CHANGE OUR MINDS IF IT SOUNDS LIKE GOOD NEWS!

All of this means that strongly held false beliefs are very hard to change, but there is one important exception: when the counter-evidence is exactly what you want to hear, you're more likely to change your mind. For example, in a 2011 study in which people were told that others see them as much more attractive than they see themselves, they were happy to change their self-perception. And in a 2016 study in which people learned that their genes suggested that they were much more resistant to disease than they thought, the participants were again quick to change their beliefs.

What about politics? Back in August 2016, 900 American citizens were asked to predict the results of the presidential election by putting a little arrow on a scale that went from Clinton to Trump. So, if you thought Clinton was highly likely to win, you put the arrow right next to Clinton. If you thought the odds were 50/50, you put the arrow in the middle, and so on. They were first asked: 'Who do you want to win?' to which 50 per cent said they wanted Clinton to win and 50 per cent said they wanted Trump to win.

When they were asked who they thought *was* going to win, both groups of supporters put the arrow closest to Clinton – indicating that they believed she would win. Then a new poll was introduced, predicting a Trump victory. And everyone was asked again who they thought was going to win. Did the new poll change their predictions?

Indeed, it did. But it predominantly changed the predictions of the Trump supporters – because it was exactly what they wanted to hear. They were elated that the new poll was suggesting a Trump victory, and were quick to change their predictions.

The Clinton supporters didn't change their predictions much, and many of them ignored the new poll altogether.

DON'T ATTACK BELIEFS, INSPIRE NEW ONES

Tali Sharot concluded that in order to change beliefs, 'the secret is to go along with how our brain works, not to fight against it', which is what most people try and fail to do.

Don't try and break or argue with someone's existing evidence; **instead focus on implanting completely new**

evidence, and make sure you've highlighted the incredibly positive impact this new evidence will have on them.

One example of this is of parents' reaction to the false link drawn up between the mumps, measles and rubella (MMR) vaccine and autism, in a now-debunked journal article that was published in 1998. As news of the article's theory spread, many parents refused to vaccinate their children, and held on to their beliefs stubbornly. Eventually, a group of researchers changed their minds, not by trying to break their existing beliefs – they didn't focus on their existing beliefs at all – but by offering the parents new information about the very positive benefits of the vaccine – true information about how it prevents kids from encountering deadly disease. And it worked – parents agreed to have their children vaccinated.

★ DETAILED SELF-REVIEW CAN REDUCE ANY BELIEF

Interestingly, people won't lower the conviction of their beliefs when you attack them or try to convince them with data, but they will lose conviction when asked to explain or analyse the *details* of their beliefs. This is a technique cognitive behavioural therapists know well.

The *New Yorker*'s Elizabeth Kolbert described a study conducted at Yale where graduate students were asked to rate their understanding of their own toilet at home. They were then asked to write detailed, step-by-step explanations of how the device works. Once they'd attempted to explain the inner workings of a toilet, they were asked to rate their understanding again. Their belief in their understanding of toilets dropped significantly.

In a similar study conducted in 2012, people were asked about their stance on political proposals relating to health care. As Kolbert describes, 'Participants were asked to rate their positions depending on how strongly they agreed or disagreed. Next, they were instructed to explain, in as much detail as they could, the impacts of implementing each proposal. Most people at this point ran into trouble.' Asked once again to rate their views, the conviction of their beliefs decreased and they either agreed or disagreed less vehemently.

Asking someone to explain the detail and logic underpinning their strongly held beliefs is a profoundly powerful way to reduce their conviction. This works for limiting beliefs too. If someone is struggling with their self-belief and believes they're worthless, having them explain in as much detail as they can, why they feel that way, and questioning their responses, is an effective way to get them to relinquish that belief.

★ THE GROWTH ZONE IS WHERE NEW EVIDENCE EXISTS

As you learned in Law 2, when I was younger, I struggled with awful stage fright, which itself is underpinned by a set of limiting beliefs. Telling me it was 'all going to be OK' was not enough to change my preconceptions about speaking on stage, how I would perform and what the reaction would be – my beliefs were too stubborn.

The reason my stage fright eventually vanished – to the point that now I feel 99.9 per cent less nervous when speaking in a packed arena or live on TV – is simply because I carried on speaking on stage. And doing so gradually gave me new, positive, first-party evidence that replaced the existing evidence I had about my on-stage abilities – the more I spoke on stage, the stronger my confidence in this new evidence became, and with it, the belief in my inability and the fear it created diminished.

'Do the thing you fear, and keep on doing it. That is the quickest and surest way ever yet discovered to conquer fear.'

Dale Carnegie

This, for me, is maybe the most important fundamental truth about belief change and how to increase a person's self-belief – even your own; **beliefs change when a person gets new counteracting evidence** that they have a high degree of subjective confidence in.

If a friend of yours has a limiting belief about themselves, or you have a limiting belief about yourself, the best chance you have of changing that belief isn't by reading self-help books, inspirational quotes or watching motivational videos, it's by **stepping out of your comfort zone** and into a situation where that limiting belief will be confronted head on with new first-party evidence.

This is how you change even the most stubborn beliefs. This is how I went from being deeply religious to agnostic in the space of 12 months, from low confidence to self-believing in my transition from childhood to adulthood, and from being a terrified public speaker to having unshakeable confidence on any stage.

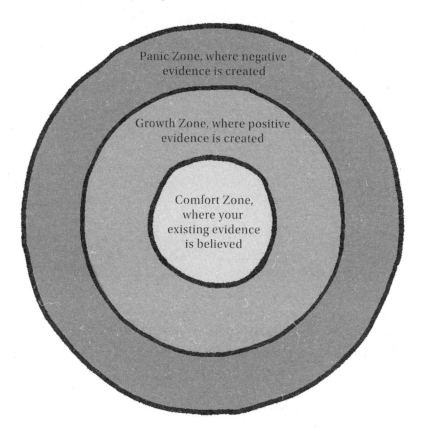

★ THE LAW: YOU DO NOT GET TO CHOOSE WHAT YOU BELIEVE

Beliefs are stubborn, but they are malleable. To change a belief, a person must find a way to attain convincing new evidence that they can trust. They're more likely to believe the validity of this new evidence if its source agrees with their other existing beliefs. Evidence that offers positive outcomes is the easiest evidence for someone to believe. If you interrogate the validity and detail of one of your own limiting beliefs,

your conviction in it will weaken. If you want to change someone's belief, don't attack it, make them a direct witness to
positive new evidence that will both inspire them and coun-
teract the negative effects of their old beliefs. Unchallenged
limiting beliefs are the greatest barrier between who we are
and who we could be.

Stop telling yourself you're not qualified, good enough or worthy.

Growth happens when you start doing the things you're not qualified to do.

LAW 5

YOU MUST LEAN IN TO BIZARRE BEHAVIOUR

This law is responsible for every successful company I've ever built – it teaches you how to stay at the forefront of the rapidly changing world we live in, how to capitalise on change and how to avoid ever being left behind by any of the incoming technological revolutions.

★ THE STORY

'People love music; that's why we'll always be in business.'

These were the fateful words uttered by the former CEO of one of the world's largest music stores as he peered over the second-floor balcony out on to his bustling shop floor.

Years later, his global music store was out of business.

He was right; people do love music. But they don't love travelling for an hour, in the rain, wrestling through a busy shop floor to get a plastic disc and then queuing to pay for it.

He misjudged what his customers wanted: they wanted music, they didn't want CDs.

iTunes, the digital music platform built by Apple, had emerged in the spring of 2003, allowing his disc-buying customers to get what they wanted – music – without all the inconvenience.

I'm told on good authority that this particular CEO was so cynical about digital music that he wouldn't even entertain conversations with his senior leadership team about its introduction or the threat it posed.

One of his professional associates told me that he had '**leaned out**', because he didn't understand it, he thought the space was rife with piracy and that it wouldn't directly impact people's love of CDs.

I believe writer Clifford Stoll had also 'leaned out' when he made the following scornful prediction about the future of the internet, which was published in *Newsweek* in February 1995:

> I'm uneasy about this most trendy and oversold community. Visionaries see a future of telecommuting workers, interactive libraries and multimedia classrooms. They speak of electronic town meetings and virtual communities. Commerce and business will shift from offices and malls to networks and modems … Baloney … The truth is no online database will replace your daily newspaper.

Newsweek would end up discontinuing their print magazine and moving their entire business onto the internet.

In 1903, the president of a leading bank had certainly leaned out when he told Henry Ford – the founder of Ford Motor Company – 'The horse is here to stay but the automobile is only a novelty – a fad.'

In 1992, Andy Grove, the CEO of Intel, had clearly leaned out when he said: 'The idea of a personal communicator in every pocket is a pipe dream driven by greed.'

And the former CEO of Microsoft Steve Ballmer had certainly leaned out when he laughed at Apple and said, 'There's no chance that the iPhone is going to get any significant market share.'

At 19 years old I had a meeting at the beautiful London offices of one of the world's leading fashion brands. It was 2012 and social media had caught on among consumers, but brands were lagging behind – as they always seem to do with new technology.

My mission that day was to persuade the brand's marketing department – namely their marketing director – to take social media more seriously – to lean in – and more specifically to launch their own social media pages. I failed. I was berated, mocked and dismissed. The marketing director I was pitching to was visibly terrified: 'So people will be able to comment on our posts and criticise us?' he questioned. 'I don't want our brand to go viral – how would we control that?' he continued. 'Magazine advertising is doing well for us and social media is just too dangerous.' He ended the meeting midway through my presentation and needless to say, he never called me back.

My company would go from strength to strength, arguably becoming the most influential marketing company in its market.

The brand I met that day filed for bankruptcy in 2019.

✱ THE EXPLANATION

Leaning out, as I define it, isn't about being 'wrong' – it's about being so arrogantly sure that you're right that you refuse to listen, learn and pay attention to new information.

This isn't just a symptom of arrogance – unfortunately, it's often a symptom of being human; the psychological reason why people lean out of important, potentially vital information is because of the incredibly well-studied psychological phenomenon known as **cognitive dissonance**.

Coined by the American psychologist Leon Festinger in the 1950s, 'cognitive dissonance' describes the tension you experience when your thoughts conflict with your behaviour. Being a smoker, for example, is dissonant – it conflicts with the evidence that smoking is incredibly harmful. To resolve this tension, the smoker must either give up or find a way to *justify* their behaviour. We can all think of the excuses smokers use, from 'I only smoke on occasion' to 'there are far worse things you can do to your body' to 'why shouldn't I be free to behave as I choose?'

For Festinger, cognitive dissonance helped explain why so many of us live with contradictory ideas or values. But it can also stop us from changing our minds when we should, even when it could save careers, jobs, businesses or lives.

> Research has shown that cognitive dissonance is most painful for us when we encounter facts or evidence that destabilise or conflict with how we see ourselves, that undermine our identity and confidence in ourselves, or that make us feel in some way threatened.

In business, anyone who is too rigidly fixed to an ideology probably won't provide the solution, because resolving a problem often requires enough humility to disregard your initial hypothesis and listen to what the market is telling you.

★ WE WOULD RATHER BE DEAD THAN WRONG

Making a public statement about your views on something, as the CEO of Intel did about mobile phones, or the CEO of Microsoft did about the iPhone, risks putting an additional nail in your coffin, because once we've made a commitment to a belief, our brains will fight tirelessly to prove that we were right, even when we're clearly wrong.

Time and time again, research shows that as soon as we make any decision – I will vote for this party; I'm going to buy a house in this area; I think Covid-19 is serious; no, I'm sure the risks are being exaggerated – we automatically begin justifying and rationalising it. Quite quickly any doubts we initially had will disappear.

The American psychologist Elliot Aronson, who studied this phenomenon, famously assembled a discussion group of pompous, dull people. Some of the participants were made to endure an arduous selection process; others were allowed to join immediately, without expending any effort. Those who were given the runaround reported enjoying the group far more than the ones who were simply let in. Aronson explained what was happening here: whenever we've invested time, money or energy into something and it ends up being a complete waste of time, this creates dissonance, which we try to reduce by finding ways of justifying our bad decision. Aronson's participants focused unconsciously on what might be interesting, or at least bearable, about being part of a deliberately boring group. The people who had invested very little effort in joining therefore had less dissonance to reduce, and more readily admitted what a waste of time it had been.

✶ WE WON'T LISTEN TO THE OTHER SIDE

It wasn't just that fashion brand's marketing director that dismissed me. For the first three years of my social media marketing company's existence, we were attacked, berated and criticised daily.

Commentators called us 'parasites', said our business was a 'fad' and predicted we'd be 'bankrupt in a few months'. I remember consoling my tearful co-founder, Hannah Anderson, in 2015, when BuzzFeed News wrote a critical article challenging our character, practices and credibility.

Unsurprisingly, the attacks always came from people from the 'traditional' media and marketing world – TV, print and radio. They viewed us as the annoying 'new kids on the marketing block'. One commentator said we were 'mysterious social media hackers' and another journalist wrote that we were making millions from our 'less than savoury advertising practices'.

The truth is, we weren't doing anything that revolutionary – they just didn't understand it, and on some level it threatened their sense of identity that a 'group of twenty-somethings in Manchester' was taking over marketing, as one journalist described it.

When we don't understand something, someone, a new idea or technology, and when that new thing challenges our identity, intelligence or livelihood, instead of listening and leaning in – in an attempt to ease our cognitive dissonance – we too often lean out and attack them. This might make us feel good, but an ostrich with its head in the sand is at great risk of being eaten.

This explains why the most important innovations in our lives received the most criticism when they were first introduced – they threatened to disrupt people's sense of identity, intelligence and understanding. For this very reason I've long held the belief that passionate criticism of a technology is usually a positive indicator of its potential – it's a sign that there's something worth leaning in to, someone is threatened and innovation is coming.

This is why I leaned in to what is known as 'Web 3.0', 'blockchain technology' or 'crypto', and founded a software company in this space called thirdweb – because all the right people were dismissing, attacking and angry about it. This wave of pessimism gave me flashbacks to 2012 when I first launched a Web 2.0 (social media) company, and so I reserved judgement and did my own research. Beneath all the nefarious money-grabbing and short-sighted behaviour – which is common when a new technology emerges – I found an underlying technological revolution in blockchain that I believe will make many functions of our lives easier, better, faster and cheaper. Thirdweb was recently valued at $160 million in our latest investment round and we now have hundreds of thousands of clients using our tools.

Even if a new innovation doesn't beget a wave of critics, it's important to remember that innovation disrupts because it's different. By definition, it should look weird, it should feel unconventional, it should be misunderstood, and it should sound wrong, stupid, dumb or even illegal.

I interviewed advertising legend Rory Sutherland, vice chairman of the Ogilvy advertising group, on this very topic, and he told me: 'All too often, what matters to people is not whether an idea is true or effective, but whether it fits with the preconceptions of a dominant convention or incumbent. New things put ego, status, jobs and identities at stake.'

You see this cognitive dissonance and avoidance every-where you look. Whenever we feel an affinity with an ideology, politician, newspaper, brand or technology, that very allegiance distorts evidence that conflicts with those loyalties. If we believe someone is 'on the other side', there is dissonance before they've said a word.

★ HOW TO BECOME A 'LEAN-IN PERSON'

To quote the education entrepreneur Michael Simmons: 'If someone is 40 years old today, the rate of change they exper-ience in 2040, when they're 60, will be four times what it is now. What feels like a year's worth of change by today's stan-dards will occur in three months. When someone who is 10 today is 60, they'll experience a year of today's rate of change in just 11 days.'

To summarise the profundity of this extreme acceleration of change, Ray Kurzweil, arguably the world's pre-eminent futurist, says: 'We won't experience one hundred years of technological advance in the twenty-first century; we will witness in the order of twenty thousand years of progress (when measured by today's rate of progress), or about one thousand times greater [rate of change] than what was achieved in the twentieth century.'

Change is only going to get faster – so expect your feelings of cognitive dissonance – the feeling that something doesn't make sense and conflicts with what you already know, to increase.

As discussed in Laws 3 and 4, admitting we're wrong – rather than reflexively jumping to self-justification or dismissal – requires self-reflection and, at least temporarily, dissonance.

You don't want to be the entrepreneur that misses the next technological revolution, you don't want to be the CMO that dismisses the next big marketing opportunity, you don't want to be the journalist that dismisses the next frontier of media. You don't want to be a 'lean out' person. With the aforementioned rate of change in mind, there's going to be a lot more things that tempt you to lean out.

Thankfully, there are a few practical and mental techniques we can adopt to reduce this dissonance and the 'lean out' behaviour it creates.

One technique is to default to believing that two seemingly conflicting ideas can be true at the same time and having a bias to keep them separate, a technique Elliot Aronson and his fellow social psychologist Carol Tavris refer to as the 'Shimon Peres solution'. Former prime minister of Israel Shimon Peres was angry when his friend Ronald Reagan, the American president, made an official visit to a cemetery in Germany where former Nazis were buried.

Peres was asked how he felt about Reagan's decision to visit the cemetery. He could have chosen one of two ways to reduce dissonance:

1. Renounced the friendship.

2. Dismissed Reagan's visit as trivial and not worth worrying about.

Yet Peres resorted to neither of these responses, instead simply saying, 'When a friend makes a mistake, the friend remains a friend and the mistake remains a mistake.'

Peres managed to 'hold' the dissonance, and resisted the urge to force two things to make perfect sense. It's a lesson in avoiding easy, knee-jerk responses or being pressured into a binary choice, and instead accepting nuance and recognising that two apparently conflicting things can be true at the same time. Despite what passionate online tribalism might tempt you to believe – your most important beliefs should not be binary; lean-in people can see the merit of the old way and the new way at the same time, without the compulsion to reject or condemn either.

In moments of dissonance, when we're faced with ideas, innovations and information that we don't understand, which challenge our conventions or threaten our identity – Web 3.0, AI, virtual reality, social media, opposing political ideologies and social movements – the key is to reserve the temptation of judgement – which is often just an attempt to ease our cognitive dissonance – to **lean in**, to study and to ask honest questions: Why am I believing what I believe? Is it possible that I'm wrong? Do I know what I'm talking about? Am I leaning out because I don't understand? Am I following the party line? Are these my own beliefs or the beliefs of the people like me?

Those that have the patience and conviction to do this will undoubtedly own the future.

Those that don't will continue to be left behind.

THE LAW: YOU MUST LEAN IN TO BIZARRE BEHAVIOUR

When you don't understand, lean in more. When it challenges your intelligence, lean in more. When it makes you feel stupid, lean in more. Leaning out will leave you behind.

Don't block people that you don't agree with, follow more of them. Don't run from ideas that make you uncomfortable, run towards them.

Taking no risks will be your biggest risk.

You have to risk failure to succeed.

You have to risk heartbreak to love.

You have to risk criticism for the applause.

You have to risk the ordinary to achieve the extraordinary.

If you live avoiding risk, you're risking missing out on life.

LAW 6

ASK, DON'T TELL – THE QUESTION/ BEHAVIOUR EFFECT

This law reveals one of the most simple and effective psychological tricks that you can use to motivate someone to do something, form a habit or perform a desired behaviour. You can use it on yourself or someone else!

It's 1980 in America. Ronald Reagan is running for president against Jimmy Carter, who'd been elected in 1976. The economy is in a horrific state, and Reagan must convince voters that it's time to kick Carter out of the White House.

In the last week of the 1980 presidential campaign, on 28 October, the two candidates held their one and only presidential debate and 80.6 million viewers tuned in to watch – making it the most-watched debate in American history at the time.

Going into the debate, incumbent President Carter had an eight-point lead according to polls.

Reagan knew he needed to use Carter's abysmal economic performance against him but, instead of doing what every presidential candidate before him had done and stating the economic facts, he did something that no one had ever done, but every presidential candidate seems to have done since: he asked a simple but now legendary question, 'Are you better off now than you were four years ago?' He said:

> Next Tuesday, all of you will go to the polls, you'll stand there in the polling place and make a decision. I think when you make that decision, it might be well if you would ask yourself, are you better off than you were four years ago? Is it easier for you to go and buy things in the stores than it was four years ago? Is there more or less unemployment in the country than there was four years ago? Is America as respected throughout the world as it was? … And if you answer all of those questions yes, why then I think your choice is very obvious as to who you will vote for.

A televote poll carried out by ABC News immediately after the debate received about 650,000 responses – and almost 70 per cent of respondents said Reagan had won the debate. Seven days later, on 4 November, Reagan defeated Carter by ten points, in a historic landslide victory, to become the 40th president of the United States.

Just a question? No, political magic backed by science. Why? **Questions, unlike statements, elicit an active response – they make people think.** That's why researchers at Ohio State University have found that when the facts are clearly on your side, questions become extremely more effective than simply making a statement.

★ THE POWER OF THE QUESTION/ BEHAVIOUR EFFECT

We all make commitments we fail to honour. How many times have you said, 'I'll eat better this year' or 'I'll exercise every morning this week', only to fall short of your plan? Of course we intend to follow through, but good intentions aren't enough to create meaningful change. A well-designed *question*, however, might be.

After combing through more than 100 studies spanning 40 years of research, a team of scientists from four US universities discovered that asking is better than telling when it comes to influencing your own or another's behaviour.

David Sprott, a co-author of the research from Washington State University said: 'If you question a person about performing a future behavior, the likelihood of that behavior happening will change.' Questions prompt a psychological reaction that is different from the reaction to statements.

This means, for instance, that a sign that says, PLEASE RECYCLE is much less likely to increase its viewers' chance of recycling than a sign that says, WILL YOU RECYCLE? Telling yourself 'I will eat vegetables today' is less likely to increase your chances of eating vegetables than asking yourself the question, 'Will I eat vegetables today?'

Will you recycle?

Astonishingly, researchers found that turning a statement into a question could influence a person's behaviour for up to six months.

The question/behaviour effect is even more powerful with questions that can only be answered with either yes or no.

The question/behaviour effect is at its strongest when questions are used to encourage behaviour that fits the receiver's personal and social ambitions (when answering yes to the question would bring them closer to who they want to be).

Starting the question with 'will' implies ownership and action, and causes the question/behaviour effect to be even stronger than starting your question with a word like 'can' or 'could', which imply the question is about ability rather than action. It's also stronger than starting your question with 'would', which is conditional and implies possibility more than probability.

★ USING COGNITIVE DISSONANCE IN YOUR FAVOUR

In Law 5 I explained how harmful the phenomenon of cognitive dissonance can be, I'm now going to tell you how helpful it can be.

Cognitive dissonance describes the mental discomfort you experience when the best you – the person you really want to be – doesn't match up with the person you currently are. Let's say you aspire to be an expert in Tai Chi and a friend asks whether you practise Tai Chi daily. Answering no would create cognitive dissonance because it would highlight a disconcerting mismatch between who you want to be and who you actually are. To remove that mismatch you're likely to answer yes. And, once you've done that, your aspiration is more likely to become a reality because the question has reminded you of not only who you want to be but the path to becoming that person, and you've set an intention to walk that path – all in the form of one small but powerful question.

The reason this works even more effectively when answering a yes or no question is because these binary choices don't allow for justification and excuses – both of which allow us to wriggle away from confronting the reality of who we want to be and what we need to do to get there.

If you've read my first book, you'll know that my wonderful PA, Sophie, likes to announce every week that she's 'going to the gym on Monday'. On occasion, when I've been naive and gullible enough to ask her if she went to the gym on the aforesaid Monday, she'll respond with a long, elaborate reason why it wasn't possible and follow that with a new announcement that she's going to go next Monday instead. She's continued this routine every week for eight years now.

The great thing about a 'yes' or 'no' question is it doesn't give you any wiggle room to deceive yourself. It forces you to commit one way or the other.

So, if you start making excuses for your behaviour or want to lecture someone about what they should do differently, try this instead: ask yourself or them a simple question to which the answer can only be yes or no. It works really well when focusing on an area that could benefit from some additional motivation. 'Will I go to the gym today?' 'Will I order healthy food for lunch?' Allow no explanation. Just yes or no. Recently, I went for a run near my girlfriend's house in Porto, Portugal. The area is known for its steep hills, but as I approached one particularly terrifying hill that was so steep it appeared almost vertical, the question/ behaviour effect came to my rescue. I asked myself, 'Will you keep running – without stopping – until you've reached the top?' I told myself 'yes'. I can't really explain it, but for some reason it really helped – I made it to the top without stopping; it killed any possible excuses I might have used to stop and it created a promise to myself that I didn't want to break.

Use the question/behaviour effect to help others: ask a friend or loved one, 'Will you eat more healthily?' or 'Will you go for that promotion?' This gentle confrontation has been repeatedly proven to lead to reliable, meaningful change and encourages people to be their best selves.

Use it in your job. If you're a waiter in a restaurant serving a table of happy customers, instead of telling them 'I hope you enjoyed your food' when you're collecting their plates, instead ask 'Did you like the food?' just as you're handing over the bill, right before it's time for them to decide on the tip.

As President Reagan taught us, when the facts are clearly on your side, questions become extremely powerful tools for encouraging the behaviour you want.

★ THE LAW: ASK, DON'T TELL – THE QUESTION/BEHAVIOUR EFFECT

If you want to create positive behaviour, don't make statements, ask binary yes or no questions. People are more likely to answer 'yes' if it will bring them closer to who they want to be, and once they answer 'yes', that yes is more likely to come true.

Ask questions of your actions, and your actions will answer.

LAW 7

NEVER COMPROMISE YOUR SELF-STORY

This law introduces a concept you've probably never heard before called your 'self-story'; it shows you how your self-story determines your success in life, and gives you the secret strategy for writing a better self-story about yourself, so you can achieve big ambitions.

'A lot of people don't know this …' Chris Eubank Jr said, as he leaned forward ominously in his chair.

Chris Eubank Jr, championship boxer and son of the International Boxing Hall of Fame legend Chris Eubank, had stopped by my house to be interviewed by me in preparation for this book.

He continued:

…but 80 per cent of being a fighter is mental. The balls, the guts and the grit that you have to have, to walk through crowds of thousands of people. And while you're walking, knowing that once you get to that ring and walk up those stairs, you're going to have to take off your jacket. The bell's going to ring and you're going to have to fight somebody. You're going to have to get hurt and you're going to have to hurt somebody, in front of millions of people watching around the world. That in itself, that walk, most people on the planet cannot do that. Just the walk, let alone the fight part, it takes huge mental strength.

Me: Do you think you can train someone to have that mental strength?

Eubank Jr: I think you can; I've seen fighters develop it, and you need it. At the end of the day, there are going to be times in training, in sparring and definitely in fighting where you're going to get really hurt. You're going to be in a position where you're questioning yourself. What am I doing here? Am I going to be OK? Can I beat this guy? Should I give up? Should I find a way out? This is too much. Every fighter experiences that moment, you know.

Me: Have you ever seriously considered quitting in a fight?

Long pause

Eubank Jr: There was this one time where I was close to giving up. I went to Cuba before I turned pro. Out there, the guys are animals. They're monsters. I get in the ring to do a casual sparring session and then the Cuban Olympic heavyweight representative walks up the stairs and gets into the ring. I thought he was coming into the ring to shadow box and warm up for his sparring session with somebody else. And they said, 'No, no, no, no, you guys are going to spar.' I was like, 'Uh, he's about three times the size of me. What do you mean?' And they said, 'No, no, he'll work with you, just a casual spar.' So I thought, *Sure. That's fine. Let's go.*

The bell goes for the first round and this guy sprints over to me and just starts laying into me. The biggest shots I've ever taken. Bang, bang, bang. I'm dodging, moving out the way, running around the ring. And he's just coming at me and I can't get this guy off me.

Bang, bang, bang. He knocks me out of the ring! It's a four-foot drop out of the ring onto solid concrete. My knee hits the concrete and my leg goes completely dead. I tried getting up and my leg is completely gone. I'm looking up and this Cuban heavyweight is leaning over the ropes, looking down at me. I'm at a mental crossroads and I have a decision to make. Do I say, 'Listen, my knee's bad. You're too big.' Or do I get back in. I'm sat there on the concrete, looking around. Everyone's looking at me, my dad is there. I made a decision. I was like, you know what, let's fucking go. I got back in, and the Cuban just started laying into me again for another two painful rounds ... But the only thing I could think was: *I have to finish the three rounds, because I said I was going to do the three rounds. I'm not leaving this gym with everybody knowing that I quit. Because I couldn't live with myself. I've got to go home and go to sleep. I can't go to sleep knowing that another man made me quit.* So I got back into that ring and I took my beating like a man. And from that day on, I was never scared again. It was the worst experience of my life, but it was also the best experience of my life because I now knew what I was capable of. I knew I had it inside me to not give up. If he can't make me quit, who's going to make me quit? Nobody. And that belief stayed with me for the rest of my career.

Me: That's incredible. You're talking about a story you're writing about yourself, for yourself, and how important that story is in determining how you behave in the future.

Eubank Jr: Exactly. In training it happens the most: there are times I'll be on the treadmill, where I'll be running, and I'll get cramp in my calf and I've still got 8 minutes to go, because I've set the timer for 40 minutes and I'm on 32 minutes. The cramp starts and I will run with one leg, literally limping, because if the treadmill can make me quit, what happens when I get into the ring with a guy who's hit me, and I'm hurt? He's going to make me quit too. It's hugely important because it teaches you to believe that no matter how hard things get, you are the type of person that will find a way.

It doesn't matter if people are watching, or if nobody would know I quit. You can't quit when no one is watching – you don't ever want to put that, that spirit inside yourself, you've got to keep those demons out. They are demons and if you let them in often enough, they will take over!

'I hated every minute of training, but I said, "Don't quit. Suffer now and live the rest of your life as a champion."'

Muhammad Ali

★ YOUR SELF-STORY CREATES 'MENTAL TOUGHNESS'

The US military is the most powerful on earth. Each year, roughly 1,300 cadets join its famously demanding military academy at West Point. Part of their initiation involves a series of extremely difficult challenges called 'Beast Barracks'. These, according to researchers who studied West Point cadets, are 'deliberately engineered to test the very limits of cadets' mental capacities'.

When I read about their study, I, like most people, assumed that the cadets with the most stamina, intelligence, physical strength and athleticism would be the most successful. But when Angela Duckworth, a researcher at the University of Pennsylvania, studied their achievements, and more specifically, how mental toughness, perseverance and passion impact ability to achieve goals, she found something very surprising.

Duckworth tracked almost 2,500 cadets spread across two initiation classes. She compared several metrics including their high school rank, SAT scores, Physical Aptitude Test results and Grit Scale (which measures perseverance and passion for long-term goals with a grade from one to five).

It turned out that it wasn't physical strength, intelligence or leadership potential that gave the most accurate indication of whether a cadet would make it through Beast Barracks – it came down to mental toughness, matched with determination to reach a long-term goal. Perseverance was the most important thing. Believe it or not, cadets who were just one standard deviation point higher on the Grit Scale were *60 per cent* more likely to make it through Beast Barracks.

Research continues to reveal that your self-story and the 'mental toughness', 'grit' or 'resilience' that you have is more important than anything else for achieving your goals in business and in life. That's very good to know because while you can't do much about your physicality or the innate abilities you are born with, you *can* do a lot to develop your self-story.

Unfortunately, our self-story isn't just influenced by the first-party evidence we've collected about ourselves, it's also influenced profoundly by the stereotypes around us. For instance, if the society you live in holds the stereotype that Black people are less capable than white people – and you're a Black person – you will likely internalise that belief and it will become part of your self-story; the science shows how this stereotype alone can significantly impact your self-story, your performance and ultimately your results.

At eight years old, I was eagerly putting on my swimming shorts in the school changing room ahead of my first swimming lesson, when a fellow pupil turned to me and casually said, 'Did you know Black people can't swim? Their bodies are different, so it won't be easy for you today!' I am of English and African heritage, so in that moment, with that one casual comment, not only did my excitement evaporate, but so did my belief that I would ever be able to swim. Needless to say, that swimming lesson did not go well – I flapped around like a drowning dog and ultimately gave up halfway through the lesson. It would take me 18 years, and someone credible convincing me that this wasn't true, for me to finally learn how to swim.

A remarkable study published in 1995 used something called 'priming' to demonstrate the effects that this type of 'stereotype threat' can have on your self-story.

Researchers gave a group of students a difficult vocabulary test, but before the test began, they asked some of the Black students questions about their race. Astonishingly, the Black students who were asked about their race performed worse on the test, scoring lower than both the white students and the Black students who had not been questioned.

Importantly, when students were not asked these questions, the scores were comparable.

The insidious impact a negative stereotype can have on someone's self-story isn't just observed in matters of race. In another study, researchers wanted to test the pernicious myth that says women aren't as good at maths as men. Before setting both male and female undergraduates the test, some of the participants heard the researcher say that as a rule, men and women scored differently on this test; others were told that men and women had previously scored equally.

The women who heard the researcher's negative comments performed significantly worse, reported greater anxiety and had lower expectations about their performance than the men. This experiment confirmed earlier studies by finding that when participants were exposed to a comment about their gender, a stereotype threat kicked in and their performance deteriorated.

So, what would happen if a woman could escape her identity, change her self-story and pretend to be someone else while writing the test?

A researcher called Shen Zhang set out to test this. Zhang gave 110 female undergraduates and 72 male undergraduates 30 multiple-choice maths questions. Before the test, each of them was told that men do better at maths than women. In addition, some of the volunteers were then told to take the test under their real name, but others were to complete it under one of four invented names: Jacob Tyler, Scott Lyons, Jessica Peterson or Kaitlyn Woods.

- The men outperformed the women in the test. But astoundingly, women who assumed an alias, whether it was male or female, outperformed the women who didn't. And –

importantly – the women adopting an alias did just as well as the men!

This demonstrated once and for all the merits of tests and interviews using alternative identification methods that avoided names – in the researcher's words, this would potentially 'allow stigmatised individuals to disconnect their self from a threatening situation', and crucially, 'disarm negative stereotypes'.

★ THE SCIENCE OF DEVELOPING A STRONG SELF-STORY IN YOUR HEALTH, WORK AND LIFE

The 'self-story' Chris Eubank Jr was describing is a theory scientists and psychologists know well and refer to as your 'self-concept'. It is our personal belief of who we are, encompassing all our thoughts and feelings about ourselves – physically, personally and socially. It includes our beliefs about our capabilities, our potential and our competence.

Your self-story develops most rapidly during early childhood and adolescence, but it continues to form and change as we collect more evidence about ourselves throughout our adult life.

YOUR SELF-STORY CREATES MENTAL TOUGHNESS

Psychology professor Fatwa Tentama states that individual 'resilience' is influenced by having a positive self-story. Individuals with a positive self-story will be more optimistic, persevere for longer in the face of adversity, handle stress better and achieve their goals more easily.

'Individuals with a low self-concept will believe and view themselves as weak, incompetent, unwelcome, lose interest in life, be pessimistic about life and give up easily.'

Laura Polk, scientist and leadership expert

One study on students, conducted by Eka Aryani, a scientist at Mercu Buana University of Yogyakarta in Indonesia, sought to understand the relationship between self-story and resilience, and concluded that 'self-story' is almost 40 per cent of what makes a student 'mentally tough'. The other 60 per cent of factors that can affect individual resilience include actual abilities, family factors, and community factors.

So how do we improve our self-story so that we can be resilient and optimistic, achieve our goals and persevere in the face of adversity?

CREATING A STRONGER SELF-STORY

You've probably heard this quote by legendary college basketball coach John Wooden: 'The true test of a man's character is what he does when no one is watching.' This is true, but according to science, it's also true that a person's character is created, built or destroyed when no one is watching.

Everything you do – with or without an audience – provides evidence to you about who you are and what you're capable of.

As we discovered in Law 4, first-party evidence – that is, everything you observe with your own senses – is by far the strongest evidence when it comes to creating or changing a belief.

You're in the gym alone lifting weights, you're on your last set and you've got to do ten repetitions to complete the workout. You get to the ninth rep and your muscles are burning – what do you do?

Your choice, in this moment, may seem inconsequential – but every decision we make writes another line of powerful first-party evidence, about who we are, how we respond to adversity and what we're capable of, into today's chapter of our self-story.

That evidence will not only become self-fulfilling in the gym, it will permeate the rest of your life and relentlessly influence your behaviour.

That evidence will whisper to you when things are difficult – 'just drop the weight', 'just give up', 'remember, you can't do this' – and science shows that in the face of adversity, negative self-evidence will cause you more stress, more worry and more anxiety than a story full of perseverance, overcoming and victory.

What we believe about ourselves creates our thoughts and feelings, our thoughts and feelings determine our actions, and our actions create our evidence. To create new evidence you must change your actions.

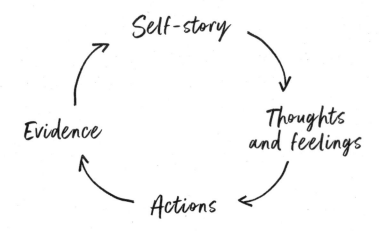

Choose to do the tenth rep when it would be easier to stop at nine. Choose to have the difficult conversation when it would be easier to avoid it. Choose to ask the extra question when it would be easier to stay silent. Prove to yourself – in a thousand tiny ways, at every opportunity you get – that you have what it takes to overcome the challenges of life. And if you do – only then will you actually have what it takes to overcome the challenges of life – a robust, positive, evidence-based self-story.

★ THE LAW: NEVER COMPROMISE YOUR SELF-STORY

Mental toughness is required for enduring success, and it's principally derived from having a positive self-story. To build your self-story, you need evidence, and that evidence is derived from the choices you make in the face of adversity. Be wary of counter-evidence and the insidious long-term impact it can have on your self-belief and behaviour. If an eight-year-old tells you that you can't swim, tell him to fuck off.

The most
convincing sign
that someone
will achieve
new results in
the future is
new behaviour
in the present.

LAW 8

NEVER FIGHT A BAD HABIT

This law reveals some surprising truths about how to make and break any bad habit you have. It shows you why fighting bad habits is a failing strategy which often leads to rebounding – and what you should do instead.

I grew up worrying that my dad was going to die.

At some point before I turned ten, my siblings and I discovered that Dad was a secret smoker – presumably he'd hidden it from us to stop us replicating his habit. But once we'd found his miniature cigars, he began smoking in front of us.

Surprisingly to me, he only ever smoked in the car. Never at parties, never at home, never at work, only in the car. I made a few subtle attempts to get him to quit, but nothing worked. Until one day, ten years later, when I inadvertently led him to finally quit his 40-year habit.

In order to explain what happened, I first need to briefly explain how habits are held in place.

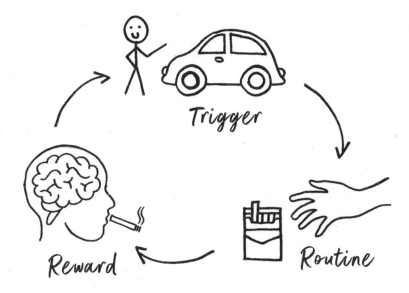

The concept of **habit loops** was introduced by Charles Duhigg in his book *The Power of Habit,* in which he explores how and why habits develop, why they stick and how we can break them. Simplified, a habit loop consists of three key elements:

- CUE: The trigger for habitual behaviour (e.g. a stressful meeting or negative event).

- ROUTINE: The habitual behaviour (e.g. smoking a cigarette or eating chocolate).

- REWARD: The result/impact on you of the habitual behaviour (e.g. a feeling of relief or happiness).

When I was 18 years old, after dropping out of university to build my first tech start-up, I read a book called *Hooked* by Nir Eyal which explains how big social media companies and tech companies get their users addicted to their products by exploiting this habit loop. While I was reading the book, I happened to stop off at home, and accidently left it in my dad's bathroom.

My dad loves to read while he's on the toilet, and picked the book up. It taught him about his habit loop, and he finally understood the cue (his car), routine (reaching into the car door, grabbing the cigarettes and lighting one), and reward (nicotine creating a dopamine release in his brain) that were causing him to smoke.

The next day he went to his car, took the cigarettes out, put miniature lollipops into the cigarette case, and never smoked again. The habit loop had been interrupted. A new, less-addictive habit had taken its place, and with that my father's health outcomes had drastically improved.

Whether my father realised it or not, the science shows that the most important thing he did was not trying to fight the habit, but **replacing the final step of the habit loop with a much less addictive reward** – the lollipops.

Some incredible new scientific research has revealed just how foolish it is to try and fight your bad habits – and why people always seem to rebound when they do.

Have you ever noticed that when you focus too much on stopping something, you ultimately end up rebounding and do it more?

This is because we are action-oriented creatures, not inaction-oriented creatures. Tali Sharot, who we met in Law 3, said to me:

> To get something good in life – whether it's a chocolate cake or a promotion – we usually need to take

action and do something to earn it. Consequently, our brain has adapted to understand that action is related to reward. So when we expect something good, a 'go' signal is activated, which makes us more likely to act – and act fast.

Sharot describes an experiment where volunteers were told they could either press a button to get a reward (one dollar) or press a button to avoid a negative action (losing one dollar). Perhaps unsurprisingly, the volunteers who pressed the button to get the reward did so much more speedily than the volunteers who pressed the button not to lose the dollar.

The brain associates rewards with action, so you need to pair an action with a reward.

Additionally, some studies have shown that the more you try to suppress an action or thought, the more likely you are to take the action, or think about that thought. This is great evidence for the power of manifestation – you get what you think about – but it's also further evidence that trying to fight or not think about a habit is a foolish strategy.

A 2008 study in *Appetite* found that the group of volunteers who tried not to think about eating ate more than the group who didn't. The first group exhibited what is called a 'behavioural rebound effect'.

Similarly, a 2010 study in *Psychological Science* found that the group of smokers who tried not to think about smoking actually thought about it even more than the group who didn't.

This reminds me of a small piece of advice my driving instructor said to me when I was 18: 'Steven, the car will go where your eyes are looking. If you want to avoid crashing into the cars on the side of the road, don't focus on the cars on the side of the road, because you will veer towards the parked cars on the side of the road. Look forwards, into the distance, where you want the car to go.'

This seems like a fitting analogy for breaking and making habits: you will end up doing the thing you're focusing on, so don't focus on stopping smoking, don't fight it; focus on the behaviour you want to replace it with.

The director of the University of Oregon's Social and Affective Neuroscience Laboratory, Elliot Berkman, says that if you're a smoker and you tell yourself not to smoke, your brain still hears 'smoke'. Conversely, if you tell yourself to chew gum every time you want a cigarette, your brain has a more positive, action-orientated goal to focus on. This explains why those miniature lollipops caused my dad to quit smoking: he didn't just take the cigarettes out of his car door; he replaced them with a new action for his brain to focus on – sucking lollipops.

★ IF YOU WANT TO BREAK A HABIT, GET SOME SLEEP

'When do you sleep?' is a question that I've been asked almost weekly for the last ten years, by more interviewers, panel moderators and journalists than I can remember. The implied assumption behind this question – which has always perplexed me – is that I can't have accomplished extensive professional success while also getting a sufficient amount of sleep. The truth is very much the opposite – I've always slept well. I don't allow any meeting, call or appointment to be scheduled before 11am and I rarely use an alarm clock, because I've always known that sleep is the foundation of success, not an inhibitor of it.

'You're more likely to do the thing you don't want to do when you're stressed out,' said Russell Poldrack, a psychology professor at Stanford University – i.e. you're more likely to search out a dopamine hit, in the form of sugar, processed food, drugs, porn or alcohol, if you're stressed.

Therefore, one of the most important things you can do to make new habits stick, and perform enough repetitions in that early phase to make the neurons in your brain fire together and wire together, is keep your stress levels low – especially in that critical early phase while you're forming the new habit.

One of the most effective things you can do is also the simplest: get a good night's sleep. Whatever you're trying to improve, from your social life to your smoking habit, sleep will help.

If you're trying to get fit, getting enough sleep improves your speed, your strength and your endurance. If you're trying to perform better at work, a lack of sleep will lead you to be less productive – and if you're a manager, less attentive, less focused, less cheerful and even less ethical.

If you're trying to lose weight or eat more healthily, sleep deprivation will decrease leptin, the hormone that gives your body the signal that you are full. It also leads to a corresponding increase in ghrelin, known as the 'hunger hormone', which causes a surge in appetite and fat storage, and can lead to you making unhealthy food choices.

So, if you want to break old habits and make new ones, forget all the complicated tips, tricks and hacks, and focus on the basics – you'll succeed if you **feel good**, if you're **not over-stressed** and if you've had **a good night's sleep**.

★ DO NOT TAKE ON MORE THAN ONE HABIT AT A TIME

We all know that willpower is key to success, but until about 25 years ago we had a pretty simplistic view of it as a skill that, once developed, remains constant. This all changed when, during his PhD, Mark Muraven (now professor at the University at Albany, New York) argued that willpower appears to diminish the more we use it.

In 1998, he conducted a now famous experiment. In his lab, he set up a bowl of radishes and a bowl of freshly baked cookies, then brought in two groups of people who were led to believe the experiment was about taste perception. The first group was told they could eat the cookies and ignore the radishes, while the other was asked to ignore the cookies and eat only the radishes.

Five minutes into the experiment, a researcher entered the room and, after a 15-minute break, gave both groups a puzzle that was impossible to complete.

The cookie eaters, with their unused reservoirs of willpower, were incredibly relaxed, and would continue to try and solve it over and over and over again, some of them for over half an hour. On average, the cookie eaters spent almost 19 minutes trying to solve the puzzle before giving up.

The radish eaters – who'd had to restrain themselves from eating the delicious cookies, depleting their willpower – couldn't have behaved more differently. They became frustrated and expressed their annoyance. Some put their heads on the table hopelessly; others lost their temper and took against the entire thing, complaining it was a waste of their time. On average, the radish eaters worked for around eight minutes – less than half the time the cookie eaters persevered for – before they gave up.

Since the cookie/radish study, several researchers have tested and proven 'willpower depletion': the idea that rather than willpower being simply a skill, it is more like a muscle and – as with any muscle in the body – it gets tired as it works harder. In one, participants who were asked not to think about certain things during a first experiment were unable to suppress laughter when the researcher tried to make them giggle. Another experiment asked subjects to watch a tear-jerker without giving in to their emotions; in a subsequent test of something physical rather than something emotional, the subjects – just like the unfortunate radish-eaters – gave up more quickly.

So if the science here is correct, and willpower is a limited resource, it's obvious that the more pressure, restrictions and strain you put on yourself while trying to make new habits and break old ones, the less chance you have of achieving them and the more chance you have of rebounding.

Fighting habits is a bad idea – it will drain your willpower and increase your chances of yo-yoing back into the habit. This is why unsustainable crash diets do not work – any time you feel like you're depriving yourself of something that you really want, you nearly always fail. For instance, in a 2014 study, almost 40 per cent of people said they failed to keep their New Year's resolutions because their goal was too unsustainable or unrealistic, and 10 per cent said they failed because they had too many resolutions.

This is why making sure your habits are small and achievable enough to be sustainable – without the need for major sacrifice, which will deplete your willpower reserves – is incredibly important. Rather than giving up every unwanted habit you have at the same time, you should aim to have fewer goals, which increases the likelihood that you will complete any of them. With too many big, unrealistic, sacrifice-centric goals, your willpower will be under too much strain, it will run out, you'll fail, and you'll rebound.

And this is also why so many psychologists and scientists have found that the best way to create a new habit isn't by fighting an old one or depriving yourself of rewards – which is counter-productive – it's by **finding new rewards, healthier rewards and less addictive rewards, but nonetheless making sure you *are* still rewarding yourself** along the way.

★ THE LAW: NEVER FIGHT A BAD HABIT

If you want to overcome a habit, do not fight against it. Work with your habit loop and use positive action to replace it. Do not take on more than one bad habit at once; the more you try and change, the less your chances of changing anything. While you're creating your new habit, make sure you take care of yourself and get as much sleep as you can.

Sleep, Lift, Move,
Smile, Laugh, Listen.
Read, Save, Hydrate,
Fast, Build, Create.

Your habits are
your future.

LAW 9

ALWAYS PRIORITISE YOUR FIRST FOUNDATION

This law makes the case that most of us have the wrong priorities – and it urges you to re-prioritise your health, so that you can live long enough to enjoy all your other priorities.

Warren Buffett, formally the richest man on earth, sat in front of a small group of college students in Omaha, Nebraska, and gave them his most important piece of advice:

> When I was 16, I had just two things on my mind – girls and cars. I wasn't very good with girls. So I thought about cars. I thought about girls, too, but I had more luck with cars.
>
> Let's say that when I turned 16, a genie had appeared to me. And that genie said, 'I'm going to give you the car of your choice. It'll be here tomorrow morning with a big bow tied on it. Brand-new. And it's all yours!'
>
> Having heard all the genie stories, I would say, 'What's the catch?' And the genie would answer, 'There's only one catch … This is the last car you're ever going to get in your life. So it's got to last a lifetime.'

If that had happened, I would have picked out a car, but, can you imagine, knowing it had to last a lifetime, what I would do with it?

I would read the manual about five times. I would always keep it garaged. If there was the least little dent or scratch, I'd have it fixed right away because I wouldn't want it rusting. I would baby that car, because it would have to last a lifetime.

This is exactly the position you are in concerning your mind and body. You only get one mind, and you only get one body. And it's got to last a lifetime. Now, it's very easy to let them ride for many years.

But if you don't take care of that mind and that body, they'll be a wreck 40 years later, just like the car would be.

It's what you do right now, today, that determines how your mind and body will operate 10, 20, and 30 years from now.

You must take care of it.

I spent the first 80 per cent of my life prioritising work, girls, friends, family, my dog and my material possessions.

Until, that is, I was 27 years old, when I and the rest of the world watched a global virus called Covid-19 sweep through civilisation, tragically killing more than 6 million people.

Because of the privilege of my youth and the naivety that instilled, up until then, being 'healthy' was something I took for granted. If I'm totally honest, I didn't care about my health; I cared about looking good – trying to get a six-pack – but actually 'being healthy' was something I'd fortunately never had to think about.

I think the global pandemic was psychologically traumatic for most of us, but if there was a silver lining for me, it's that the trauma of those two years etched the unarguable truth into my mind that **my health should in fact be my top priority**.

An international team of researchers announced that pooled data from scores of peer-reviewed papers capturing almost 400,000 Covid-19 patients found that people with obesity who contracted Covid-19 were 113 per cent more likely to fall so ill that they would need to be hospitalised. Unhealthy individuals were significantly more likely to die.

I have a strong enduring belief that none of us actually believe we're going to die – this is so clearly evidenced by how we live our lives, the petty things we worry about and our attitude to risk. However, Covid-19 brought death to my doorstep, I got to see death up close and all too personal for the first time in my life. I was able to ponder its terrifying, liberating and uncertain features.

Staring into the clarifying face of death, I could see how poorly I had prioritised my life. I could see that my work, my girlfriend, my friends, my dog, my family and everything I owned were all just items placed on a fragile table called my 'health'.

Life could take any of those items off the table – as it often does – and I would still have everything else on the table. You could remove my dog, God forbid, and I'd still have everything else on the table; you could take my girlfriend off the table, and I would still have everything else; but if you removed the table – my health – everything falls to the floor. I would lose it all.

Everything is contingent on the table.

Everything is contingent on my health.

My health is my first foundation.

Therefore my health, logically, must be my first priority, every day, for ever.

And crucially, by embracing this reality – by having health as my first priority – my life is extended so I can enjoy all of my other priorities (my dog, my partner, my family) even more.

There is no greater form of gratitude than taking care of yourself.

This one realisation changed the trajectory of my life, and for the past three years I have made radical dietary changes – cutting down sugar, processed food and refined grains. I began exercising six days a week – without missing a week – and I have drastically increased my consumption of water, plants and probiotics.

I'm objectively healthy, which is great, but I also feel amazing – which is even better. The positive impact on every part of my life – my business, productivity, sleep, relationship, mood, sex life, confidence – has been so profound that I couldn't write this book without including taking care of your first foundation as an unavoidable law of greatness.

'Those who think they have no time for bodily exercise will sooner or later have to find time for illness.'

Edward Stanley

★ THE LAW: ALWAYS PRIORITISE YOUR FIRST FOUNDATION

Take care of your body; it is, after all, the only vehicle you get to own, the only vessel you'll use to explore the world and the only house you can ever truly call a home.

Your health is your first foundation.

PILLAR II
THE STORY

LAW 10

USELESS ABSURDITY WILL DEFINE YOU MORE THAN USEFUL PRACTICALITIES

This law shows you how to make your marketing or brand message travel ten times further and reach ten times more people, with a hundredth of the budget.

I started my first marketing company when I was 20 years old. The business grew faster than my experience could possibly have handled and a year after founding the company I accepted a $300,000 investment from our biggest client.

When you give an inexperienced 20-year-old first-time-CEO a lot of money – more money than they've ever seen in their life – there's a chance they might do something really stupid with it. And that's a fitting description of exactly what happened.

I took out a ten-year lease on a gigantic 15,000-square-foot warehouse in Manchester, in the north of England, large enough to accommodate hundreds of employees – but there were ten of us.

Before I had even purchased desks for my team to work on, I had built a mezzanine floor and installed a gaming room so that we could play video games. Uninspired by the prospect of using stairs to exit the gaming room, I decided to spend £13,000 on an enormous blue slide with a big ball pool at the bottom.

By the time the desks arrived, I had installed a basketball hoop, a fully stocked bar, beer taps, a massive tree right in the middle of the office, and several other immature fittings.

Over the next few years, even though the average age of our employees was just 21, the company became the most publicised, the most mentioned, the fastest growing and the most disruptive in its industry. Our sales grew by more than 200 per cent per year, on average, for several years in a row. Our clients were the world's biggest brands, and our workforce swelled to more than 500 people by my 25th birthday.

And the most fascinating part of this story is that we never had a sales team.

We didn't need a sales team because we had a massive blue slide.

I know this sounds crazy – like hyperbole and exaggeration – but genuinely, the single biggest driver of our media publicity for the first few years of our existence was that gigantic blue slide.

Every major press title that wrote about us, every TV channel, every blog that mentioned us always referenced, joked about or focused in on the massive blue slide.

By my company's third birthday, it had been photographed by journalists hundreds of times, and so many journalists had asked me to pose lying in the ball pool for their stories that it had become a running joke in our office. The minute a journalist would arrive at reception to interview me, someone in the office would shout 'Get in the ball pool!' at me, without fail.

The BBC, BuzzFeed, VICE News, Channel 4, Channel 5, ITV, *Forbes*, *GQ*, the *Guardian*, the *Telegraph*, the *Financial*

Times – they all queued up to come to our office, to cover our story and to interview us, and the headline image of the story nearly always featured a picture of that big blue slide. In one BBC story they called our office the 'coolest' in the country, and when VICE came to make a documentary about us, the crew spent most of their time shooting the ball pool and big blue slide from different angles.

In hindsight, our entire founding team all agree, one of the best financial decisions – albeit stupid, unintended and immature – that we made, was spending £13,000 of our investment on that big blue slide.

Admittedly, I only saw the slide used a handful of times in the seven years that I ran the company, but the slide's usefulness should never have been measured on its intended purpose, but rather on its effectiveness as a marketing message.

The slide screamed something about us to the world; it said, 'this company is different', 'this company is young', 'this company is disruptive' and 'this company is innovative'. It communicated that message louder and more convincingly than any marketing campaign we ever crafted.

If a picture paints a thousand words, our big blue slide wrote an entire book – and that book is a story of our values, who we are, what we believe and how we behave.

I'm absolutely not telling you to go and blow your money on a big blue slide, but I am telling you that your public story will be defined not by all the useful practical things that you do – in many cases, not even by the products that you sell – but by the **useless absurdity** that your brand is associated with.

My friend recently joined a gym in London called Third Space. Third Space is arguably the largest high-end gym in London, spanning three pristine floors. In an attempt to get me to join he said, 'You should come – it's so good, they even have a 100-foot climbing wall in the entrance!'

Did you see what he did there? He did what everyone does. He didn't mention their hundreds of useful exercise machines, the incredibly useful weight racks or the very useful changing rooms; he sold me the gym based on the most absurd quality it possesses.

And I must be honest, it worked. I've now been a member of that gym for more than a year, and in that year, I have never, not once, seen anyone go anywhere near the 100-foot climbing wall.

But when you hear that a gym has a 100-foot climbing wall, your subconscious mind thinks, *If the gym has a 100-foot climbing wall, then they must have everything!* or *If a gym has 100-foot climbing wall, it must be huge.* Or if you're Gen Z or a millennial, *If a gym has a 100-foot climbing wall they must have so many other fun, crazy things that I can take a picture of and upload to social media!*

> A brand's publicity is defined more by its useless absurdity than its useful practicalities; the most absurd thing about you says <u>everything</u> about you.

★ TESLA'S MARKETING STRATEGY IS ABSURDITY

In a fraction of the time that it's taken some of their competitors, Tesla has become one of the world's bestselling car companies. The Tesla Model Y is the bestselling car in Europe and the Tesla Model 3 is one of the bestselling luxury vehicles in the United States. Tesla's advertising budget is $0.

Like my marketing agency didn't need a sales team and my gym probably doesn't need a marketing team, Tesla doesn't need to advertise because it's a brand driven and defined by its absurdity.

It is riddled with intentionally absurd features to make its customers, the media and the public at large talk, laugh and spread the word about the car. Whereas most car companies have named their driving modes 'Comfort', 'Standard' and 'Sport', Tesla has amusingly embraced the power of absurd-ity by calling theirs 'Insane', 'Ludicrous' and 'Ludicrous+'.

In 2019, Teslas got a new 'Caraoke' function which allows owners to turn their car into a karaoke machine, and in 2015, Tesla famously released a 'Bioweapon Defense Mode' which protects the driver from 'bioweapons'. They introduced an 'Arcade' mode which turns the car into an arcade on wheels; they installed 'Easter eggs' – hidden features that the driver has to find, which include making the car look like Santa's sleigh, turning the road ahead into a rainbow, and even a 'farting mode' that causes the car to produce fart sounds from any passenger seat in the car.

All these things sound immature and stupid – like my big blue slide – but when you delve into the social-listening data, these absurd features produce more conversations than the useful features of all of their key competitors combined.

People have no incentive to think, talk or write about things that maintain the status quo, but they have a tremen-dous incentive to share absurd things that mock it, tear it down and laugh in the face of it.

★ BEER SHOWERS HELPED MAKE BREWDOG BILLIONS

BrewDog, the indie brewery, became the fastest-growing beer brand in the UK in 2019. They too have been in operation for far less time than most of their rivals and they have a fraction of the marketing budget of some of their global competitors –

some two centuries old or more. But once again, this financial disadvantage hasn't inhibited their marketing reach, because their strategy – for better or for worse – intentionally evokes the power of absurdity in spreading their message.

When they launched the BrewDog hotel chain in 2021, they installed beer fridges inside every shower so that customers can guzzle beer as they wash. I'm pretty sure nobody – at least no sane person – is going to use it, but a quick Google Images search shows that a significant number of photos of the hotels contain a picture of the beer fridge in the shower. The most absurd thing about the brand is saying everything about the brand.

Without directly saying anything at all, the presence of that beer fridge screams to customers: 'we are for beer lovers', 'we are a punk brand', 'we don't care about the rules', 'we are disruptive', 'we have a sense of humour', 'this hotel is for people that are different', and again, if you're in a younger generation, it's saying, 'this hotel will give you great content for your social media channels'.

★ ★ ★

If it's that powerful, why doesn't everyone lean in to absurdity? Because most business leaders, CFOs and accountants demand direct measurable ROI from their marketing, brand and product initiatives. The absurdity I'm describing is incredibly difficult to measure or quantify, and so like many things in marketing, storytelling and branding – you either believe in it or you don't.

From what I've witnessed over my decade-long tenure of advising the world's leading brands, those few people that do believe in, and act upon, the power of absurdity, are nearly always company founders (appointed CEOs are typically more risk averse, have less financial control and have less conviction about brand values). Their marketing dollar nearly always goes ten times further than their rivals', and they always seem to outpace the rest of their industry over the long term. Most importantly, they're just more fun people to work with.

If you look around you, you'll notice that the most powerful brand storytelling leverages the power of absurdity, illogicality, costliness, inefficiency and nonsensicality, because convention, similarity and rationality, for all their usefulness, convey no message about who you are and who you aren't.

> 'Meaning is conveyed by the things we do that are not in our own short-term self-interest – by the costs that we incur and the risks we take.'

Rory Sutherland, vice chairman of the Ogilvy advertising group

✶ THE LAW: USELESS ABSURDITY WILL DEFINE YOU MORE THAN USEFUL PRACTICALITIES

You'll be known for the most absurd things you do. Those absurd things will do the job of saying everything about you, and you won't have to *say* anything at all. Absurdity is more effective and more fun, but it's not for the faint-hearted: it's for the risk taker, the idiot and the genius.

Normality is ignored.

Absurdity sells.

LAW 11

AVOID WALLPAPER
AT ALL COSTS

This law will teach you the science of grabbing people's attention in everything you write, speak and produce. It's the underlying secret of all of the world's most famous storytellers, marketers and creators.

'I'm going to have to cut my arm off.'

For six days, Aron Ralston kept himself alive with fierce determination, awe-inspiring hope and a powerful innate human survival tool – which we all have built into our system – that allowed him to tune out of the extreme pain he was experiencing for long enough to cut his own arm off his body.

On a spring day in 2003, Ralston drove alone to Moab, Utah, to mountain-bike the dramatic Slickrock Trail and spend a few days solo climbing canyons in preparation for ascending Alaska's Denali (formerly known as Mount McKinley) later in the year. He climbed into Bluejohn canyon on 26 April, and 5 miles in came to a section where huge boulders were wedged between the walls of the canyon. As he slowly worked his way through, he dislodged an 800-pound rock, which slid down and crushed his right hand against the canyon wall.

Not only was his hand reduced to a bloody mess, but he couldn't move the boulder. He was stuck. He hadn't told anyone where he was, had only brought with him a pouch of water and a few snack bars, and wouldn't be declared missing for days.

Ralston was trapped.

After an agonising period of trying to free his trapped arm and going through disbelief, shock and despair, he finally composed himself.

The cheap multi-use pocketknife that he'd brought with him was his only conceivable path to freedom. Over the next few days, he attempted to chip away at the boulder, to no avail. He then tried to chip away at the canyon wall – again, to no avail. Time was running out; he had started with 3 litres of water and now he was down to 1.

As he recalls: 'I was over the pain, I was over the fear, but I couldn't get over my body's need for water.'

Ralston had been imprisoned in the canyon for five days. With no other option, he resolved to do the unthinkable. With his free hand he assembled his things, took a deep breath, and set about cutting off his arm.

He stared momentarily at the dirty blade of his pocketknife, and then plunged it into his trapped arm. The amputation took over an hour, and it worked: he was conscious, he was alive, and he was now free.

Exhausted and bloodstained but overcome with relief and adrenaline, he made his way back out of the canyon. After 6 miles, he was met by some tourists who led him to safety.

It is striking that in Ralston's own book, and in the film *127 Hours*, which portrays his ordeal, just how curiously unemotional, focused and calm he was about his predicament.

'Everything else – the pain, the thought of rescue, the accident itself – recedes. I'm taking action,' he said.

This, while an extreme example, highlights one of the many in-built survival tools of the human brain: its ability to tune out information that it doesn't consider to be relevant, so that we can focus on the new and unfamiliar information that is more important for our survival and wellbeing, even – as in Ralston's case – if that information comes in the form of inconceivable pain, a dire situation or feelings of hopelessness.

When describing parts of his injuries, Ralston remarked in his book: 'Perhaps the strangest thing is that I didn't feel pain from the injury – so many other things were wrong with my circumstances that it wasn't important enough to warrant my brain's attention'.

What Ralston is describing is the incredible psychological phenomenon of habituation.

★ HABITUATION

Habituation is an in-built neurological device that helps us to focus on what matters, and tune out of things that our brain doesn't need to focus on.

Holocaust survivor Elie Wiesel, who was imprisoned in Auschwitz and Buchenwald concentration camps during the Second World War, described how he and his fellow prisoners were exposed to the constant threat of violence and death, as well as the horrific sounds and ghastly smells of the camps. As they spent more time in the camps, their brains underwent habituation: becoming desensitised to the dangers, the sounds, the smells and other hardships they faced.

Pavel Fischl, a young Czech poet who arrived in the Nazi-controlled Theresienstadt ghetto, described how people there quickly got used to their horrific new surroundings:

We have all gotten used to the noise of steps in the barracks' hallways. We have already gotten used to those four dark walls surrounding each barracks. We are used to stand[ing] in long lines, at 7am, at noon, and again at 7pm, holding a bowl to receive a bit of heated water tasting of salt or coffee, or to get a few potatoes. We are wont to sleep without beds, live without radio, record player, cinema, theatre, and the usual worries of average people. [W]e have gotten accustomed to see[ing] people die in their own dirt, to see the sick in filth and disgust [...] we are habituated to wear one shirt one week long; well, one gets used to everything.

Habituation is a phenomenon in which the brain adjusts to repeated stimuli by ignoring or downgrading their significance.

For example, if you are in a room with a constant low-level hum, it might annoy you at first, but you probably won't even notice the sound after a few minutes, because your brain has adapted to it and is no longer processing it.

This cognitive phenomenon frees up mental capacity that we need for other things – new things that might aid in our survival – and it can be observed in any animal with a brain. In one study, researchers put rats in a maze that had chocolate hidden at the end of the maze. They then monitored the rats' brain activity: 'The first time the rat entered the maze sniffing the air and scratching the walls, its brain exploded with activity, as if analysing each new scent, sight, and sound. Although the rat looked calm, the rat's brain was furiously processing everything.'

But once the rat had found the chocolate, when placed back into the maze to find a second piece of chocolate hidden in the same place, the brain activity completely disappeared. The rat was now on autopilot. It no longer needed to process things – it had habituated to the maze – and so it glided on autopilot straight to the chocolate without pause, in the same way that we all glide unconsciously through our habituated lives, to work, to the gym or to a familiar part of our house, without thinking, processing or even noticing familiar environmental information.

Because the rat's brain was now on autopilot, it had freed up cognitive capacity to think about other things. So theoretically, the rat could glide to the chocolate while also pondering a complex problem it was having at work that day. In a world where we didn't habituate to our environment, our brains might implode from the amount of sensory stimuli it's required to process.

★ SEMANTIC SATIATION

Father. Father.

Have you ever noticed that if you repeat any word over and over and over again, it begins to become just a sound? Even when you look at the same word written repeatedly, as seen above, the brain will eventually tune out its meaning. This loss of familiarity sometimes makes a word look like it belongs to another language. Stare longer and it may appear as merely a collection of letters, stare even longer and it'll look like meaningless marks on the paper.

You've probably had your own experiences where the repetition of a word suddenly made it feel weird, alien and confusing – where you've used a word so frequently that you've had to pause for a second, to check the word made sense.

This is all because of a form of habituation called **semantic satiation** – a term coined by Leon James, a professor of psychology at the University of Hawaii's College of Social Sciences – in which the meaning of a word or phrase becomes temporarily inaccessible due to repetition and the brain's inclination to tune out of things it doesn't need to commit resources to.

This effect can be seen in our optical senses too. When patients are given a drug that paralyses their eye muscles, after a few seconds the world in front of them will begin to fade away. They haven't gone to sleep, but the inability to move their eye muscles means that the exact same pattern of light is falling on the receptors in the back of the eye, and for all of our senses, when a certain input is constant, we gradually tune out of it by a process of habituation that cancels out the constant, which in this case is the entire visual world. A hand waved in front of their face (or anything moving) would be enough to bring back the patient's visual world.

HOW HABITUATION HAPPENS

Neuroscientist Eugene Sokolov says that when a stimulus is experienced – words, sounds or even physical sensations – the nervous system essentially creates a 'model' of what caused it, what it is and how the brain should react to it. With most sensory stimuli, no reaction is needed, so when an unimportant stimulus occurs, the model that the brain creates includes instructions to ignore that stimulus in future.

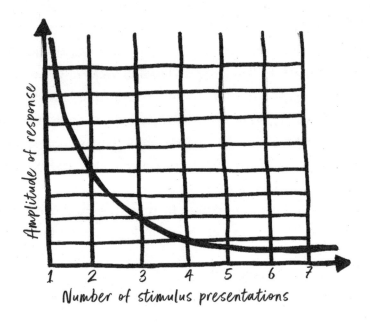

A hypothetical habituation curve in response to repeated stimuli.

★ FEAR SLOWS HABITUATION

WARNING. WARNING. WARNING. WARNING. WARNING. WARNING. WARNING. WARNING. WARNING. WARNING. WARNING. WARNING. WARNING. WARNING. WARNING. WARNING. WARNING.

Interestingly, any word can be affected by semantic satiation, but the amount of time before words begin to lose their meaning varies. For example, emotive words or those that have dramatic connotations – like 'WARNING!' – appear to lack the satiation effect because our brain draws up other strong associations with the word, making it unlikely that its meaning becomes lost.

★ ★ ★

Of all the facial expressions, those related to threats seem to make the biggest impact. For obvious, survival-orientated reasons, it's important for us to distinguish a threatened face from a calm face. Even at just seven months old, babies have been shown to pay more attention to fearful faces when compared with neutral and happy faces.

Having A/B tested more than 200 YouTube thumbnails across my YouTube channel over the last two years, I've consistently found that the more animated, threatening or scary the face on the thumbnail, the more clicks the video will get. Neutral faces – which the brain has become attuned to ignore and deems 'wallpaper' – perform significantly worse in terms of clicks, across all channels.

★ YOU BECOME HABITUATED TO MUSIC AND SOUND

Over the years, Leon James showed that semantic satiation is more than just something that has an impact on things we read: it's at work on every sight, scent and sound in our life.

If you've got a cat or dog, you may have noticed how easily they seem to fall asleep while you're watching Netflix, talking or blasting music – this is due to the same process of habituation. In one study, a loud sound was played to a sleeping cat, and the cat immediately woke up. But as the sound was played more and more, the cat took a little longer to wake up each time, until it just remained sleeping. However, if the tone was varied slightly, the cat was immediately awake.

James also explored this phenomenon in music. He found that the songs that made it into pop charts the fastest – and thus were played on the radio more often – were also the ones that fell out of the charts the fastest – they had reached habituation. While the songs that slowly climbed the charts to the top spots dropped away just as slowly, fading away versus burning out.

With this notion in mind, one might understandably wonder why we like to listen to a song more than once. This question brings me to another psychological phenomenon called the '**mere exposure effect**', referring to the tendency of people to develop a preference for things or people that are more familiar to them, because of repeated exposure.

In a 1968 experiment conducted by social psychologist Robert Zajonc, participants were exposed to a variety of nonsense words, each presented either 1, 2, 5, 10 or 25 times. Participants rated words they had heard 5, 10, and 25 times as more positive than the ones with 1, or 2 exposures. The mere exposure effect has since been proven in several further experiments.

So if new things grab our attention, but we like things when they're familiar, is it possible that there's an optimal level of exposure to something, where it's both new enough to engage our brain, but old enough for us to like it? The answer is yes, and scientists call it '**the optimal level of exposure**'.

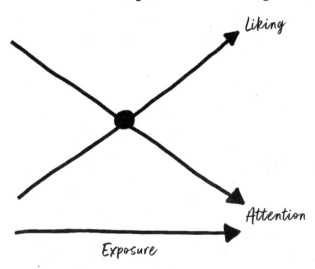

Creating products that hit that sweet spot of new enough to grab the brain's attention, but familiar enough to be loved is the plight of most record labels and producers. This is why they will create several remixes of a hit song, why new artists sample old-school classics, and why most songs have familiar riffs, sounds and melodies.

★ WE BECOME HABITUATED TO SMELLS

Your brain habituates to smells too; the reason why people often ask the friend stood next to them if they smell is because receptors in their nostrils have become habituated – they can no longer smell their own stench – and signals are no longer being sent from their nasal receptors to their brain.

If you've ever sampled perfumes in rapid succession, you'll be familiar with this phenomenon. Perfume sellers will sometimes prompt you to smell coffee beans between samples in an attempt to reduce the effects of this nasal habituation.

In one habituation study, researchers gave people a bedroom air freshener that dispensed a strong but pleasant pine-like smell, in an equal quantity, every day for three weeks. Researchers remarked that 'every day, the participants became less sensitive to the odor, and they would increasingly ask us, "Are you sure it's still working!?"'

★ HABITUATION AND SEMANTIC SATIATION IN MARKETING

There's irony in the fact that I spent so long reading research on the term 'semantic satiation' – literally thousands of articles, studies and videos – that the term slowly lost its meaning and became wallpaper in my mind.

On several occasions, while writing and researching this law, I had to stop to double and then triple check I was using the right phrase, because my brain had seemingly become numb, desensitised and unfamiliar with it.

Similarly, marketers are rethinking their sales ploys thanks to the new research on this concept. One timely example is what people are calling 'Black Friday numbness'. Thanks to tremendous overuse, 'Black Friday' is no longer the valuable hook it once was. We've repeated it so much that for many, the term has become as indistinct as the wallpaper in their bedroom.

In marketing, any word or phrase that is effective will eventually be exploited, abused and disempowered. Author and journalist Zachary Petit said:

Another interesting example can be the word 'revolution'. In 1995, a journalist colleague of mine and I took up a project after noticing the frequency of the word revolution/revolutionary in press ads. We scanned various editions of a newspaper from 1950 till 1995. Our findings indicated that the word 'revolution' was only sparsely used till the late 1960s, mainly for actual political revolutions.

However, by the late 1960s, the word was frequently repeated by both, left and right mainstream political parties, and even youth groups. Then in a mid-1970s edition of the newspaper, we came across a press ad of a furniture brand that claimed its office chairs were made with 'revolutionary Swedish technology'. After that we came across ad after ad for electronics, medicines, chocolates, milk, cooking oils and detergent brands, all claiming that they were 'revolutionary'.

A couple of decades later, the word 'revolution' had been used so often that it lost its meaning, both politically and from a marketing standpoint. Its power had effectively vanished.

★ BYPASSING THE HABITUATION FILTER

Here's a secret that I would like you to keep to yourself in order to avoid the exploitation, overuse and disempowerment of the words.

When I launched my podcast *The Diary Of A CEO* on YouTube, we were generating millions of monthly views to the channel, but about 70 per cent of those that watched the podcast frequently didn't subscribe. In a lazy attempt to get them to subscribe I added the phrase 'please like and subscribe' to my introduction, which is the phrase that every YouTube creator I've ever watched adopts.

It had virtually no impact on my view to subscription rate, and my channel continued its painfully slow trickle of new subscribers. Thinking more deeply about why this might be, I hypothesised that because the phrase 'like and subscribe' is the default call to action for all creators, maybe viewers' brains had habituated to it. Maybe that phrase is so overused, they didn't even hear me saying it.

I crafted a new phrase based on the laws of habituation. In the opening seconds of my YouTube videos, I said:

'Seventy-four per cent of you that watch this channel frequently do not subscribe.'

(This is so specific, revealing and thought-provoking that the brain pays attention to it, bypassing the habituation filter.)

'If you've ever enjoyed our videos, please could you do me a favour, and hit the subscribe button?'

(This is a call to reciprocity – a psychological phenomenon that shows people will do something for you if they feel you've done something for them.)

'It helps this channel more than you know, and the bigger the channel gets, the bigger the guests get.'

(This is a promise of a future reward – if you subscribe, you'll be rewarded with bigger guests.)

After saying this new 'call to action' just once, the channel's viewer to subscriber rate increased by a staggering 430 per cent! The channel has become the fastest growing YouTube podcast in the world, outpacing the legendary Joe Rogan. It went from 100,000 subscribers to millions of subscribers in months, and SocialBlade.com forecasts predict it will exceed 30 million subscribers in the next five years.

'**Wallpaper**' as I call it – the overuse of popular terms, phrases and calls to action to the point that the brain habituates to them and tunes them out – is the enemy of effective and successful storytelling and marketing. Marketing teams default to using common phrases through laziness, risk-aversion and a lack of creativity. But this law shows that if you have an important message and you want to infiltrate the brain's circuitry, grab its attention and be received with meaning, use terminology that is unexpected, unusual and unsaturated.

REPETITION ISN'T KEY

In marketing, we're told that repetition is key. A cherished principle in mass-media advertising seems to be that the more your customer sees your advert, the more likely they are to act upon it. This is true in principle, because all learning does depend on the repeated presentation of a certain stimulus, but it's important to understand the conditions that make a repeated stimulation constructive, as in learning, or disruptive, as in satiation.

In multiple studies, researchers have found that the relationship between frequency of exposure of an advertising message and its meaningfulness can be represented by an inverted U.

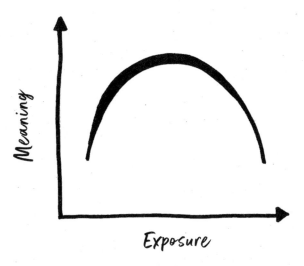

The rising part of the curve (which indicates *increase* in meaning) is called 'semantic generation' and the descending part (*loss* of meaning) is 'semantic satiation'. The sweet spot for advertisers is where the curve *changes* inflection. This is where the term, message or phrase has reached optimal meaning and effectiveness in the mind of your customer.

Once it's reached this critical point – even if it's still memorable – it's no longer an effective message to create action, drive sales and evoke an emotional response. At this point – if the phrase, words and sounds were originally employed to drive action – it's time to get creative and think of a new way to pierce the brain's habituation filter.

Great marketing is <u>uncomfortable</u>. It springs a dormant brain into a neurological frenzy.

Strong marketing demands an opinion, a response and an emotion. It doesn't want to be liked – it calls for either love or hatred. And once it's finally reached a point of habituated familiarity, it changes shape, ensnaring its audience's attention once again.

✶ THE LAW: AVOID WALLPAPER AT ALL COSTS

Words really matter, and the fate of ideas, politicians and brands can be decided by them. Knowing how to communicate in a way that cuts through, grabs attention and beats our habituation filters, will be the difference between success and failure in many endeavours in our lives. Your brain has a profound prehistoric survival tool, its habituation filter, which allows it to adapt to and tune out of even the most unthinkably painful, annoying or smelly stimulus. In order to be heard, tell stories in an unrepetitive, unfiltered and unconventional way.

Make people feel something, either way.

LAW 12

YOU MUST PISS PEOPLE OFF

This law will explain why pissing people off is an unavoidable consequence of building a brand that matters and why 'hate' is a signal that you're saying the right things.

In preparation for this book, I wandered through a Barnes & Noble bookstore in Los Angeles conducting a bit of observational research on trends within the publishing world. One of the clearest and most striking observations I had was that a huge number of self-help books are now covered in curse words!

This trend of swearing on the front cover of books exploded in 2016 with Mark Manson's *The Subtle Art of Not Giving A F*ck* – which Manson, who I interviewed in preparation for this book, tells me has sold more than 15 million copies. It is one of the clearest signs that authors – who are competing in saturated genres – are trying to avoid 'semantic satiation' and grab your brain's attention by bypassing its 'wallpaper filter'.

By 2018, the top 25 books on Amazon's bestseller list included – as well as *The Subtle Art of Not Giving a F*ck* – books titled *What the F*@# Should I Make for Dinner?*, *50 Ways to Eat Cock*, *Unf*ck Yourself* and *Calm the F**k Down*. Archive data shows that ten years ago, none of the books at the top of the charts had a profanity in their title.

Sarah Knight's editor Michael Szczerban – who published several of her cuss-covered, multi-million copy selling books, including *Calm the F**k Down*, said:

> Publishers and authors are trying to find ways to cut through all the noise and reach people. This seems to be one way that some books can do that, and when that happens, other people try to follow in those footsteps. Some people don't like it, some retailers don't want to carry a book because it has a swear word on the title. But the upside more than wins out.

When he says, 'but the upside wins out', he's touching on one of the most foundational principles of marketing, avoiding semantic satiation, and being heard.

It's a principle that all my marketing teams have exploited, preached about and executed for more than a decade, so much so that we wrote it on our office walls: 'Make people feel something – either way.'

Indifference – when people don't love you or hate you – is the least profitable outcome for a marketer.

Indifference to your words, your message or your calls to action is the surest path to the dreaded habituation filter mentioned in the previous law.

I interviewed Jane Wurwand, the illustrious founder and chief visionary of Dermalogica and The International Dermal Institute. Wurwand is one of the most recognised and respected authorities in the beauty industry. Under her leadership, Dermalogica has grown to be a leading skincare brand, used by more than 100,000 skin therapists in more than 100 countries around the world, and consequently she's become one of the richest women in the beauty industry.

Her number one marketing secret to avoid her customers' habituation filter is to say things and do things that 'piss people off'. She explained:

> We have to be prepared to piss off 80 per cent or we'll never turn on 20 per cent. If we don't, we'll be middle of the road, mediocre, average, palatable, but not definable. That's a product. That's not a brand. A brand triggers an emotional response. And so that became our watchword in marketing: 'We need to piss off 80 per cent and turn on 20 per cent.' We don't need everyone to like us. And if we're not being slightly disruptive, then everyone's going to like us, but they're not going to love us. If some people hate us, some people will love us.

But be wary; all emotional tactics have a shelf life – emotional hooks have diminishing returns as the brain habituates and downgrades its meaning.

When comparing the chart dominance of cuss-covered books between 2018 and now, it's clear that the effectiveness of this swearing tactic is starting to wane. The thing that makes any emotional messaging effective, ultimately makes it popular, which by the power of habituation quickly turns it into wallpaper.

★ THE LAW: YOU MUST PISS PEOPLE OFF

Don't be afraid of alienating people with emotional, bold or even divisive marketing approaches – triggering an emotional response that engages 20 per cent of your audience and enrages 80 per cent can be more valuable than an approach to which 100 per cent is indifferent.

Some people will love you.

Some people will hate you.

Some people simply
won't care.

You will only connect to
the first two.

But not to the third.

Indifference is the least
profitable outcome.

LAW 13

SHOOT YOUR PSYCHOLOGICAL MOONSHOTS FIRST

This law will show you how to create huge perceived value in your customers' minds with shockingly tiny, often free, superficial changes to your product and it reveals the psychological tricks your favourite brands are using on you right now.

My hairdresser has been manipulating me for three years.

He comes to my house at the same time on the same day, every week, and delivers the same haircut. I've stuck with him because I've always believed he has the greatest attention to detail, he's a perfectionist, and so I've always trusted him to cut my hair.

One day, on one of his routine visits, we had our first ever issue. After finishing my haircut, he took the apron off me and announced, 'You're done, mate.'

Instinctively, something just didn't feel right to me. For a reason I couldn't quite articulate, it felt as if he had rushed my haircut, and like he hadn't paid his usual attention to detail.

I replied, 'Really? That was quick!' I dubiously walked over to my kitchen mirror and began to examine my scalp in search of the patch that he must have missed. Surprisingly, the haircut was perfect, as usual.

Still believing he had rushed the haircut, I walked over to my phone to check the time – he'd spent the same amount of time cutting my hair as he did every week.

Confused as to why I felt so inexplicably short-changed, I said to him, 'For some reason that felt really rushed.' For a moment he looked back at me totally confused, and then, as if struck by a hilarious joke, he burst into an uncontrollable fit of laughter. 'My bad, my bad, mate; because we were talking so much, I forget to do my "end-of-trim routine"!' he explained.

End-of-trim routine? He went on to tell me about a psychological trick he calls 'one last snip', which he's been using on me and all his clients for the last ten years.

He said he's noticed that clients always feel like he's done a better job if at the end of the haircut he pretends to inspect their finished haircut before doing one last – fictitious – snip.

So at the end of every haircut – including all of my previous haircuts – he's done an 'end-of-trim routine' that involves turning off the electrical hair clippers, taking a long pause, walking around the client as if inspecting their hair closely, and then pretending to do one tiny final snip on their hair, before announcing that he's done.

Today, he had simply forgotten this little routine, and I had instinctively felt it. I felt that my haircut was worse, rushed or negligent because he had simply forgotten a ten-second psychological trick which had subconsciously convinced me he has tremendous attention to detail.

In reality, his 'one last snip' trick does nothing to improve my hair – he admitted he doesn't even cut any hair during this routine, but it does a lot to improve my perception that he's done a thorough job. This is the power of a 'psychological moonshot', a term coined by Ogilvy's Rory Sutherland.

> *A psychological moonshot is a relatively small investment that drastically improves the perception of something.*

Psychological moonshots prove that it's nearly always cheaper, easier and more effective to invest in perception than reality.

★ UBER IS A PSYCHOLOGICAL MOONSHOT

'What if you could request one on your phone?'

That's the question Travis Kalanick and Garrett Camp asked each other one freezing night in Paris. They were over from the United States for a tech conference, waiting endlessly for a cab, experiencing a misery many of us will be familiar with: not knowing if, or when, your cab is coming sucks. The simple question they asked that night, borne from uncertainty and frustration, would lead to the creation of Uber, now the default taxi app for more than 100 million people every month, in 600 cities and 65 countries.

In high-stress situations, when we're late for a flight, a meeting or an event, every second feels like a minute, every minute feels like an hour and every hour feels like a day. The feelings of angst this scenario creates is one we can all relate to; this is the awful anxiety of customer uncertainty.

Reducing their customers' psychological friction became Uber's key challenge, and so they launched an entire in-house team of behavioural (data) scientists, psychologists and neuro-scientists in what would be called 'Uber Labs'.

In their research, Uber Labs discovered several key psychological principles that impact a customer's satisfaction with Uber and their perceptions of the overall experience: the peak–end rule, idleness aversion, operational transparency, uncertainty anxiety and the goal-gradient effect. Understanding these five powerful psychological forces allowed Uber to completely redesign an entire industry and create a business valued at $120 billion.

1. THE PEAK-END RULE: THE TWO MOMENTS THAT MATTER MOST

The peak–end rule is a cognitive bias that describes how people remember an experience or event. Simply put, we judge an experience according to how we felt at its peak and at its end, rather than by some perfectly aggregated average of every moment of it. Crucially, this applies to both good and bad experiences! Businesses and brands take note: **customers will judge their entire experience on just two moments – the best (or worst) part, and the end**.

This perspective helps us to understand why a terrible flight at the start of a holiday has less negative impact on satisfaction than a terrible flight at the end of a holiday. Why a wonderful dinner can be tainted by a surprise surcharge on the bill, and why a two-minute disagreement at the end of a positive date night with your spouse will taint your memory of the whole evening.

It also explains why Uber drivers are trained to be exceptionally kind to you at the end of a ride, moments before you rate them and offer them a tip.

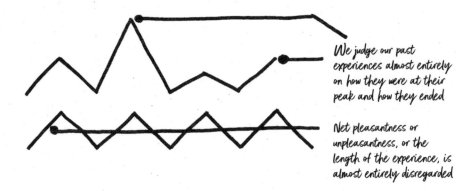

We judge our past experiences almost entirely on how they were at their peak and how they ended

Net pleasantness or unpleasantness, or the length of the experience, is almost entirely disregarded

2. IDLENESS AVERSION: OUR NEED FOR JUSTIFIABLE BUSYNESS

Uber Labs cited research that **people who are busy are happier than people who are idle** – even if they are not busy of their own volition (i.e., you've coerced them into some activity). In fact, even a false justification – a spurious reason – can motivate people to action, such is our appetite for distraction and activity. The implications of this research are that many of the 'goals' we pursue are really just excuses to keep ourselves busy.

For Uber, this meant that if they could keep waiting customers busy by giving them something to watch or to engage with, those customers would be significantly happier, and less likely to cancel rides.

Instead of merely letting users know what time their driver was due, the Uber Labs team installed several engaging animations – including a moving car on a map that gives customers something to watch while they wait – in an effort to avoid 'idle unhappiness'.

Remarkably, Uber's cited research shows that the majority of people would choose a wait time that was long – if they're able to do something during the wait – over a short wait time in which they're not able to keep themselves busy. This, in part, explains why restaurants bring you freebies while you wait, why streaming sites like Netflix and YouTube play previews when you hover over videos, and why Google Chrome installed a T-rex game that appears when you lose connection.

Studies show keeping your customer busy can improve customer happiness, retention and conversion by more than 25 per cent!

3. OPERATIONAL TRANSPARENCY: BRANDS SHOULD BE GLASS BOXES

Getting a cab back in 2008 came with a lot of uncertainty. A customer had no way of knowing when their taxi would arrive (or even *if* it would arrive), who was picking them up, or why it was taking so long. Back then, if you got into a cab without a meter, the driver would effectively pluck the price out of the air, based on their own guesstimate. Even when you got in a cab *with* a meter, you'd worry that the driver was intentionally taking a longer route to increase the fare.

This lack of transparency is poison to customer experience; it breeds distrust, and distrust makes us sceptical, resentful and disloyal to a brand.

Given these insights, Uber Labs used a psychology principle called **operational transparency** and began explaining each step going on behind the scenes to show the rate of progress during the wait. They included the arrival time estimate calculation, gave a detailed breakdown of how the fare was calculated, justified estimates for everything and provided quick updates – with an explanation – when something changed.

These changes resulted in an 11 per cent reduction in the post-request cancellation rate, which to Uber, with more than 7 billion trips taken per year, is a multi-billion-dollar improvement.

4. UNCERTAINTY ANXIETY

In 2008, Domino's Pizza experienced an interesting operational and customer experience challenge. Customers who were waiting longer than they expected for their pizza would phone Domino's to ask where it was. The whole process of pizza making would then be interrupted, because the person making the pizza would be asked why there was a delay by the person who'd answered the phone, and the customer would ultimately be given a vague and uncertain answer. A calling customer was unwittingly delaying the delivery of their own pizza, because of the lack of operational transparency they'd been given.

Some pizza chains responded to this challenge by investing in warming bags to keep the pizzas hot, hiring more staff and drivers, launching money-back guarantees on delivery times and offering free breadsticks for slow deliveries, but their phones carried on ringing.

What they were all missing was the psychological frustration at the heart of the problem – people didn't want faster delivery – **they wanted less uncertainty** about their delivery.

Domino's understood this, and in 2008, using their pre-existing in-house order-management software, they created the now famous 'Domino's Pizza Tracker', which shows customers exactly where their order is in a five-step process.

This small psychological insight and the innovation it produced changed Domino's business. Angry phone calls plummeted, customer satisfaction and retention skyrocketed and Domino's saved and made hundreds of millions in the process.

Research published in the journal *Nature* showed that it's less psychologically stressful to know something negative is about to happen (e.g., our pizza is going to be 30 minutes late) than to be left in uncertainty (e.g., we have no idea where the late pizza is). That's because the area of our brain that tries to anticipate consequences is most fired up when we're faced with uncertainty – it's on edge. As Rory Sutherland explains in his book *Alchemy*, a 'DELAYED' alert on your scheduled flight is much more mentally irritating than a 'DELAYED 50 MINUTES' alert.

Every day, more than 300 Shinkansen (bullet) trains arrive and depart Tokyo Station's four platforms, at an average interval of roughly four minutes. The trains only stop at the station for ten minutes and it takes two minutes for the passengers to disembark and three minutes for new passengers to board.

'TESSEI', a subsidiary of Japan Railway, is in charge of cleaning these bullet trains, making them hygienic for the more than 400,000 passengers that use the service every day. Customers would often complain about the cleanliness and hygiene of these trains, in light of these fast turnaround times – assuming the trains couldn't possibly be properly cleaned in such a short window of time.

Teruo Yabe, TESSEI's CEO, wanted to change this perception; he believed that the trains were in fact very clean – but some customers didn't have enough visibility to believe it. So instead of hiring more cleaners, Yabe decided to make the cleaners stand out: he changed the colour of employee uniforms from pale blue shirts to unmissable bright red jackets, and he asked cleaners to put on a show – which is now internationally known as the 'seven-minute Shinkansen theatre' – to greet incoming and outgoing customers.

As the train pulls into the platform, cleaners line up by the doors and bow as it pulls in. Holding open bags, they greet the arriving passengers and thank them for handing over their rubbish. Staff then whizz through the train, picking up rubbish, sweeping and sanitising surfaces, and once complete, the cleaners line up by the train and perform a second bow to show respect for the departing train and its new passengers.

Not only did hygiene complaints plummet, but it is reported that the cleaners – with their newfound pride in their work inspired by the increase in respect they received from passengers – cleaned more thoroughly, with more joy, and more motivation. What would become known as the '7-minute miracle' repositioned the train line as being one of the cleanest in the world.

This shows that even hygiene uncertainty can be rectified with a psychological moonshot, and offers further evidence that **it's nearly always cheaper, easier and more effective to invest in perception than reality**.

5. THE GOAL-GRADIENT EFFECT: SPEEDING UP NEAR THE FINISH LINE

In 1932, a behavioural scientist named Clark Hull was studying rats in a maze. Using sensors attached to the rats, he monitored their speed as they ran towards a food reward. Hull observed that the nearer the rats came to the end of the maze – and its accompanying prize – the faster they moved.

He called this principle 'the goal-gradient effect'.

It's been repeatedly proven that what motivates us most is how close we are to achieving a goal: we work faster the closer we are to success.

Participants collecting stamps as part of a café's reward programme buy coffee more frequently the closer they get to earning a free drink; internet users who rate songs in return for gift certificates rate more songs as they approach the reward goal, and LinkedIn users are more likely to add profile information if they're shown a 'profile strength' bar that details how close they are to completing their profile.

Uber Labs solved this problem with the design of their map, which goes to great lengths to emphasise just how close the car is from arriving at both the pick-up and the destination.

All of these psychological hacks have made Uber the most famous taxi company in the world, dominating their industry internationally. And because of the work done by the psychology experts in Uber Labs, the company now says it only takes 2.7 rides before someone becomes a permanent customer.

☆ THE POWER OF PSYCHOLOGICAL MOONSHOTS

The term moonshot is derived from the Apollo 11 spaceflight project, which landed the first human – Neil Armstrong – on the moon in 1969, and which was described by Armstrong as 'a giant leap for mankind'. A psychological moonshot, is a giant leap forward using the power of psychology.

When I interviewed Rory Sutherland, he said:

It's hard to increase customer satisfaction by making a train ten times faster; it's much easier to increase customer satisfaction by using psychological principles to make it feel ten times more enjoyable. I don't think governments like the UK government would need to spend £50 billion on faster trains if they just made the Wi-Fi work better while you're on it. It seems likely that the biggest progress in the next 50 years won't come from improvements in technology, but in psychology and design thinking.

Remarkably, the 'close' button in most lifts doesn't actually work. Lift doors are designed to close after a certain amount of time, for safety and legal reasons. According to Karen Penafiel, former executive director of National Elevator Industry Inc., 'The riding public cannot make elevator doors close any faster.' But this illusionary placebo creates the impression of control, decreases uncertainty, makes you feel safer and in doing so increases customer satisfaction.

Some hand soap manufacturers put menthol, peppermint or eucalyptus in their products solely for the purpose of producing a tingling effect on your hands, which creates a powerful psychological effect – also seen in medicine and supplements – that something is working because you can *feel* it.

McDonald's recently deployed their own psychological moonshots, installing self-service kiosks and large screens that show where orders are in the process, and giving customers tickets once they've placed an order – leveraging the goal gradient effect – and diminishing uncertainty, wait times and frustration in the process. This change produced a series of moonshot-sized results for the brand.

As McDonald's former president Don Thompson said, 'people eat with their eyes first', visually seeing every item – as opposed to words on a list – makes you more likely to want it, which was a possibility not previously achievable with the limited space of in-store displays. Additionally, research showed the use of a touchscreen creates novelty and fun, which leads to an enhanced consumer preference towards more self-indulgent purchasing. Furthermore, without the potential shame of having to directly tell the cashier your embarrassingly long, gluttonous and potentially detailed order, customers felt psychologically safer to order more food.

This relatively small change delivered multi-billion-dollar results for the global franchise: sales rose almost 10 per cent, customer satisfaction improved and although the production process didn't change, people's perceptions of how 'fast' the 'fast food' restaurant is were impacted positively.

★ THE LAW: SHOOT YOUR PSYCHOLOGICAL MOONSHOTS FIRST

Psychological moonshots allow brands to create huge perceived value with tiny, often free, superficial changes. They are the first place entrepreneurs, marketers and creatives should look in their attempts to create – the illusion of – value.

Do not wage a war on reality, invest in shaping perceptions.

Our truth is not what we see.

Our truth is the story we choose to believe.

LAW 14

FRICTION CAN CREATE VALUE

This law will show you the counterintuitive truth that sometimes your customers will want your products more ... if you make their experience worse.

During my time as a marketing CEO, I sat in numerous brand marketing meetings with our client Coca-Cola where their marketing executives were seemingly dumbfounded by the success of Red Bull and the wider energy drink industry.

Sugary drink sales were plummeting, yet the equally unhealthy, rancid-tasting energy drinks category was skyrocketing. What was making one category grow so much more successfully than the other? Our research revealed that customers in different categories had different expectations, and with different expectations come different psychological moonshots.

In my conversation with Rory Sutherland, he pointed out that Red Bull delivers on its psychological expectation of enhancing your performance and 'giving you wings' by intentionally making it taste bad. Because it tastes more like medicine than a pleasant fizzy drink, they've convinced their customers that it's packed with powerful, effective chemicals.

Making things taste 'better' can make them less desirable – depending on expectations.

One of my closest friends founded and ran one of the fastest-growing performance nutrition brands in Europe. He often confessed to me that the biggest product challenge they had was that their products tasted so good that customers simply didn't believe they were good for them. At one point, they had seriously considered making products taste worse in an attempt to increase sales.

These examples prove that making things easier isn't necessarily the path to a psychological moonshot; sometimes you have to do the opposite: increase friction, wait times and inconvenience, to achieve the same increase in perceived value.

General Mills launched several cake mixes in the 1950s under the famous Betty Crocker brand. To make the cake, you had to add water, mix it and bake it. It was a foolproof cake mix. It included powdered milk and eggs and was impossible to get wrong. When the cakes were launched, expectations were high. But the product didn't take off and reception was luke-warm at best.

General Mills didn't understand what had gone wrong. It had wanted to save time for busy wives and mothers, but somehow that had fallen flat. It hired a team of psychologists to investigate. Their conclusion was that although the product saved time and effort compared to making a cake from scratch, American wives and homemakers felt guilty about the assumption that they had spent hours baking when they hadn't, or about having to admit that they had taken a shortcut and hadn't put the work in, so they went back to traditional baking.

General Mills might have considered an advertising campaign to address the issue but, driven by psychology, they went in another direction – against all marketing conventional wisdom and towards a psychological moonshot. They took the egg out of the mix and printed 'Add an egg' on the front of the package. This 'subtraction technique' caused more friction, made the product less convenient and cost its customers more time – objectively resulting in a less valuable product – but in doing so it made the baker feel more valuable themselves, and consequently sales soared.

Similarly, every time a restaurant brings me a raw steak and a hot stone to cook it on, it's clear to me that they're intentionally or unintentionally employing a powerful psychologic moonshot.

Everyone's steak preference is notoriously specific – meaning steaks are one of the most returned food items to even the most high-end kitchens. It appears illogical that asking a customer to cook their own food might increase their satisfaction and perception of value of the overall experience, but that's precisely what happens when a hot stone is presented.

By bringing the meat raw, they're bringing down my wait time, saving their chefs time, increasing my chances of satisfaction by allowing me to cook my own steak the way I like it (medium rare), giving me a sense of having invested effort in my meal, reducing complaints and returns and avoiding customer idleness by keeping me busy. In this psychological moonshot, operational transparency, idleness aversion and the goal-gradient effect are all at work at the same time!

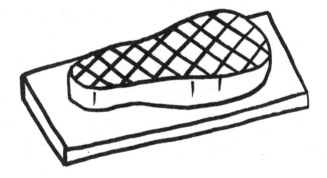

Flight, hotel and insurance aggregator websites understand that friction can create value. They found that faster search times on their websites often resulted in fewer sales. They now artificially increase search times and show all the sites they're searching in an attempt to convince you that they've done a thorough search, so you don't have to look elsewhere. This tactic has resulted in more sales, better retention and higher customer-return rates.

★ THE LAW: FRICTION CAN CREATE VALUE

It seems nonsensical that friction can create value, but companies that deploy psychological moonshots understand that humans aren't logical – they're irrational, unreasonable and fundamentally illogical in their decision-making and behaviour. Therefore, if you are to successfully influence them, sometimes you must create, produce and say things that don't make sense.

'Value' does not exist.

It's a perception we reach with expectations we meet.

LAW 15

THE FRAME MATTERS MORE THAN THE PICTURE

This law explains how the way a product is presented to consumers drastically affects their perception of its value.

A single, trivial mistake shattered my love affair with my favourite brand.

You would typically find me covered in this one particular brand of clothing from head to toe. A few years ago, I fell for the brand after discovering the founder's story, his vision, his unrelenting devotion to detail, creativity, artistic flair, and the technical wizardry he poured into each masterpiece. This brand crafted one-of-a-kind designs for everyday wear, all at a rather premium price point.

One fateful day, as I casually scrolled through social media, I stumbled upon a video the founder had posted. In it, he toured the production line in China where his creations came to life. The video aimed to flaunt the vast scale of the operation and the meteoric rise of the brand by illustrating how many products were being made, how they made them, and the process that governed the production line.

In that very instant, the spell was broken; the enchanting illusion the brand had cast over me evaporated.

It wasn't the fact that the brand was produced in China, nor the faces of the workers creating the clothes, or even the conditions of the production line that jolted me. Rather, it was the sight of the very shoes I was wearing as I watched the video, regurgitated from a monstrous machine and tossed into a heap of thousands of identical pairs. It was the sight of the exact T-shirt I had on at that moment, haphazardly piled atop thousands of others in a gargantuan, dumpster-like container, with a cascade of shirts spilling over the edge like an overflowing rubbish bin.

Although the brand never explicitly made such claims, my infatuated mind had always perceived their products to be unique works of art, each lovingly handcrafted by the devoted founder himself. Logically, I would have guessed that mass production must have been involved somewhere, but these things aren't governed by logic – they're stories we choose to believe based on the evidence presented to us. Up until then, the only narrative the brand had woven was one of artistry, exclusivity and romance.

> The way that something is packaged has a big impact on how it's received. How something is framed affects how consumers perceive and value the brand. In this moment, the frame of my favourite brand changed irreversibly.

This isn't a recent behavioural discovery. The famous Pepsi Challenge campaigns of the 1970s required customers to blind taste Pepsi and Coca-Cola out of plain white cups and their branded cans and bottles. People preferred Pepsi when they were drinking it from the cups but, surprisingly, they preferred Coca-Cola when it was served in the bottle or can.

The framing of the drink actually changed how it tasted to the consumer.

If you go into your local electronics store, you'll likely find yourself in an overwhelming jungle of wires, gadgets and batteries stacked on top of each other from floor to ceiling. Conventional thought in product merchandising was that the more items you displayed, the more chance you'd have of making a sale. This is a very logical way of thinking, but Apple knows that humans are anything but logical, and that there are other dominant psychological forces that matter much more.

Every Apple Store in the world evokes the astonishing power of framing to unconsciously persuade shoppers that spending several thousands of dollars on a small electronic gadget – like an iPhone – is worth it.

They've designed their stores to feel more like art galleries – known for their high-value, unique pieces – than a cluttered electronic retailer. Their behavioural scientists know that the frame they create will sway the value of the gadget within it. By displaying only a small quantity of their items, they evoke the power of scarcity – a form of framing – which dictates that demand, and therefore the perceived value of a product, is increased when supply appears limited. We all intuitively know retail space is expensive, and so by giving each individual Apple product lots of empty space around it, they're signalling that each item is so valuable that it warrants that expense. Psychologically we pour the value of the free space around the product into the product itself – like a piece of art. Apple frame their products on an alluring psychological stage.

To illustrate how powerful the frame around something can be on altering perception, check out this visual example:

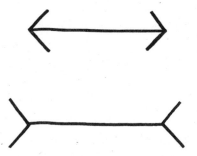

The lines between the two arrowheads are the same length.

I'm an investor in, and ambassador for, a company called WHOOP, a health-monitoring wearable that tracks your key health metrics. The company was recently valued at $3.6 billion, it dominates its category and its customers include everyone from Cristiano Ronaldo to LeBron James and Michael Phelps.

It has won in a category packed with giants and their colossal marketing budgets – Apple, Fitbit, Garmin – in part because of their genius focus on framing.

The CEO of WHOOP told me that the company has continually resisted all calls to add a time display to their wristband, despite how easy it would be to implement, for this very reason. WHOOP is now the only leading health wearable or wristband in its category that has no screen and doesn't show its wearer the time.

Why? Because they believe adding a screen would change the customer's perception of the device from being an elite health device that athletes use, to a watch. Adding something that is objectively valuable – the ability to know the time – would decrease the psychological value of the product. In the world of psychological moonshots, less is so often more, and one word, tweak or decision can make a huge difference to the perception of a product's value.

In 2019, I advised a large global B2B company to ban the job title 'salesperson', to stop using the term 'sales' and replace it with a 'partnerships' team. More people responded to their emails, and their sales rose by 31 per cent. As I suspected, a job title with the word 'sales' in it, primes the people you contact to believe you're going to pester them to buy something they don't want – conversely, the framing of the word 'partner' suggests the person is on your team.

✶ ✶ ✶

A few years ago, Elon Musk made a promise to animal rights associations: no more leather in Tesla cars. The entrepreneur has kept his word and, starting with the Tesla Model 3, its cars' interiors have been made of what is curiously called 'vegan leather'.

Rory Sutherland, the advertising legend that coined the phrase 'psychological moonshot', told me that Tesla instinctively understand the powerful impact of psychological moonshots on the perception of value: instead of calling its new car seats 'plastic' – which they are – they eagerly clung on to the word 'leather' and its luxury connotations to maintain the perceived value of their cars' upholstery. Framing like this is one of the most common ways people achieve psychological moonshots, without improving the reality of a product or experience at all.

Framing isn't about lying and deception; it's about knowing how to present your product or service through the most factual and compelling lens.

For example, it's more appealing to say a food product is 90 per cent lean than to say it contains 10 per cent fat. Both are true, but one frame is more psychologically alluring.

These examples illustrate an important but too often forgotten principle in branding, marketing and business: **reality is nothing more than perception** and **context is king**.

★ THE LAW: THE FRAME MATTERS MORE THAN THE PICTURE

What you say, is not all that you say. What you say is determined by the context in which your message, product or service exists. If you change the frame, you change your message. Your customers will hear everything – including the things you didn't say. Don't just focus on what you say, focus on how the frame around what you're trying to say is positively or negatively distorting your message.

A smart frame will transform the plain.

LAW 16

USE GOLDILOCKS TO YOUR ADVANTAGE

This law shows you the powerful yet simple sales trick that you can use to make the thing you're selling appear to be better value, without changing the price.

'Why does he want to show me properties that I'm not interested in?' I asked my PA, Sophie, as she read out the itinerary for my house-viewing trip with my estate agent, Clive, scheduled for the following day. 'I'm not sure; he insists that you see a variety of options,' she replied.

A few days later, I submitted an offer to purchase the second of the three properties that Clive had shown me. Thank you, Clive.

But that's not the end of the story; some months later, while researching different psychological tricks brands and marketers deploy to influence our behaviour, I stumbled across something called the Goldilocks effect.

The Goldilocks effect is a type of '**anchoring**'.

Anchoring is a cognitive bias where individuals rely too heavily on seemingly irrelevant information (the 'anchor') when making decisions.

In the context of the Goldilocks effect, by presenting two 'extreme' options next to the option you're hoping to sell, you can make the middle option appear more attractive or reasonable.

In most contexts the 'true' value of something is nothing more than opinion – so we search for cues within context and pricing to help us make our decisions; when the Goldilocks effect is in play, we perceive the most expensive option as an excessive luxury. In contrast, we see the cheapest option as risky, insufficient and lower quality, and in the middle we have what we assume is the best option – we believe it must have the combined benefits of the other two: it's a safe bet, cost-efficient and of good quality.

Reflecting on the property viewings I'd had with Clive, I realised that I had only asked him to show me the second property, but he had insisted on showing me three. The first property he showed me was far too small and arguably over-priced. The second property was spacious and only slightly more expensive than the first, while the third property was extremely expensive, in the same area, and seemed to be vastly overpriced. Like a puppet under Clive's control, I, of course, instantly chose to make an offer on the second property.

Curious to know if Clive had intentionally manipulated me, I sent him a text asking if he was familiar with the Goldilocks effect. He replied first with a laughing face and a wink, and then went on to say, 'Never show people only one option!'

Crafty #@$%.

Clive isn't the only person, brand or organisation using the Goldilocks effect to influence your behaviour. Panasonic utilised it in 1992, by offering a $199.99 premium microwave as well as its existing microwaves at $179.99 and $109.99.

Sales of what then became the mid-priced option – the $179.99 microwave – skyrocketed, which pushed Panasonic up to a 60 per cent market share!

An experiment asked participants to choose between an all-inclusive holiday to Paris or an all-inclusive holiday to Rome. Paris won.

Experiment 1

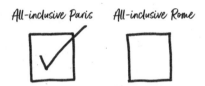

But then a second survey was run, this time adding an option for a holiday to Rome that's all-inclusive for everything except coffee. The totally all-inclusive deal to Rome wasn't just more popular than the version without coffee, it was also more popular than the all-inclusive trip to Paris.

Experiment 2

With little information provided, the brain will search for context cues about the value of the three options. The presence of the 'Rome without coffee' option provides one such cue, and implies that the Rome trip is so valuable that they removed something from it, because it is such a good deal.

To make the Goldilocks effect work, brands usually price the medium option higher than the lowest price, but far away from the most expensive price. For example, an airline selling return flights to New York would charge £800 for economy, £2,000 for business class and £8,000 for first class. Many customers will perceive the £2,000 ticket as the best value, even though it's clearly not the best price.

Everything described in the psychological moonshot law serves to highlight a fundamental fallacy that drives how we tell stories and deliver experiences: we believe that we're rational – the cognitive dissonance created every time I tell you that your decisions don't make sense is evidence of that – so when we create marketing for others we assume they are too and so we lean towards the hard work of improving reality, instead of the easier task of leveraging psychology.

Our decisions aren't driven by sense, they're driven by the nonsense created by social cues, irrational fear and survival instincts.

Great marketers, storytellers and brand-builders understand that pursuing a psychological moonshot isn't a malevolent, unethical or disingenuous undertaking. It's fair that these psychological perceptions work against you to create shortcuts to unfavourable perceptions – so it's also fair that you have a chance to use the same forces to turn these words, contexts, stigmas and perceptions in your favour, creating shortcuts to a perception that allows the world to see a truer representation of the true beauty, value and importance of the things you've created.

All is fair in psychological moonshots.

★ THE LAW: USE GOLDILOCKS TO YOUR ADVANTAGE

People are inclined to make value judgements based on context, so offering a range of options – including an economy, standard and premium version of your product – can tell a story and affect potential customers' perception of your standard offering.

The context
creates
the
value.

LAW 17

LET THEM TRY
AND THEY WILL BUY

This law reveals the easiest way to get someone to love a product instantly.

'No, Uncle Steven! It's mine!' my niece exclaimed, her eyes brimming with tears, as I sheepishly asked her to return the Christmas present I had just given her.

In the frenzy of wrapping presents for my entire family, including my niece and nephew, I had made the rookie mistake of neglecting to label each gift with the recipient's name. Consequently, I had inadvertently presented my niece with a toy figurine of Buzz Lightyear – my nephew's all-time favourite character. I was now on the verge of watching my nephew unwrap a present containing an Elsa doll – the apple of my niece's eye.

The room fell silent as I fumbled for words, attempting to rectify the situation. My niece clutched Buzz Lightyear to her chest, her eyes narrowing with fierce determination. 'But … but,' I stammered, 'you see, there's been a tiny mix-up. Buzz is actually meant for your brother!'

The tension in the room was palpable as my niece's eyes darted between me and her treasured toy. My nephew, sensing the drama unfolding before him, froze mid-unwrapping, craning his neck to get a better view of the spectacle.

I conceded defeat.

'All right, you keep it.' I wasn't prepared to negotiate with the steely resolve of a tearful three-year-old girl – the drama simply wasn't worth it.

To my surprise, my nephew, who had now unwrapped his brand-new Elsa doll, seemed content too. He didn't complain, made no attempt to swap, and he clutched the doll with the same fondness that his sister held her new Buzz Lightyear toy. They both adored what they had been given, but I knew if I had given them both a choice in the toy shop, they would have opted for the other toy.

This Christmas present wrapping blunder taught me a powerful psychological lesson about a phenomenon behavioural psychologists call '**the endowment effect**'. The endowment effect is a cognitive bias that causes people to overvalue an item simply because they own it, regardless of its objective value. In other words, individuals tend to be

much more attached to items they believe they own than they are to similar objects they do not possess. This is a potent psychological trick that brands deploy on all of us, all the time.

Apple is one such brand: every store provides an inter-active experience for customers, with all products displayed openly and touchable.

Moreover, they insist that every device on the floor is plugged into a power supply, loaded with apps and connected to the internet, and they tilt all the screens to the exact same angle in order to attract more potential experiences. They rigorously train staff not to press customers to buy (ensured by the fact that floor staff don't earn sales commissions) or to ask customers to leave, thus offering an unlimited time to play with the products.

In their 'One to One' workshops, the aim is to empower the customer to find the solutions themselves; they do not touch the computer without the customer's permission.

This might just sound like kindness or good manners, but I assure you it's something much more calculated. Apple is evoking the power of two subconscious psychological spells – the mere exposure effect we saw in Law 11, which increases a fondness for the product by increasing consumer exposure to the product, and the endowment effect, which increases a product's perceived value by giving a consumer possession of the product. Put simply, the mere exposure effect makes you like it more, and the endowment effect makes you value it more highly.

Apple believes that creating an '**ownership experience**' is more powerful than driving a hard sell. The multisensory experiences built into Apple Stores deliver exactly that.

So powerful, in fact, that the Illinois state attorney general's office issued a warning to holiday shoppers in 2003 to be careful of holding products as if they were their own when shopping. Although this warning sounds slightly bizarre, the basis of it is supported by 30 years of research.

In a 2009 study conducted by the University of Wisconsin, groups of students were asked to evaluate two products: a Slinky toy and a mug. In the first experiment one group was allowed to touch the items and the other group wasn't. In the next experiment one group was allowed to imagine they owned the item, and the other group wasn't. Extraordinarily, touching the items or even just imagining you owned it increased the participants' value estimates.

Apple's strategy of allowing customers to stay and play for an unlimited amount of time is also deliberate, based on further research that shows the longer a customer experiences the product, the greater their willingness to buy it.

A global company with 400 locations, Build-A-Bear is centred on offering a highly multisensory, engaging and interactive experience. In the stores, children can choose, design and participate in the creation of their own stuffed animals in-store. Although Build-A-Bear is not a 'store'; they call their locations 'workshops', and above every bear hangs a sign that evokes the mere exposure and endowment effects, to encourage the children to touch the bears: DRESS ME, HUG ME, HEAR ME, FLUFF ME, CHOOSE ME!

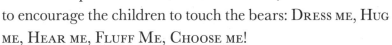

More evidence of the effects of ownership comes from a study in 1984, where researchers gifted participants either a lottery ticket or two dollars. Later, each of them was offered an opportunity to swap the lottery ticket for the money or the money for the lottery ticket. Only a few participants were willing to make the trade.

How about in real-world conditions? Dan Ariely and Ziv Carmon from Duke University examined the endowment effect in everyday life. The most popular sport at Duke is basketball – there is not enough space at the court for all the people who want to watch the games. Consequently, the university created a randomised lottery system to distribute tickets to each game.

Crucially, Carmon and Ariely conducted their experiment during the final round of the college basketball tournament March Madness, when the demand for tickets was higher than usual. The students surveyed by the economists all waited patiently on the university grounds in order to enter the lottery.

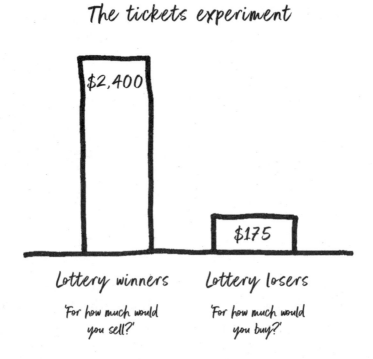

The tickets experiment

$2,400

$175

Lottery winners   Lottery losers

'For how much would   'For how much would
you sell?'   you buy?'

After the lottery, the ticket winners were asked how much they would sell their tickets for if someone wanted to purchase them. Those who hadn't won a ticket were asked how much they would be willing to pay for a ticket.

On average, those who didn't have a ticket said they would pay up to $175. Those who had won a ticket said they would not sell theirs for less than $2,400! So, those with tickets valued them nearly 14 times as much as those who didn't have them.

✱ THE REASON FOR OUR POSSESSIVENESS

Possessiveness can be traced back thousands of years in human history and is still observed today in some of our primate cousins.

In 2004, two economists conducted an experiment using chimpanzees, fruit juice ice lollies and nut butter inside a tube. The food was chosen specifically because it couldn't be eaten too quickly and would last long enough for the purpose of trading. When given a choice, 58 per cent of the chimpanzees preferred the nut butter to the ice lollies. Unsurprisingly, of the chimpanzees who were given the nut butter, nearly 79 per cent opted not to trade it for the ice lollies. But of the chimpanzees who were given the ice lollies, 58 per cent refused to trade for the nut butter.

The economists concluded that the endowment effect probably became rooted within humans early on in our evolution. But why were early humans so protective of what they had and reluctant to trade or pay for what they did not yet have? The answer seems that the risk associated with trading – particularly if the other party didn't act fairly – was a serious deterrent. Our ancestors had no reliable way of enforcing the conditions of a deal, so they reduced the price they were willing to pay for things (the value of the trade) to compensate for the risk of ending up with nothing or less than they should have got.

★ THE LAW: LET THEM TRY AND THEY WILL BUY

Getting your product into customers' hands remains an incredibly powerful tool for salespeople, marketers and brands. Next time you're trying to make someone love something and pay a good price for it, don't just tell them how great it is, use the power of the endowment effect and take a page out of Apple's book: let them touch it, play with it, test drive it and try it out. If you do, like my niece, they just might not want to give it back.

Through the lens of ownership, the ordinary becomes the extraordinary.

LAW 18

FIGHT FOR THE
FIRST FIVE SECONDS

This law proves why in marketing, business and sales, your success often depends on just five seconds. If you get those five seconds right, you'll succeed. If you don't, you'll fail.

Awkward ten second pause, staring ominously at the audience.

"'This is exactly why you were expelled from school; you are INCAPABLE of sticking at anything you don't believe in. And you always think you know a better way. DO NOT CALL ME or any of the family, until you go back to university!" And with that, my mum hung up the phone.'

These four sentences are the first words I uttered on more than 300 stages, in every corner of the world, between 2015 and 2020. They are the very emotional words my mother said to me on the day I called her to tell her I was dropping out of university to start a company.

I didn't introduce myself. I didn't say my name or the company I was presenting on behalf of. I knew, that in the first five seconds, the audience's habituation filters were going to either tune in and give me their attention, or decide I was wallpaper, tune out and take their attention somewhere else.

For this very reason, **the first five seconds, in any story, is do or die**.

As I said earlier, my marketing companies have never had an outbound sales team, yet we've attracted the world's biggest brands as clients – Amazon, Apple, Samsung, Coca-Cola – and generated nine-figure revenues.

If I could put our success down to just one thing – although the blue slide mentioned in Law 10 would be close – undoubtedly it would be that we told the most captivating, surprising and emotional stories. I never, ever 'pitched'. I never bombarded an audience with graphs, stats or data. Every talk I delivered started, sounded and ended more like something out of Harry Potter than a sales presentation.

I, like most people, have a horrifically short attention span when I'm bored of something – so much so that I was expelled from school for sleeping in lessons, skipping classes and had a 31 per cent attendance record. I then went off to university, fell asleep in the first lecture, dropped out the next day and never went back. I think because of this, I've naturally always understood how important it is to tell stories that demand attention – someone talking at me in a monotone voice for a prolonged period of time triggers my brain's snooze button.

But for some reason, most stories delivered on stage are still horrifically boring. After spending years shedding blood, sweat and tears while creating something, the creator of that thing nearly always falls into a delusional, self-centred bubble. They begin to believe that the thing they've created is so revolutionary, fascinating and important, that it's inherently worthy of the world's undivided attention.

From this distorted, self-absorbed perspective, one of the most common and treacherous traps the creator of that thing can fall into when telling their story to the world is believing that their audience cares about them, their product, their hard work and their 'innovation' as much as they do. When this happens, the story they tell becomes logical, long, and lacklustre.

Conversely, when a storyteller understands that nobody – absolutely nobody – cares about them as much as they care about themselves (nobody cares that their toothpaste is a little mintier, their marketing agency is a little bolder or their clothing brand is a little more fitted) they tell captivating, emotional, punchy stories that leave you no choice but to commit your undivided attention to every word they say.

MrBeast, if you're unfamiliar, is arguably the most famous YouTuber in the world: at the time of writing, he has over 150 million subscribers, he has 30 billion video views, and he's reportedly generating hundreds of millions of dollars from his videos every year. He's recently announced that he will become the first billionaire YouTuber – and I tend to believe him.

How has he done it? In his own words, the first few seconds of every video is the most important – in the opening five seconds of every video he's made, he delivers what he calls 'a hook' – a clear, compelling promise, explaining why you should watch the video, that bypasses your brain's habituation filter, makes you think *WTF?* and in doing so prevents the viewer from tuning out and clicking away.

He says you shouldn't start with anything else; you shouldn't introduce yourself, 'overexplain anything' or even have the typical B-roll footage overlaid with music that most video creators opt for. He essentially screams a compelling promise in his audience's face, which holds their attention long enough for him to deliver upon that promise. Here are some examples of the first five seconds of his videos:

Video 1, first five seconds:

I RECREATED EVERY SINGLE SET FROM *SQUID GAME* IN REAL LIFE, AND WHICHEVER ONE OF THESE 456 PEOPLE SURVIVES THE LONGEST, WINS 456 GRAND! (350 million views)

Video 2, first five seconds:

I PUT 100 PEOPLE INSIDE OF A GIANT CIRCLE, AND WHOEVER LEAVES THE CIRCLE LAST WINS $500,000! (250 million views)

Video 3, first five seconds:

I SPENT $2.5 MILLION DOLLARS ON THIS PRIVATE JET AND HAD 11 PEOPLE PUT THEIR HAND ON IT. WHOEVER TAKES THEIR HAND OFF THE JET LAST, WINS THE PRIVATE JET! (100 million views)

Over the last ten years, I've become known for repeating one hypothetical scenario, over and over again. Whenever I'm faced with a marketing team that has regrettably fallen into that delusional self-centred bubble – when they've fallen into the trap of overestimating how much the world cares about them – I tell them this:

Imagine, the customer you're trying to reach is called Jenny. Imagine right now, she's just left home for work, after a long sleepless night and an argument with her husband. FUCK, she's got a flat tyre and has just broken down on the motorway in the pouring rain; she's now late for work, she's angry, she's tired, and she's time-poor. She pulls out her phone on the side of the road to call the breakdown service and the first thing she sees is your marketing message, your advert, your content. What would you have to say to her, in that moment, to get her to pay attention to you? To get her to click, to get her to buy. Whatever that message is, it's exactly what you need to say to all your customers, because if you can get Jenny, on the side of the road, in that situation, you'll get everyone else.

When you're thinking about storytelling, cater to your most uninterested customer first. For this very reason, you may have noticed that every law in this book starts with a compelling five-second statement about why you should read it. I know most of you will skip sections of this book, but by making you a compelling promise in the first five seconds of each law, I imagine chapter retention increases by at least 25 per cent – and in business, 25 per cent, especially in areas with compounding returns, will completely change your trajectory. If I did 300 talks on stage, a 25 per cent increase in enquiries means potentially hundreds of millions of dollars over the course of ten years – simply by focusing on the first five seconds.

STOP INSULTING GOLDFISH

'You have the attention span of a goldfish.'

This phrase has always been used to mock people with short attention spans, but if recent research is correct, it might actually be a compliment.

In a study led by Microsoft in 2015, Canadian researchers monitored the electrical brain activity of 2,000 participants. The research showed that, in the last 15 years, the average human attention span had dropped from 12 seconds to 8.

To place this in perspective, it was reported in the same article that goldfish have an attention span of 9 seconds:

one whole second longer than humans! So if someone ever compares your attention span to that of a goldfish, an appropriate response is now, in fact, 'thank you'.

> We are increasingly distracted. On average, an office worker will pick up their phones more than 1,500 times per week, amounting to 3 hours and 16 minutes a day, and will check their email inbox 30 times every hour.

The average web page visit lasts for just 10 seconds or so, and Ofcom, the UK's communications regulator, reported in August 2018 that people check their smartphones almost every 10 minutes while they're awake.

I interviewed Johann Hari, bestselling author of *Stolen Focus*, a book about dwindling human attention spans, and he said to me:

> I ended up travelling all over the world. I interviewed 250 of the leading experts in the world about attention and focus, from Moscow to Miami; from a favela, a slum in Rio de Janeiro, where attention had collapsed in a particularly disastrous way; to an office in New Zealand. We are facing a real crisis. Our attention span really is shrinking. There are changes in the way we live that are pouring acid on everyone's ability to pay attention. We have an attentional pathogenic culture, a culture in which it is very hard for all of us to form and sustain deep focus. This is why activities that require deep forms of focus, like reading a book, have just fallen off a cliff in the last 20 years.

Over the last ten years I've produced thousands of videos, and the retention graphs on those videos tell a predictable and often disheartening story: I lose 40–60 per cent of my viewers within the opening seconds in pretty much every video I make that is longer than five minutes, on every social platform.

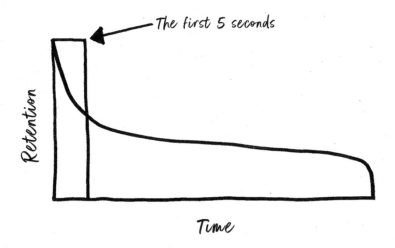

This serves to prove that those first five seconds disproportionally dictate the fate of every second that follows. This is true for social media content, speeches, videos and any other medium that's fighting for your attention.

Five years ago, my marketing company was tasked with promoting a campaign. It was a hilarious two-and-a-half-minute video that had cost hundreds of thousands of dollars to produce and it was our job to make sure it got seen.

When the company sent us the asset to distribute, we initially suggested that they re-edit the video to make the opening five seconds more compelling. In the asset they had sent us, the first five seconds featured an establishing shot of the location overlaid with the brand's logo.

We were instructed that the video needed to be shared as it was, and so we followed their instructions and shared it across a variety of highly engaged social media channels. The results were underwhelming to say the least.

When the client asked me why it had underperformed, we told them that the opening five seconds were killing the entire video. We offered to re-edit the first five seconds and assured them that those five seconds were changing the fate of the proceeding two and a half minutes.

Thankfully they obliged. The re-edited video went viral, racking up more than 3 million views across our social media channels within seven days. A tiny change to the first five seconds had meant that 150 per cent more people continued watching past the ten second mark and stayed watching long enough to enjoy the video, engage with the video (which makes the algorithms share it) and directly share it on their own feeds.

THE LAW: FIGHT FOR THE FIRST FIVE SECONDS

I could give you a hundred more client case studies that prove those first five seconds are do or die for any great story. If you want your story to be heard, you must aggressively, passionately and provocatively design those first five seconds to be thumb-stoppingly compelling, annoyingly magnetic or emotionally engaging. Drop the warm introduction, the pleasantries and the musical B-roll footage, and urgently get to the most compelling promise, point or provocation that you can. No matter the medium, you must earn the right to the attention you're seeking within those first five seconds.

Attention might just be the most generous gift that anyone can give.

PILLAR III
THE PHILOSOPHY

LAW 19

YOU MUST SWEAT THE SMALL STUFF

This law reveals what every great entrepreneur, athlete and coach seems to instinctively know: your success will be defined by your attitude towards the small stuff – the things most people overlook, ignore or don't care about. The easiest way to do big things is by focusing on the small things.

In 2023, my podcast, *The Diary Of A CEO*, became the most downloaded podcast in the UK, according to Apple's end-of-year ranking. It reached the number one spot in the USA Spotify business podcast charts, and for the first time ever, in January gained more subscribers – 320,000 – on YouTube than the legendary podcaster Joe Rogan did in the same month.

Our podcast is relatively new compared to many of our peers. We only started producing the podcast weekly and in video form just over two years ago. I actually don't believe the podcast has been successful because of me as a host; I don't believe that my questions are significantly better, or that our editing is the best, or even that we have the most famous guests in the world. I'm not saying we're bad at these things, but there are others doing those things better.

The secret, in my opinion, is that we <u>sweat the small stuff</u> more than any other team I have ever encountered. <u>We obsess over thousands of small details</u> that I believe most people would dismiss as trivial, crazy or a waste of time.

To offer just a few examples: before a guest arrives, we research their favourite music and play it softly in the background when they arrive – no guest has ever mentioned this, but we believe that it will put them in a better, more open mood. We've researched the optimal room temperature for a conversation – not too hot, not too cold. We A/B test the title, thumbnail and promotion of each podcast episode using AI and social media ads weeks before the podcast is published to the public. We've even hired a full-time in-house data scientist and had him create an AI tool that translates the podcast into multiple languages, so if you click on the YouTube version of the podcast while you're in France, for example, both mine and the guest's voices will be automatically translated into French. We've built a data-driven model that informs us which guests we should book, the best-performing topics the guest has previously discussed, the optimal length for a conversation, and even how many characters long the title of a podcast should be.

Our success can't be attributed to being the best at any one thing, but it *can* be attributed to our relentless focus on the smallest stuff. Searching for minor, seemingly trivial ways to improve has become our religion. This same meticulous philosophy is embodied by all my companies and is a shared characteristic among the world's most innovative, fast-growing and disruptive brands.

★ KAIZEN

For 77 years, through ups and downs, General Motors (GM) had led the way, with higher car sales annually than any other company globally. But in recent years they've been dethroned by Toyota and its unique approach to building cars, a company and a culture.

Toyota was announced as the world's leading automaker in terms of sales for another consecutive year in 2022. Their year-on-year growth of 9.2 per cent increased the gap with their closest competitor, Volkswagen, by almost 2 million cars sold, compared to the 250k gap the year before.

Central to the company's success is something called the 'Toyota Production System'. It was developed during the post-Second World War era in Japan, when the country was undergoing reconstruction and facing a shortage of capital and equipment. In response to these challenges, Toyota engineer Taiichi Ohno formulated a philosophy that allowed the company to extract the maximum potential from each component, machine and employee.

The secret to Toyota's philosophy is a principle known by its Japanese name, '**kaizen**', which means 'continuous improvement'. In the kaizen philosophy, innovation is seen as an incremental process; **it's not about making big leaps forward, but rather making small things better, in small ways, everywhere you can**, on a daily basis.

The kaizen philosophy vehemently rejects the notion that only a select few members of a company's hierarchy are responsible for innovation; it insists that it has to be an everyday task and concern of all employees, at all levels.

Because of the kaizen philosophy, Toyota reportedly implements a staggering one million new ideas each year – the majority of which are suggestions made by ordinary factory-floor workers.

Remarkably, Toyota's US facilities are said to receive a hundred times fewer suggestions from their workers than their Japanese counterparts.

These suggestions are often tiny, including things like increasing the size of water bottles to better hydrate employees, lowering a shelf to make tools slightly easier to reach or making the font on a safety warning just one point size bigger to reduce accidents.

These suggestions may sound insignificant in nature, but the kaizen philosophy believes that it is in fact the smallest of improvements that will cumulatively push the business forward and keep it ahead of competitors that don't care about sweating the small stuff.

Kaizen philosophy says you must create a standard, make sure everyone meets the standard, ask everyone to find ways to improve the standard, and repeat this process for ever.

Create a standard

Everyone follows the new standard

Everyone searches for ways to improve the standard

Implement the improvement

★ KAIZEN VS. CONVENTION

Because Toyota is one of Japan's most successful companies, many have assumed its success is down to 'Japanese' culture, pay dynamics or employee attitudes. But history tells another story.

In the early 1980s, during Ronald Reagan's presidency, tensions had been mounting between the United States and Japan over the large number of imported cars flooding American roads. American industry had been struggling. The General Motors plant in Fremont, California, was a prime example of this deterioration. With regards to quality and productivity, it was GM's worst plant by far: it took much longer on average to assemble a vehicle compared to any other plant and defects in finished cars ran into double digits.

The lack of Fremont-built cars in the employee car park clearly showed the absence of employee pride and confidence. The plant had a backlog of some 5,000 union grievances and there had been a number of strikes and 'sickouts' by the United Auto Workers; labour conditions were toxic and unsustainable.

Huge amounts of temporary workers were needed on any given shift to cover absenteeism rates which exceeded 20 per cent. While special cleaning crews were hired to clear the liquor bottles and drug paraphernalia from the employee car park after each shift.

GM viewed the plant as irreversibly broken, and in February, they closed the factory and laid off the entire workforce.

Toyota spotted an opportunity to resolve the wider trade frictions and test its kaizen philosophy on its competitor's home turf. In 1983, Toyota approached GM with the idea of a joint partnership. The Fremont factory would reopen and be renamed New United Motor Manufacturing Inc. (NUMMI), making the Toyota Corolla and Chevrolet Prizm as its primary products.

Toyota offered to invest cash, oversee the smooth running of the plant and implement their philosophy. They even agreed to rehire the same workers, use the same workers' union, the same facilities and the same equipment, despite the terrible failure of the plant just a year earlier.

Toyota's former chairman, Eiji Toyoda, believed that this was the necessary first step towards having a wholly owned Toyota manufacturing factory in North America. But he also saw it as the perfect way to test the viability and transportability of the Toyota Production System.

Toyota hired back almost 90 per cent of the Fremont hourly union workforce and implemented a 'no lay-off policy', preventing anyone from being fired. They sent 450 group and team leaders to Toyota City to be trained in their unique kaizen-inspired 'Toyota Production System', at a cost of over $3 million. Under the Toyota philosophy, workers would have a strong voice in plant operations. The workers' old, 100-line job descriptions were replaced by two words: 'team member'. Management hierarchy was simplified, reduced from fourteen levels to just three: plant management, group leader, team leader.

As if by magic, employees who had previously been so disillusioned that they turned against their employers began participating in work-related decisions. They received training in problem solving and kaizen practices, so that they became true experts in their respective areas. The parameters of their jobs radically changed as well: rather than being expected to simply do their bit, they were tasked with proactive thinking and improving.

Team members were empowered to quickly implement ideas for improvement, and anything that worked was replicated as best practice. All team members could also stop the entire line at any time to fix a problem by pulling a cord that was accessible from any location in the factory.

Within a year of launching in 1985, the NUMMI factory had the highest quality and productivity of any GM plant in the world.

Rather than an average of twelve defects per vehicle it was now just one, even though cars were assembled in half the time it had previously taken the disgruntled workers. Just 3 per cent of workers was absent at any time, a reflection of the fact that worker satisfaction and engagement had soared. Operational innovation also took off: employee participation in new ideas exceeded 90 per cent and management recorded the implementation of nearly 10,000 new ideas.

By 1988, NUMMI was winning awards, and by 1990, the Toyota Production System and its kaizen philosophy became the global industry standard for manufacturing. All in under two years. The building, workforce and equipment was unchanged. The philosophy was new and the outcome was radically different.

1 PER CENT CAN CHANGE YOUR FUTURE

The great illusion in life and business that makes the kaizen philosophy of incremental improvements so poorly adopted, disregarded and overlooked, is that small things are just small things.

This is objectively true, but a large number of small things is a large thing, and it's easier, more inclusive of all team members, and therefore more achievable to aim at

improving a large number of small things than it is to galvan-
ise people to find and implement big things.

It's an unfortunate reality of life that things that are easy
to do are also very easy *not* to do. It's easy to save $1, so it's
also easy not to save it. It's easy to brush your teeth, so it's
also easy not to brush your teeth. When things are easy to
do, and not to do, the outcome of doing or not doing them is
invisible in the short-term, so we often choose not to do them.
But maths and economics clearly illustrate how our smallest
decisions have the biggest impact on our future position.

Over time, the difference between allowing something to
worsen by 1 per cent each day vs. improve by 1 per cent each
day becomes extremely significant. Consider this:

Year	Year Start	Year End: 1% better each day	Year End: 1% worse each day
1	£100	£3,778	£2.5517964452291100000
2	£3,778	£142,759	£0.0651166509788394000
3	£142,759	£5,393,917	£0.0016616443849302700
4	£5,393,917	£203,800,724	£0.0000424017823469998
5	£203,800,724	£7,700,291,275	£0.0000010820071746445
6	£7,700,291,275	£290,943,449,735	£0.0000000276106206197
7	£290,943,449,735	£10,992,842,727,652	£0.0000000007045668355
8	£10,992,842,727,652	£415,347,351,332,000	£0.0000000000179791115
9	£415,347,351,332,000	£15,693,249,374,391,300	£0.0000000000004587903
10	£15,693,249,374,391,300	£592,944,857,206,937,000	£0.0000000000000117074

If you start the year with £100 and manage to improve that
value by 1 per cent each day for 365 days, you will have
multiplied that value by 37. Over ten years, assuming the
same 1 per cent per day incremental improvement, that
value balloons to £15 quadrillion!

Conversely, letting that £100 degrade by 1 per cent each day quickly reduces your money to £2.55 after one year, 6p after 2 years and 0p thereafter.

1% better each day vs. 1% worse each day

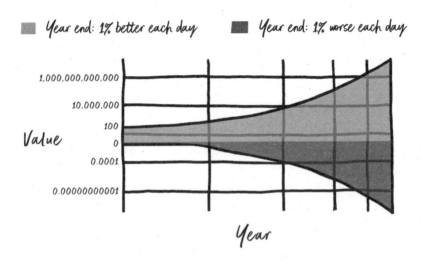

Not brushing your teeth today will have no visible impact. Not brushing your teeth every day this week might cause a slight smell but there will be no significant consequences. Not brushing your teeth every day for five years will have you screaming in a chair as a dentist rips the molars from your mouth. When did this dental problem occur? It began today, by overlooking something that was easy to do and easy not to do.

For Toyota, the kaizen culture didn't happen overnight. It took 20 years for two suggestions per person per year to become standard across the business.

Kaizen philosophy takes time, investment and tremendous belief.

★ THE ART OF INCREASING SUGGESTIONS

You've seen it everywhere: the company suggestion box – a small opening on top for employee suggestions, a padlock, a general look of neglect. Though it comes from a good place and is well intended, its failure to yield any meaningful results is usually down to two factors. One: a large number of 'suggestions' are usually not 'creative ideas' by Toyota's standards but anonymous complaints, unconstructive criticisms or passive-aggressive attacks on how the company operates. Two: the few proactive suggestions are either never actioned or cannot possibly be actioned because they are impractical. It is the deadly mix of complaining by the workforce and lack of follow-through by management that leads sadly to the destruction of trust and the dusty death of the suggestion box.

So what's different about Japanese companies' *teian*, or suggestion systems? Why do they work where other systems fail? Are their employees smarter or more sensible? Are the managers more open to finding useful suggestions among the unhelpful ones? Is it to do with Japanese culture? The answer is much simpler, and unconnected to any national culture.

The answer lies with the person we will call the 'idea coach' and any company can take advantage of this. When Toyota's manager of domestic public relations in Japan, Ron Haigh, was asked how they can accept 99 per cent of the ideas that arrive in their suggestion system, he had a telling answer.

Ron explained that supervisors reviewed their employees' ideas with them one on one, coaching them on the practicalities, giving them direction and support to make the idea well-rounded and effective, and helped it to succeed. This sits in stark contrast to most Western suggestion-box systems where the manager says 'yes' or – perhaps more often – 'no', then explains why an idea will 'never work'.

Under the kaizen system, your supervisor is your idea coach. It remains the employee's idea, but through working with someone who is more experienced with a deeper understanding of the art of the possible, 99 per cent of ideas are accepted and collaboratively developed into something that could work.

All employees at Toyota are tasked with coming up with at least one idea per month – making it a central part of everyone's role. Supervisors are also tasked with making sure each of their team members succeeds in coming up with at least one idea per month. This ensures that everyone is rowing in the same direction – it's in everyone's best interests to help ideas succeed.

Coaches also have coaches – each supervisor has a coach above them, who is incentivised to help the supervisor develop enough new ideas each month. In this way, everyone from the top to the bottom of the company is positively encouraged to listen, to refine and to support all new suggestions.

Critically, the person who implements the idea has to be the one who had it in the first place. You can imagine how this principle alone alters the types of suggestions people make. A criticism is no longer an idea; 'I hate the office music' can't be a suggestion, as under this principle every idea must be practical, productive and focused on a solution.

Finally, Toyota employees are all provided with an education in kaizen, the Toyota Production System, and how the idea-suggestion process works. It's exceptionally rare for Western counterparts to educate their teams on the philosophy of incremental gains, how to properly formulate suggestions and the rationale behind their philosophy.

✱ AVOID PAYING FOR SUGGESTIONS

Companies tend to treat employees like rats in a maze sprinting after cheese by paying them for the behaviour they want to reinforce. This is the easy, less-effective, short-term, costly approach. The harder, more effective, cheaper approach is to create a culture where people care enough, are motivated enough and are recognised sufficiently enough to step forward, contribute and invest their energy in the betterment of the company.

Under the kaizen philosophy, you need lots of ideas, very often, to make meaningful progress over time. And in order to get lots of ideas, you need people to be driven by their own curiosity, motivation and care. There's a famous fable that illustrates this idea well:

There was once an old woman, who lived alone. Every afternoon, her peace and quiet was disrupted by children playing noisily on the street outside her house. As time went on, the children got noisier and noisier, and the woman became more and more infuriated. One day she had an idea: she called them over and explained to them amiably that hearing them playing joyfully outside was the highlight of her day, but that there was a problem: in her old age and isolation, she was going deaf. So, she asked, would they be willing to make even more of a racket, just for her? She went one step further, offering them each a quarter for their trouble.

The next day, the kids eagerly returned and made a huge din outside her house, as requested; they were each paid their 25 cents and asked to return the next day. But this time, the woman only paid them 20 cents. And the following day it was just 15 cents! The poor old woman explained that she was running out of money, and that their fee would drop to a nickel a day from now on. The kids were appalled at the prospect of earning a fifth of what they were earning just days before. They stormed off and pledged never to return. It was simply not worth the effort, they said, for just five cents a day.

The woman's clever idea was to take the joy out of the thing the children loved doing and were doing for free. The bigger lesson is clear, though: it's possible to replace a genuine motivation with a synthetic one. This phenomenon is also known as 'motivation crowding': if you attach a financial reward to ideas, it can interfere with or even eliminate people's genuine creative energy and ambition.

This is more than a fable; this is science. I interviewed motivation expert and author Daniel Pink about the impact financial rewards have on our motivation and he shared a plethora of research that shows that paying someone to do something that they once did for fun will cause them to lose the intrinsic joy of doing that task. When a hobby becomes a job, motivation drops.

Scholars at the London School of Economics and Political Science looked at 51 studies on pay-for-performance schemes and stated: 'We find that financial incentives may indeed reduce intrinsic motivation and diminish ethical or other reasons for complying with workplace social norms such as fairness. As a consequence, the provision of financial incentives can result in a negative impact on overall performance.'

★ INNOVATION DISTORTION

Innovation is often portrayed as a miraculous occurrence, something that only arises from the genius of a select few or the luck of a fortunate accident. The light bulb, Velcro, penicillin and Post-it notes are just a few examples that perpetuate this misleading belief.

The painful, incremental process behind the breakthrough is nearly always neglected in the retelling of these stories of invention, which only highlight the final outcome.

> Don't let these myths deceive you – true innovation is nearly always born from the sweat and determination of persistent individuals and great teams bound together by the right culture and philosophy, not from eureka moments, accidental fortune or intentional genius.

In all the companies I've founded that have reached the summit of their industry, there was no one decision, invention or innovation that got us there. My central focus has always been to get our teams to 'out-care the competition'. Creating a culture through recognition, celebration and evidence, which continually proved to all of us that the smallest of things – the easiest and most accessible things – can have the biggest of impacts.

'One per cent' is the most repeated phrase in my companies, and one of my key responsibilities as CEO is identifying and encouraging those 1 per cent gains, wherever they might arise within the company.

★ THE LAW: YOU MUST SWEAT THE SMALL STUFF

I've always felt that I have a cheat code. While our competitors think consistency or big wins are the paths to the podium, I know – without a shadow of a doubt – the correct route is to be found by making consistently small improvements, sweating the smallest stuff and fighting for tiny gains.

If you don't care about tiny details you'll produce bad work because good work is the culmination of hundreds of tiny details. The world's most successful people all sweat the small stuff.

LAW 20

A SMALL MISS NOW CREATES A BIG MISS LATER

This law reveals why most people end up lost in their relationships and work because they've overlooked one simple, ongoing discipline in their lives.

Asked to explain how Tiger Woods became one of the greatest golfers of all time, most of us would reel off the same well-known facts: he was a child prodigy, his talent already apparent when he was just two years old; he devoted his life to training, famously spending hours analysing footage of his performance; his own father described him as 'The Chosen One' and had unshakeable belief in his potential.

But those who really know Woods will tell you it's his kaizen philosophy of obsessive, continuous tiny improvements that deserves the credit for his accomplishments.

In 1997, after the Masters tournament and just seven months after turning professional, Woods told his coach, Butch Harmon, that he wanted to rework – effectively rebuild – his entire swing from scratch. Harmon warned Woods that there were no shortcuts, that it would be a long journey, and that his performance at tournaments would get much worse before he saw any improvement.

Friends, fellow players and experts agreed, but Woods knew his swing could be marginally better, so he ignored them. He viewed reinventing his swing not as a threat to his game, but an opportunity to incrementally improve it, and so he took the chance and started his kaizen journey.

Woods was directly inspired by Toyota's quest for perfection, and began to speak of the kaizen philosophy as if it were his religion. He and his coach went on to create their own kaizenesque sequence of: hitting practice balls repeatedly; reviewing footage of his swing to discover improvements; implementing any improvements in the gym and on the course. And repeat.

Just as his coach predicted, it was a long road. Woods stopped winning – in fact he didn't win anything for 18 months – and pundits began to say it was all over for him. But Woods and his coaches had faith that small improvements would show up after longer periods of time. He told his critics, 'Winning is not always the barometer of getting better.'

Woods's kaizen attitude paid off. His new swing would develop into a lethal weapon: more precise, more accurate and more versatile than ever before. He enjoyed a record six straight wins starting in late 1999 and since then, Tiger Woods has arguably become the best golfer of all time, with 82 PGA tour wins – more than anyone has ever achieved before.

Woods proves that the pursuit of perfection is a matter of discipline, not heroism.

Charles Darwin's theory of evolution and 'survival of the fittest' posits that not making small adaptations can result in extinction, while small mutations create a survival advantage. This idea serves as a fitting analogy for the kaizen philosophy.

As Charles Darwin argued, an individual's success won't be determined by a single stroke of genius. Instead, it will be the by-product of a philosophy that fosters gradual evolution, mutation and adaptation in any and every aspect of an organism, over an extended period of time.

In aviation there's a principle called the '1 in 60 rule', which means that being off target by 1 degree will lead to a plane missing its end destination by 1 mile for every 60 miles flown. This concept also applies to our lives, careers, relationships and personal growth. Just a small deviation from the optimal route is amplified over time and distance – something that feels like a small miss now can create a big miss later.

This highlights the need for the real-time course corrections and adjustments that the kaizen philosophy provides. If we are to be successful, we all need simple rituals to assess our course and make the necessary small adjustments, as frequently as possible, in all aspects of our lives.

John Gottman, the acclaimed relationship psychologist, concluded from decades of research that the existence of 'contempt' in a relationship is the biggest predictor of divorce. Contempt is the subtle disrespect and disregard of your partner – like an aircraft being one degree off course, the harm happens slowly, over time, in relationships where the couple fail at conflict resolution because of poor or infrequent communication.

This insight led me to establish one of the most important kaizen-style rituals I have in my romantic relationship: a scheduled weekly check-in with my partner. We sit down, talk openly and seek marginal ways to improve, align and resolve unaddressed issues – both small and large.

In one of our recent check-ins, she mentioned that my response of 'Sorry, I'm busy with something' when interrupted while working can come across as blunt and irritated. She asked if I could add a loving word to my response to soften the message – my unintentional bluntness had been making her feel subtly rejected.

Now, instead of sounding like a grumpy workaholic, I say, 'Sorry, love, I'm busy with something.' Although it seems like a minor change, expressing and rectifying this issue has prevented it from compounding over time and causing a big problem later. Like a plane slightly off course, we've nudged our relationship back on track by one-degree so that we can continue in the right direction.

I apply the same principles to business, friendships and my relationship with myself. I have weekly check-ins with my directors and friends, and even a self-assessment in my diary to ensure everything is on course, aligned, and that any necessary course corrections are identified and implemented.

Week after week, my inbox is flooded with messages from individuals who have found themselves lost in their careers, businesses, relationships and friendships. In nearly every instance, it eventually becomes evident that their present circumstances are a consequence of neglecting small things for an extended period of time. They failed to check in with themselves and others, speak up, engage in difficult conversations or address the seemingly trivial issues in their lives. Consequently, they veered off course ever so slightly – by a mere one degree – which ultimately led them to a destination they didn't want to go to.

★ THE LAW: A SMALL MISS NOW CREATES A BIG MISS LATER

The kaizen philosophy isn't just about business, efficiencies or improvements; it's about continually ensuring you're on the right path and heading to the destination that you intend to, want to and desire to visit.

The smallest
seeds of
today's
negligence
will bloom into
tomorrow's
biggest
regrets.

LAW 21

YOU MUST OUT-FAIL THE COMPETITION

This law proves that the higher your failure rate, the higher your chances of success. It will inspire you to start failing much faster than you currently are!

Thomas J. Watson was president of IBM for an incredible 38 years, was one of the most notable entrepreneurs in the USA in the first half of the twentieth century – alongside Henry Ford – and he became one of the richest men of his time because of his enormous success at IBM. His core principle of innovation could be summed up in a simple sentence: 'If you want to increase your success rate, double your failure rate.' He also said, 'Every time we've moved ahead in IBM, it was because someone was willing to take a chance, put their head on the block, and try something new.'

When he was asked if he was going to fire a male employee who made a mistake that had cost the company $600,000, he swiftly replied, 'No, I just spent $600,000 training him. Why would I want somebody to hire his experience?'

He instinctively understood that failure was both an opportunity for progress, and that the opposite – a lack of failure – would be the death of IBM. He warned against complacency, even when IBM reached the top of their industry, and in line with the kaizen approach, he said, 'Whenever an individual or a business decides that success has been attained, progress stops.'

Even before I had heard about Thomas J. Watson and his unconventional perspective on failure, I spent ten years encouraging, measuring and driving up my team's failure rate. We all know failure is feedback, and we can agree that feedback is knowledge, and as the cliché asserts, knowledge is power. Therefore, failure is power, and **if you want to increase your chances of success, you must increase your failure rate**. Those who fail to constantly fail are destined to be the eternal followers. Those that out-fail their competition will be followed for ever.

★ HOW TO INCREASE YOUR FAILURE RATE

Booking.com is the largest and most successful hotel booking site in the world. But, like every industry leader, it started small, broken and behind.

Gillian Tans, Booking.com's former CEO, said: 'Many companies start with a nice product and market it all over the world. Booking did the opposite. We had a basic product and then worked hard to figure out what customers wanted. We failed so many times.'

A few years after launching, a Booking.com engineer attended a conference in 2004, where he heard Microsoft's Ronny Kohavi speak on the importance of experimentation and failure. He took the learnings back to his team at Booking.com, where there were constant, time-wasting disagreements about the next step forward, the right features to implement and the direction to take.

They began to learn what customers wanted through simple experiments, and then used those insights to build a product – the Booking.com we know today. As Tans says, 'We grew like this, without any marketing or PR, just constant testing and experimentation of what our customers liked.'

Having seen the success that increasing experimentation and failure had had on the firm, Booking.com developed and launched its own 'experimentation platform' in 2005 that allowed it to tremendously scale up the amount of tests it was running.

Adrienne Enggist, senior director of product development at Booking.com, recalled:

> I came from small businesses where CEOs launched a big product redesign every six months, and by the time you rolled it out, it was hard to figure out what worked and what did not work. Here, the team was small, fitted on one floor, and it was exciting to see everyone take risks, fail, push small changes very quickly, and use experiments to measure the impact.

Booking.com would go as far as appointing a 'director of experimentation', who has publicly evangelised about how critical it is for companies to fail more, fail more often and measure those experiments, saying: 'We believe that controlled experimentation is the most successful approach to building products that customers want.'

Today Booking.com has 20,300 employees and $10 billion in annual revenue. The website is available in 43 languages and features over 28 million listings in every corner of the world. And in the moment that you're reading this, 1,000 experiments are being run by Booking.com – led and devised by every single product and technology team they have. They credit their culture of out-failing their competition as being a key reason why they've overtaken their competition.

Amazon follows the same fail-faster religion. Jeff Bezos, founder of the trillion-dollar e-commerce platform, sent the following memo to his shareholders when the company became the fastest ever to reach annual sales of $100 billion:

> One area where I think we are especially distinctive is failure. I believe we are the best place in the world to fail (we have plenty of practice!), and **failure and invention are inseparable twins. To invent you have to experiment**, and if you know in advance that it's going to work, it's not an experiment. Most large organisations embrace the idea of invention, but are not willing to suffer the string of failed experiments necessary to get there.
>
> Outsized returns often come from betting against conventional wisdom, and conventional wisdom is usually right. Given a 10 per cent chance of a 100 times payoff, you should take that bet every time. But you're still going to be wrong nine times out of ten. We all know that if you swing for the fences, you're going to strike out a lot, but you're also going to hit some home runs. The difference between baseball and business, however, is that baseball has a truncated outcome distribution. When you swing, no matter how well you connect with the ball, the most runs you can get is four. In business, every once in a while, when you step up to the plate, you can score 1,000 runs. This long-tailed distribution of returns is why it's important to be bold. **Big winners pay for so many experiments.**

In a related interview, Jeff Bezos expanded upon this idea:

> To be innovative, you have to experiment. You need to do more experiments per week, per month, per year, per decade. It's that simple. You cannot invent without experimenting. We want failures where we're trying to do something new, untested, never proven. That's a real experiment. And they come in all scale sizes.

Amazon has one of the biggest business graveyards of failure – something I'm sure Bezos is proud of – A9.com (the Amazon search engine), the Fire Phone and their Endless.com shoe website are just some of the notable projects that were so unsuccessful you've probably never heard about them.

However, when one of their experiments pays off, it completely changes the trajectory of their business, and covers the losses of all of their failures combined: Amazon Prime, Amazon Echo, the Kindle and, most notably, Amazon Web Services (AWS).

AWS was launched as an experiment unrelated to Amazon's e-commerce business, but in 20 years has become the fastest-growing B2B company of all time. It is the world's top cloud computing platform. It has operations in 24 geographical regions and boasts over 1 million active users in 190 countries, $62 billion in revenue and $18.5 billion in annual profit. In 2022, that little experiment from 20 years ago was the single biggest contributor to Amazon's total profit. In 2011, Amazon created its very own experimentation platform, Weblab, which now runs more than 20,000 experiments each year to continuously innovate and improve on customer experiences.

Jeff Bezos explained how Amazon decides which experiments a company should pursue in his 2015 shareholder letter:

> Some decisions are consequential and irreversible or nearly irreversible – one-way doors – and these decisions must be made methodically, carefully, slowly, with great deliberation and consultation. If you walk through and don't like what you see on the other side, you can't get back to where you were before. We can call these Type 1 decisions.
>
> But **most decisions aren't like that; they are changeable, reversible – they're two-way doors**. If you've made a suboptimal Type 2 decision, you don't have to live with the consequences for that long. You can reopen the door and go back through. Type 2 decisions can and should be made quickly by high-judgement individuals or small groups.
>
> As organizations get larger, there seems to be a tendency to use the heavyweight Type 1 decision-making process on most decisions, including many Type 2 decisions. The end result of this is slowness, unthoughtful risk aversion, failure to experiment sufficiently, and consequently diminished invention.

★ A BATTLE BETWEEN FATHER AND SON

For six years I advised an industry-leading, multi-billion-dollar e-commerce company in the food industry that had two brands underneath it. One brand was run by the father, who had founded the whole group, and the other, much newer brand had been launched by the son. When my company was appointed to help them scale their marketing, customer acquisition, social media and innovation efforts, I initially spent up to four days a week in the boardroom with both the father and the son, understanding their brands, their goals and their objectives.

I visited both brands every week without fail; I travelled the world with them; I was in the room, doing everything from advising their crisis-management press releases to producing their social media strategy and advising them on which marketing activities to pursue. When they went to Paris to launch a new product, I was on the plane; if they had an event in America, I was there; if they had an important meeting in Singapore, I travelled with them; and when they launched in the Middle East, I was on the ground.

In the six years that I advised them and acted as a member of their extended family, I watched the son's part of the company go from an unknown, small, unprofitable brand to the best-loved, most culturally relevant, highest grossing brand in its industry. At the same time, I saw the father's brand falter, stagnate and slow down. Ultimately the son's brand would overtake his father's – generating more than a billion dollars in revenue.

I had front-row seats to both businesses, their decisions and their philosophy, and I can say with total confidence that the most significant reason why the son overtook his father is that the son had a failure rate that exceeded that of his father by a factor of ten.

When my teams made a technological discovery relating to marketing, growth or social media, we brought it to both brands at the same time, on the same day, but we were greeted with very different responses. I recall one such innovation where we found a way to grow their social media following

20 times faster than usually possible using a technique we'd discovered with a particular platform. I personally took this discovery to both the son and the father in 2016, in two separate meetings.

The father's team listened to the idea, requested a bigger presentation, scoffed at our fee and they informed me that they would need various layers of sign-off to proceed. Nine months later, they were still 'discussing it internally'.

The son didn't put me in front of a team at first; he wanted to hear the idea himself. Before I could even finish my explanation, he called out to his assistant, 'Bring all of the marketing team into the room asap.' When the marketing team arrived, he told me to repeat what I had just said, and upon finishing my explanation, he looked at his team and remarked, 'We're going to do this today.' He looked back at me and said, 'Steven, whatever you need, it's sorted – full steam ahead, right now!'

No contracts, no lawyers, no layers of sign-off, no delays – trust, speed and empowerment.

That one idea resulted in the son's brand adding 10 million more followers to one of its social media channels over the following months. In the end, it cost them 95 per cent less to grow their social media page using our discovery, than all the strategies that the brand had adopted in the past.

The son instinctively knew that this was a 'Type 2' decision – the sort of decision that wouldn't have irreversible harm if it failed, could be reversed, but also could ultimately change the course of the brand if it succeeded. And he knew that in the face of a Type 2 decision, Jeff Bezos's words should be followed: 'Type 2 decisions can and should be made quickly by high-judgement individuals or small groups.'

The son knew that the biggest cost wasn't failing, it was missing an opportunity to grow and wasting time to learn a new lesson regardless of the outcome. If the experiment had failed, it would have cost them one day and a little money, and we'd be on to the next experiment within 24 hours, one failure closer to the right answer.

By the time the father's brand had decided to cautiously proceed with the idea, some ten months later, it no longer worked – the platform loophole we were using had been closed, and growing a social media channel had once again become expensive, complicated and difficult.

It's important to note that most of the ideas we brought to the son didn't have such astonishing results. Most experiments fail, no matter how well-designed. I would estimate that three in ten were tragic failures, three in ten were average failures, three in ten were good, and one in ten was great – so great that it changed the fortunes of their business and paid for any losses incurred by the other nine.

Get to 51 per cent certainty, and make the decision.

Many years later I would have the honour of sharing the same stage as Barack Obama in Brazil, and Obama would remark that when facing tough decisions – like whether or not to fly into Pakistan unannounced at night in the hope of assassinating Osama bin Laden – he turned to probability instead of certainty.

He said every decision was painstakingly difficult: 'If it was an easily solvable problem, or even a modestly difficult but solvable problem, it would not reach me, because, by definition, somebody else would have solved it.'

Instead of saying, 'Will X or Y happen if I make this decision?' he would say, 'What is the chance of X or Y occurring?' He insisted that having smarter people in the room was key: 'Having the confidence to have people around you who were smarter than you or disagreed with you is critical.' And he would weigh each decision not just on the probability of being right, but the impact it would have if he was wrong: 'You don't have to get to 100 per cent certainty on your big decisions, get to 51 per cent, and when you get there, make the decision quickly and be at peace with the fact that you made the decision based on the information you had.'

As I came to learn from working with the father and son's companies, from my more than ten years advising the world's leading brands, and from Barack Obama, the truth is that **perfect decisions exist only in hindsight**; dwelling too long on potential outcomes, and procrastinating in the process, is futile. The real cost of indecision in business is wasted time. That time could have been used failing your way to knowledge that would ultimately help you to succeed. Instead, some brands freeze in fear, and in their attempt to avert *any* losses, they end up losing the most expensive and important things: opportunity, knowledge and time.

Nassim Taleb, author and researcher, sums it up in this graph:

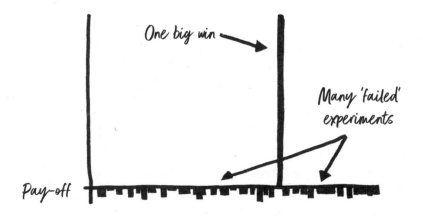

CREATING A PRO-FAILURE PHILOSOPHY

Some of the companies I worked with got this right: they had lightning-fast experimentation cycles, they viewed change as an opportunity, they out-failed their competition and they nearly always outpaced their industry. Some of the companies I worked with believed in this philosophy, tried it and failed; they asked their teams to innovate more, wrote it on the office wall, but it simply never happened. And some companies didn't believe in it at all; those companies were almost never founder-led, they were either stagnant or in decline, and they viewed the changing world as nothing more than a threat.

I discovered five consistent principles that the most innovative companies naturally embodied, which I believe enable teams to out-fail their competition:

1. REMOVE BUREAUCRACY

'It is a villain,' says Walmart CEO Doug McMillon. 'Its tentacles should be treated like the cancers they so much resemble,' says Berkshire Hathaway vice chair Charlie Munger. 'It's a disease,' says Jamie Dimon, the CEO of JPMorgan Chase.

All of these esteemed business leaders are talking about 'bureaucracy' – a word that seems to have no successful fans. In simple terms, the worst corporate bureaucracies are companies with lots of rules, long and painful sign-off processes, and several layers of hierarchy between the bottom and the top.

These systems disempower employees, slow companies down, disincentivise experimentation, delay innovation and stifle the goldmine of ideas that exist in the minds of the workforce.

Systems like this are a tax on human ingenuity, energy and entrepreneurism.

As Laurence Peter, author of *The Peter Principle*, put it: 'Bureaucracy defends the status quo long past the time the quo has lost its status.'

Bureaucracy is often seen by company leaders as an unfortunate necessity for businesses operating in complex regulatory and international environments. The US workforce is an example of this: since 1983, the number of managers, supervisors and administrators has increased by over 100 per cent, in comparison to an increase of roughly 40 per cent for all other occupations.

In recent years, nearly two-thirds of workers said their organisations had become more bureaucratic, according to a *Harvard Business Review* survey. Meanwhile, productivity growth has stalled. In the bigger companies that have come to dominate Western economies, bureaucracy is particularly detrimental. In the US labour force, over one-third of workers are employed in firms of 5,000 or more employees – and frontline workers are generally overseen by eight management levels.

Considering the astounding speed of change happening in the world – as revealed in Law 5 – doing anything to slow down your company's rate of experimentation at this point in history is a death wish.

Haier Group, a Chinese appliance business that generates more than $35 billion in annual sales, understands this better than anyone. To avoid the toxic consequences of bureaucracy, they've divided their 75,000 employees into 4,000 micro-organisations, most of which have just 10 to 15 employees. Decisions are made at lightning speed by small, autonomous teams and subsequently they've managed to out-fail their competition, innovate at the speed of the market, and dominate their industry.

And Steve Jobs, co-founder and CEO of Apple, when speaking about bureaucracy at the company, said:

> We are organised like a start-up. We're the biggest start-up on the planet and we all meet for three hours once a week and we talk about everything we're doing. Teamwork is dependent on trusting the other folks to come through with their part without watching them all the time, but trusting that they're going to come through with their parts. And that's what we do really well.

The key, as I've witnessed in all of my own companies, clients and case studies, is to make project teams as small as they can possibly be, to give them more authority, trust and access to resources when making decisions, and to cut back all sign-off processes, especially when a team is seeking to make a Type 2 – low-consequence, reversible – decision.

2. FIX THE INCENTIVES

In 2020, my company was tasked with resuscitating a faltering fashion e-commerce company that was on the brink of financial collapse. The Covid-19 pandemic had prompted the closure of their physical stores, resulting in a reduction of staff and wages. Employee morale was on its knees and a new CEO had recently been appointed to steer the company in a new direction.

During my first presentation to the CEO, I outlined the need for the company to increase their rate of failure by an order of magnitude in all areas, including marketing. They were lagging behind their competitors, missing opportunities and squandering resources on ineffective traditional tactics.

Upon hearing my proposal, the CEO mentioned that the company already encouraged their team to experiment more, citing the inclusion of 'fail faster' as one of their four core values in the employee handbook, and two of the words prominently displayed on the office kitchen wall.

Following my presentation, I held private sessions with staff – from managers to interns – for several hours. During a meeting with the brand's marketing team, I posed the question, 'What reason do you have to fail more often?' A prolonged, revealing silence ensued before I rephrased the question, asking, 'What reason have you got not to fail more often?' The marketing manager's previously paralysed mouth sprang to life as she drowned me with a series of responses, including 'I don't want to be embarrassed', 'I won't receive a pay increase', 'people will think less of me', 'I might be fired', 'I'm too busy to try new things'.

As she rattled off more and more reasons, it became increasingly apparent that the organisation was plagued by a disease called 'misaligned incentives' – what the company expected of its employees was not in line with what it incentivised them to do. The company wanted innovators, risk takers, entrepreneurs – but, upon close inspection – as is the case in most slow, dying companies – people were simply incentivised to … do their job, no less, no more.

It is startling to me, still, that any CEO would believe that the cute words, clichéd slogans and aspirational values they put in employee handbooks matter at all.

Words need evidence, incentives and example to bring them to life. Human behaviour is not driven by platitudes, slogans and wishful thinking.

If you want to predict what a group of people will do over the long term, you need to look at their incentives, not their instructions.

To redesign the incentives of the marketing department, one of the many systems I implemented was a recognition process designed to celebrate an employee or team when an experiment was successfully executed, regardless of the outcome. After all, executing the experiment is the controllable factor; whether it's successful or not in the market is impossible to control, so it's not where our incentives should focus.

3. PROMOTE AND FIRE

I told the CEO of the fashion company to identify the employees that were failing the fastest and to promote them as high in the organisation as she could. Companies don't have one company culture; every manager in an organisation creates a sub-culture underneath them.

At my first marketing company we had almost 30 managers, and I observed time and time again how one team's satisfaction, attitude and philosophy could be starkly different to the team they were sat next to, purely because of their manager. With 30 managers, we really had 30 company cultures.

Influence trickles down: you need the people at the highest point in the company to be the most avid disciples of your cultural values.

When you promote those employees – or give them pay rises – let all team members know why they're being promoted, and point out their exceptionally high failure rate.

Conversely, it's important to swiftly remove individuals from the team that stand in the way of the flow of new ideas, fast failure and experimentation. Especially if those employees are managers – one bad manager can destroy the morale, motivation and optimism of a great team of perfectly capable, hopeful and entrepreneurial employees.

4. MEASURE ACCURATELY

While advising the fashion e-commerce business, I asked the CEO to establish, educate and continually communicate to all team members an 'experimentation process' that everyone should follow, use to measure, and use to communicate a new idea or experiment that they wanted to pursue.

> Too often employees don't step forward with new ideas because they're unclear on the process they should follow. Education is the easiest way to remove operational psychological friction.

And lastly, I told the CEO to measure – team by team – the organisation's failure rate, with a clear goal of increasing every team's failure rate by a factor of ten by year end.

In business, you don't improve what you don't measure, and what you focus on grows. By establishing visible KPIs (key performance indicators) and clear goals, and making them everyone's responsibility, nobody at the fashion business could be 'too busy' for experimentation – as is the case under the kaizen philosophy – it became a central part of everyone's job.

The organisation slowly changed direction, breaking even for the first time in seven years in the first year, and turning a sizeable profit in the second.

Its newfound creativity, innovation and empowered workforce made it feel like a brand-new company. Staff retention rates improved, employee satisfaction scores soared and the company innovated more than ever before.

5. SHARE THE FAILURE

If you want to maximise the return from every failure, it is crucial to disseminate the details of each failed hypothesis, experiment and outcome throughout your organisation. This information represents a form of intellectual capital that can serve as a foundation for future experiments. By openly sharing failures, you can prevent the duplication of unsuccessful efforts, stimulate the development of new ideas, and foster a culture of continuous experimentation. As Thomas Edison said, 'I have not failed. I've just found 10,000 ways that won't work.'

THE LAW: YOU MUST OUT-FAIL THE COMPETITION

Failure is not a bad thing, and to increase your chances of success you need to increase your failure rate. Every time something is tried and found not to work, valuable information is gained that can be shared with your team. Businesses that experiment faster, fail faster, and then continue to experiment, nearly always outpace the competition.

Failure =
Feedback.

Feedback =
Knowledge.

Knowledge =
Power.

Failure gives
you power.

LAW 22

YOU MUST BECOME A PLAN-A THINKER

This law will demonstrate why your Plan B in life might just be the biggest hurdle to the success of your Plan A.

The story I'm about to tell you changed my life.

On Friday, 13 October 1972, Nando Parrado woke up after being unconscious for 48 hours. He wasn't coming round after an operation or emerging from some two-day bender: he was surrounded by dead bodies and injured friends, thousands of feet above sea level in a glacial valley in the Andes, amidst the wreckage of an airplane crash, with no means of calling for help or even working out exactly where they were.

Of the 45 passengers, members of a Uruguayan rugby team on their way to Chile for a match, 29 survived the crash. Initially they did what they could, drinking melted snow and eating whatever they could salvage from their luggage. 'On the first day,' recalled Parrado, 'I slowly sucked the chocolate off the peanut … On the second day … I sucked gently on the peanut for hours, allowing myself only a tiny nibble now and then. I did the same on the third day, and when I finally nibbled the peanut down to nothing, there was no food left at all.'

A full week later, facing the threat of starvation and knowing, after finding a transistor radio, that the Chilean authorities had called off their search efforts, Nando and his fellow survivors did the unimaginable: they decided they had no choice but to eat the dead bodies.

Among the few women on the plane had been Parrado's mother and little sister, whom he had invited on the trip to watch him play. His mother, Xenia, 49, died instantly on impact; his little sister, Susy, initially survived the crash but died in her brother's arms a week later.

The first body they ate was the pilot's, since they held him responsible for the crash. Other bodies, the survivors agreed, were off limits, including those of Xenia and Susy. But Parrado became tormented by the idea that someone would violate their agreement, and he couldn't live with himself if that happened.

Two months after the crash, Parrado announced that he was setting off to find help. He was starved, had no mountaineering experience, and no idea where he was going, but somehow this was a better option than eating the bodies of his mother and sister: 'I didn't want to have to eat their bodies, I didn't want to face that moment,' he said.

Nando and his friend Robert sewed together material for a sleeping bag and knocked together a sled, then set off. They decided to ascend rather than descend, since a higher vantage point would give them a better chance of working out an escape route. It took them three gruelling days and they somehow made it to the top of a 15,000-foot peak three days later, but didn't find what they were hoping for.

What I saw when we reached the peak of the first mountain really froze me. I couldn't breathe, speak or think, what I saw was horrible; instead of green valleys, we saw mountains and snow-covered peaks, 360 degrees around us, stretching as far as we could see into the horizon. And that's when I knew I was dead … But there is no way that I can go back, and eat the bodies of my mother and sister, the only way is forward, we will die, but we will die trying … I will keep on going until I stop breathing.

They staggered down the other side of the mountain and began to force themselves along the glacier below, growing ever weaker day by day. The pair limped on for ten days through the ice-cold mountains, deep snow and deadly crevasses.

'It was a blurry, continuous, painful effort, the mountains were so huge that it feels like you're not making any progress, you would set yourself a target location in the distance, and you would think it would take two or three hours to get there, but it was so huge that you never seemed to get there,' he said.

Sickness set in, the men's bodies began to shut down, and then on 18 December, they came upon a river. As they followed it, they saw signs that someone had been there recently: a soup can, a horseshoe, even a herd of cows, until finally on 20 December, they spotted a man on horseback on the other side of a huge river.

The men couldn't make themselves heard above the roar of the river, so Parrado mimed an aeroplane crashing to try to explain who they were, though he worried the man would think he was mad and ride off. Instead, the man tied a note to a rock and threw it across the river: 'Tell me what you want.'

Parrado wrote back, 'I come from a plane that fell into the mountains. We have been walking for ten days. We have no food, and I can no longer walk.' He explained that he had

14 friends remaining in the mountains alive, and that they desperately needed help.

The man received the note and was shocked, but believing what he read, he travelled for ten hours on horseback to the nearest civilisation and returned the next day with a rescue team. Miraculously, 72 days after the plane crash, Parrado and his friend were saved, and the next day he took the rescue team back to the crash site in a helicopter, where the 14 other survivors would be found and rescued.

'The only way you go forward, is because you can't go back,' he explained.

Parrado's story is a story of human perseverance, fortitude and courage, in the face of hopeless desperation. I stumbled across his story at 19 years old, while I was in a dire financial situation, trying to pursue my first business idea, disowned by my parents for dropping out of university, shoplifting and scavenging food on my worst days, while living in a deprived area of the country, alone and broke.

His story changed my life. It gave me hope in my darkest time, wind in my sails when I needed it the most and more reason to push on despite the circumstance I was in. After several years of perseverance, I too had escaped my situation: I had built a successful company, I was financially free, and my life resembled that of my wildest dreams.

'The only way you go forward, is because you cannot go back.' I couldn't go back. I had nowhere 'back' to go. Not having a Plan B became the most incredible motivational force in my life. When the human mind excludes all other possibilities and fixates on a single path, that path draws in every available ounce of your passion, perseverance and power, leaving no room for hesitation or deviation.

'The first step before anybody
else in the world believes it
is you have to believe it —
there is no reason to have a
Plan B, because it distracts
from Plan A.'

Will Smith

Had I had an alternate path available to me, it's entirely possible that those darkest of hours might have lured me down it. This might sound like cute but meaningless motivational words or an unrealistic platitude, but amazingly, researchers have recently revealed that having a Plan B – in any ambition – has a net negative impact on our chances of succeeding with our Plan A.

MAYBE WE SHOULD PUT ALL OUR EGGS IN ONE BASKET

You've probably heard the advice 'Don't put all your eggs in one basket'. When it comes to choosing a career or applying to university, or even applying for a new job, having a back-up plan is widely thought to be a good idea. Studies have shown that this approach does help to alleviate some of the psychological discomfort associated with uncertainty, but astoundingly new research has also shown that it comes at a big cost.

Having a back-up plan, or even considering one, has been shown to potentially hinder your performance by making you less driven to hit your primary goal.

Across three studies, almost 500 students were asked to solve a difficult word puzzle that involved unscrambling muddled sentences. If they were successful, they would be given a delicious snack. Before attempting the puzzle, some groups of students were told to think through a back-up plan – other ways they could get a free snack on campus – if they couldn't unscramble the sentences.

Researchers found that the groups that had no Plan B performed radically better than the back-up plan groups; they had higher levels of motivation, valued success more, and solved more of the puzzle. Subsequent experiments have replicated the results in other contexts with different rewards (e.g., money, other prizes and saved time), and the results were always the same.

One of the researchers, behavioural scientist Katy Milkman, concluded: 'This suggests that thinking through a back-up plan will actually make you want to achieve your goal less, which then hurts your effort, performance, and ultimately, your chances of successfully achieving your goal. These findings apply to goals where success is highly dependent on effort.'

Additionally, while some can feel frozen by their fear of failure, research shows that the fear of failure can actually provide the impetus needed to get to your goal. In a similar vein, other research has shown that the more you perceive negative emotions in the event of failure, the more driven you will be to succeed. However, if you have a back-up plan, the incentive to succeed is lessened because you have removed the fear of failure.

★ BEING RISKY DOESN'T MEAN BEING RECKLESS

If you're reading this and it's made you consider making a deadly ten-day trek across the Andes mountains, I need to provide a disclaimer. There is a difference between taking a risk – focusing your entire being on a goal – and being outright reckless.

In my story, of course, I was not at risk of death; I'm fortunate enough to live in a society that would have caught me, fed me and housed me, if I had needed catching. And many of you will have dependents, mortgages and other responsibilities that you understandably need to protect. Practicality must be a priority.

★ THE LAW: YOU MUST BECOME A PLAN-A THINKER

This law remains one of those uncomfortable, unavoidable realities of the human condition. The amount of ourselves that we can dedicate to an outcome – mind, energy and focus – is positively correlated with the likelihood of that outcome. Some call this manifestation, but I call it Plan-A thinking. In the pursuit of your most important goals, a back-up plan is an additional weight to carry, a motivational burden to bring and distracting companion to call.

There's no greater force of creativity, determination & commitment than a person undistracted by a plan B.

LAW 23

DON'T BE AN OSTRICH

In this law you'll learn why my biggest professional mistake in business was behaving like an ostrich when I should have acted like a lion. In your career being an ostrich will get you killed. This law will teach you how to avoid being an ostrich.

'God himself could not sink this ship,' said Edward Smith, captain of the *Titanic*, as people warned him of the dangers of ice in the area.

Hours later, when the ship struck an iceberg, and began to flood and sink, First Officer Murdoch, who had been on watch at the time of the collision, is reported to have turned to chief steward John Hardy and said, 'I believe she [the *Titanic*] is gone, Hardy.'

Despite their looming fate, passengers later recalled a bizarre sense of calm, disbelief and normality on the decks. 'There were some people who were playing cards, and there was one man who was playing the violin. They were just as calm as if they were in a drawing room,' said passenger Edith Russell.

Another passenger, Ellen Bird, described how some people seemed to completely ignore their impending fate: 'I saw one or two men and women get up, look out of the window, and then sit down again, evidently with the idea that they would go back to bed.'

William Carter, who survived by climbing into a collapsible boat, one of the last lifeboats to get away, said he had tried to convince George Widener to come with him in the lifeboat. Carter said that Widener ignored his warning and said, 'I think I'd rather take my chances.'

Consequently, the already limited number of lifeboats were leaving partially empty. As the situation grew more dire, crew members began to frantically blow whistles, panic and shout orders to try to get the passengers to the lifeboats. According to survivor accounts, some of the crew members had to physically force people to board lifeboats, against their will.

Very late in the sinking, just minutes before the boat was completely submerged, when most of the decks were completely flooded, widespread panic did begin. Second Officer Lightoller had to brandish his gun and Fifth Officer Lowe actually fired shots along the side of the ship to keep people from swamping the last lifeboats as they were being loaded and lowered. One frantic crew member even entered the radio room and attempted to steal the senior wireless officer Jack Phillips's lifebelt as he was working the radio.

Consequently, of the 2,240 people on board, almost 70 per cent of them died.

Such denial is a complicated thing to understand. As you read this story, hindsight might portray these avoidant, unresponsive passengers as foolish, irrational and reckless. However, their response perfectly illustrates a very human, very common behavioural phenomena called 'the ostrich effect'.

★ THE OSTRICH EFFECT

When an ostrich senses danger, it buries its head in the sand. The idea is that if the ostrich can just hide from the threat, the danger will eventually pass. We humans are no different. When dealing with difficult information, situations or conversations, we tend to be like the ostrich and bury our heads in the sand too.

As humans, we are hard-wired to avoid discomfort. We stop ourselves from checking our bank accounts when we know we've overspent, we avoid difficult conversations that we don't want to have, and more problematically, we delay booking that doctor's appointment, to avoid receiving bad news about our health.

A report recently released by UK bank TSB revealed that indebted British people are cumulatively losing £55 million a month by not confronting their finances and making simple changes. One substantiating study found that investors were likely to check the value of their personal investment portfolios when the markets overall were rising, but would avoid looking when the markets were flat or falling.

In a more startling study of 7,000 women aged 50–64, researchers found that women who had heard a colleague had been diagnosed with breast cancer were almost 10 per cent less likely to go and get a free check-up themselves.

In the moment when the ostrich effect kicks in, we don't just have anxiety, the anxiety has us, and that anxiety presses us to avert our gaze from the thing that is making us most anxious. As psychiatrist George Vaillant notes, 'Denial can be healthy, enabling individuals to cope with rather than become immobilized by anxiety, or it can be unhelpful, creating a self-deception that alters reality in ways that are dangerous.'

In entrepreneurship, the ostrich effect is too often the difference between a company's success or failure. Research conducted by Leadership IQ, the corporate survey firm, collected data from more than 1,000 board members across almost 300 organisations that had fired their CEO. They found that 23 per cent of those boards had fired their CEO for 'denying reality', 31 per cent for 'mismanaging change', 27 per cent for 'tolerating low-performing staff' and 22 per cent for 'inaction'. These are all common corporate symptoms of the ostrich effect.

> In business, the person with the fewest blind spots stands the greatest chance of victory.

We think better, make better decisions, and achieve better outcomes when we're closest to reality. The stories of Kodak, Nokia, Blockbuster, Yahoo, BlackBerry and MySpace illustrate clearly that those who feel most invincible are often most susceptible to becoming an ostrich in the face of innovation, change and inconvenient truths.

★ HOW TO AVOID BECOMING AN OSTRICH

I interviewed world-renowned author Nir Eyal in my office in New York in preparation for this book; he's spent several years studying what motivates human behaviour at the best and worst of times. He told me:

People think they're motivated by seeking pleasure; they're wrong, they're motivated by avoiding discomfort. Even sex – and the horniness it creates – is a form of discomfort that we seek to relieve ourselves from.

Most people don't want to acknowledge the uncomfortable truth that distraction is always an unhealthy escape from reality.

How we deal with uncomfortable internal triggers determines whether we pursue healthy acts of traction or self-defeating distractions.

In my own career, none of my greatest professional mistakes and regrets were unsuccessful business decisions that I made; they were the instinctively obvious but terribly uncomfortable decisions I *didn't* make: the things I avoided confronting through fear, uncertainty and anxiety. The person I knew I needed to fire but didn't, the conversation I needed to have with a client but avoided, and the warning I needed to articulate to the board that I delayed.

Similarly, we can all relate to the toxic consequences that the ostrich effect can have on our romantic relationships: avoiding the difficult conversation, evading the awkward issues and pretending things are fine. These symptoms of co-denial and mutual avoidance hold a failing relationship in place, when neither party has the words, courage or conviction to confront their unmet needs. Arguments happen, but they're rarely the right arguments. In a relationship, if you're having the same conversation over and over again, you are having the wrong conversation. You're avoiding the uncomfortable conversation you should be having.

Pain in every walk of life is unavoidable,
but the pain that we create by trying to <u>avoid</u>
pain <u>is</u> avoidable.

In business, the pain of the ostrich effect and the unresolved conflict it creates is felt by your employees, in parenting it's felt by your children and in your own life it will be felt in your mind, your body and your soul.

A White House staff member during the Kennedy administration once commented that it was always obvious when there was conflict between the president and the First Lady versus when they were relating amicably. When met with surprise from the interviewer that their relationship would be so transparent, the staff member replied:

> They actually were quite private about their struggles, but we knew when they were fighting simply by watching the interactions of their personal staffs. When the hairdressers and the transport people were arguing we knew this was because JFK and Jackie were in some form of conflict. When these groups had their act together, we knew the first couple was getting on OK.

At the core of this story from the Kennedy administration is the notion that conflict moves around within and between levels of a social system. When something is unresolved because we've chosen to bury our heads in the sand, it doesn't sit dormant, waiting to be addressed; it becomes toxic, contagious and poisonous to those around us, and inflicts more collateral damage with every day that it remains unaddressed.

Five years ago, I realised that I needed to find a way to overcome my own ostrich-like behaviour so that I could confront the most uncomfortable of realities in life, business and love, with speed and honesty. It's my belief that you cannot reach your highest potential without a better relationship with discomfort, bad news and inconvenient truths. Using advice from behavioural economics, psychology and sociology, I created my own four-step approach to dealing with discomfort and avoiding procrastination.

STEP 1: PAUSE AND ACKNOWLEDGE

The first step is to pause and to admit to yourself that something is not right. Such moments of pause tend to come about when people notice the power and horrible longevity of their own unwanted emotions. If you don't pause, the process cannot begin and you cannot create enough space for the next step.

STEP 2: REVIEW YOURSELF

The next step is to inspect yourself in terms of feelings, behaviours and emotions. These examinations are critical. They enable people to begin to articulate what they have only sensed: that something is awry in them, something is misaligned, a need is being unmet or a fear has taken control.

People who pause and inspect themselves are like detectives that are aware that a crime has been committed – they can see the evidence in its wake, but they haven't yet identified the culprit. Solving such crimes usually involves the help of others. People need help to get outside of their own narratives and accurately diagnose themselves, rather than simply being driven by their preferred ways to frame and blame.

STEP 3: SPEAK YOUR TRUTH

The next step is to speak your truth. Share the findings of your inspection, without blame and with an emphasis on personal responsibility. This marks the moment that unaddressed interpersonal conflicts move from the wrong conversations to the right conversations.

In the ostrich effect, people turn away from and do not speak directly of the emotions that grip them. They avert their gaze, misdiagnose the issues and distract themselves with something else. The issue that lies beneath remains unspoken. That silence drives the ostrich effect. Loosening its grip begins with the moments that people speak what has not yet been spoken. Ironically, the science shows that it is in talking about our disconnections that people create more connectedness with one another.

STEP 4: SEEK THE TRUTH

In the last step, you must humbly seek the truth – a feat that is easier said than done in the presence of our cognitive biases, righteousness and ignorance. This means to listen. But not just listening to hear, listening to understand. Not from the perspective of an adversary that's looking for victory, but from the perspective of a partner, patiently intent on over-coming a difficulty.

Pause and acknowledge

Review yourself

Speak your truth

Seek the truth

When you do seek, hear and understand the truth, the discomfort it creates may tempt you to bury your head once again, but the key is to return to the first step, take a pause, and repeat the process until you reach an end.

★ THE LAW: DON'T BE AN OSTRICH

Avoiding uncomfortable realities and difficult conversations is unhelpful – in business and in our personal relationships. We must recognise what isn't right, assess what we can do about it, share our findings and get to the truth, however challenging that might be.

If you want long-term success in business, relationships and life, you have to get better at accepting uncomfortable truths as fast as possible.

When you refuse to accept an uncomfortable truth, you're choosing to accept an uncomfortable future.

LAW 24

YOU MUST MAKE PRESSURE YOUR PRIVILEGE

*This law teaches you how comfort is slowly killing us mentally, phys-
ically and emotionally. It will help you understand how and why we
must make life's pressures our privilege.*

With 39 Grand Slam titles, Billie Jean King was expected
to win. People were counting on her. The pressure might
have been too much for anyone else, but not her. She had
won a record 20 titles at Wimbledon, the entire tennis world
watched her play, every sportswriter was ready to criticise her every move. When asked how she coped with the
unthinkable burden of the world's expectations, Billie Jean
King casually replied, '**Pressure is a privilege – it only
comes to those that earn it.**'

This statement – 'pressure is a privilege' – naturally
evokes a mixed reaction, as most overly simplified mantras
do. When people hear it, they hear 'stress is a privilege',
so it's important to clarify that stress and pressure are two
entirely different things. Stress is an internal psychological
response and pressure is an external environmental force.
Of course, pressure can cause both good and bad stress,
depending on the individual, but the pressure itself is not

at fault. The pressure is a subjective situation, not an objective emotion, and in the presence of a strong pressure, one person's stress is another person's pleasure.

I don't enjoy all my pressure – especially not in the moment – and none of my pressure is easy; it's often tested me in ways I wouldn't have volunteered to be tested, but all my greatest pressure has preceded all my greatest privileges. The two concepts have a clear, unbreakable relationship that I find liberating, motivating and reassuring to understand. Pressure shines a light on who I am and who I'm not at the same time, simultaneously illuminating how far I've come and how far I'm yet to go. For me, a life without pressure is a life without purpose. The pressure isn't the problem – as I said, pressure is neither good nor bad – but our relationship, perspective and evaluation of pressure and the stress it creates can have purposeful or deadly consequences.

✱ JUST A COLD, DARK NIGHT ON THE SIDE OF EVEREST

Pressure isn't life or death, but your perspective of it might be.

At the University of Wisconsin, researchers conducted a study of stress on 30,000 American adults. They asked the participants questions like 'How much stress have you experienced in the last year?' and 'Do you think that stress is harmful for your health?' Eight years later, they used public death records to find out who was still alive. Unsurprisingly, people who experienced a lot of stress during the time covered by the study had a 43 per cent increased risk of dying. BUT – and this a big but – that was only true for the people who had said that they believed that stress was detrimental to their health. People who experienced a lot of stress but did not see it as harmful were no more likely to die. In fact, analysis showed that they had the lowest risk of dying of anyone in the study, even including people who had reported experiencing relatively little stress. The researchers estimated that over the eight years they were tracking deaths, 182,000 Americans died prematurely – not from stress, but from the belief that stress is bad for you. Kelly McGonigal is a health psychologist and lecturer at Stanford University. In a TED Talk on this study, she pointed out, if the researchers' estimate was correct, believing stress is bad for you would be the fifteenth most common cause of death in the United States, killing more people than skin cancer, HIV/AIDS and homicide.

Can you recall the last time you felt real pressure? Your heart may well have been pounding, you might have been breathing faster, you might have had clammy hands. Usually we interpret these physical symptoms as anxiety or signs that we aren't coping well with the pressure.

But what if you saw them differently – as signs that your body is energising you in preparation to face a challenge? That is exactly what researchers conducting a study at Harvard University told participants before putting them through a high-pressure test. Participants who learned to view the stress response as helpful for their performance were less anxious, felt more confident and performed better. Particularly interesting was the changes to their physiological stress response. Typically, your heart rate goes up and your blood vessels constrict in times of stress, – which is an unhealthy state to remain in.

But in the study, when participants saw their physiological symptoms as beneficial, it didn't stop their heart rate going up but their blood vessels stayed relaxed and open, meaning their cardiovascular response was considerably healthier. McGonigal remarked that participants who viewed stress as beneficial had a similar cardiovascular profile to people who were experiencing moments of joy and courage.

Additionally, Harvard Business School professor Alison Wood Brooks has shown how people who mentally reframe anxiety as excitement can improve their performance in tasks such as sales, negotiating and public speaking.

This one psychological mindset shift, and the physical transformation it creates, could be the difference between a stress-induced heart attack at age 60 and living until you're 90.

The objective isn't to try and get rid of your pressure, it's to change your relationship with it altogether.

One important way to improve your relationship with your pressure is to remind yourself of the positive privilege, meaning and context it exists in. The difference between aspirational pressures – building a business, competing in a tournament or raising a child – and the pressure faced by a low-paid production-line worker on a factory floor, under threat of being fired if they don't improve their output, is how we relate to the pressure. Pressure we view as voluntary, meaningful and high in autonomy is received as a privilege. Conversely, compulsory, meaningless, low-autonomy pressure feels more like psychological pain.

'Just another cold, dark night on the side of Everest' is a phrase I've naturally repeated for the last five years in my hardest moments to bring me back to the context of my stress.

When mountaineers commit to taking on Mount Everest, they'd be naive to expect a smooth journey. The same, of course, is true of starting a company, pursuing a university degree or raising a child: all of these things induce pressure, stress and pain, but because that pressure is subjectively worthwhile, it feels different and – dare I say – enjoyable.

You are most susceptible to feel like a victim of the pressure in your life when you forget the context of that pressure. The most meaningful challenges in your life will come with a few dark nights on the side of Everest.

★ MAKE YOUR PRESSURE YOUR PRIVILEGE

Thankfully, it is possible to change your relationship with pressure. After combining years of qualitative and empirical research in psychology, a study published in the *Harvard Business Review* drawing on their work with executives, students, Navy SEALs and professional athletes found that people who adopt a 'stress is enhancing' mindset enjoy a better performance at work and fewer negative health symptoms than those who see stress as a negative, debilitating thing.

I believe changing how you respond to stress and pressure can help you harness the creative power of stress while minimising its detrimental effects. I've done this by adopting the three-step *Harvard Business Review* approach, and share it with you here – plus a final step of my own.

STEP 1: SEE IT

Awareness is the first step in hijacking any type of cognitive cycle. Don't deny it, avoid it or let is paralyse you: speak it, name it. This literally changes how your brain responds, because it activates the more conscious, deliberate areas of the brain rather than the primal, automatic, reactive centres. As *HBR* explains:

> In one study, participants in a brain scan were shown negative emotional images. When asked to label the emotion the images invoked, neural activity moved from the amygdala region (the seat of emotion) to the prefrontal cortex, the area of the brain in which we do our conscious and deliberate thinking. In other words, purposefully acknowledging stress lets you pause your visceral reaction, allowing you to choose a more enhancing response.

In addition to this, it seems that trying to deny or ignore feelings of stress is counterproductive. *Harvard Business Review* research by Peter Salovey and Shawn Achor demonstrated that those of us who think of pressure as debilitating and strive to avoid it either overcorrect or underreact to stress, whereas those with a mindset that allows them to embrace the positives have a more moderate cortisol response to stress. What this means in practice is that they are 'more willing to seek out and be open to feedback during stress, which can help them learn and grow for the longer term.'

STEP 2: SHARE IT

A study conducted at the University at Buffalo found that every major stressful life experience increased an adult's risk of death by 30 per cent – unless they then spent a significant amount of time connecting with loved ones and their immediate community. Then, there was no increase to the risk of death.

Sharing our stress with a supportive community completely changes the psychological impact that stress has on us. When we choose to connect with others under stress, an incredible resiliency is created.

STEP 3: FRAME IT

The key to 'owning' your pressure is to recognise the positive role it plays and the powerful signal it represents. We feel pressure when something matters, when there is something at stake, when we care. Framing your pressure in this context unleashes positive motivation and calms your physiological reaction.

It reminds you that this is just another cold night on the side of Everest – a mountain that you both choose to climb and a mountain that is worth the climb.

In Navy SEAL training, former SEAL commander Curt Cronin says:

> The leadership squad designs situations that are exponentially more stressful, chaotic, and dynamic than any combat operation so that the teams learn to centre [themselves] in the most arduous circumstances. When the stress of the training seems unbearable, we can own it, knowing that ultimately it is what we have chosen to do – to be a member of a team that can succeed in any mission.

And that's a worthwhile pressure to endure.

STEP 4: USE IT

When under pressure, stress can help you to succeed. The evolutionary goal of stress is to push you to perform at your best both mentally and physically; to raise your game and meet the scenario or the problem you face. Our physical response to stress is to produce hormones, such as adrenaline and dopamine, which provide the brain and body with much-needed blood and oxygen. This results in a state of higher energy, enhanced alertness and a boost in focus.

What a wonderful way for our body to prepare us. Don't fight it, use it.

Former Navy SEAL commander Cronin recently said, 'Learning to ask, "how could these experiences serve us?" and being pushed to use them to fuel us, proved a powerful tool in helping our individuals, teams and organization thrive, not in spite of the stress but because of it.'

As Teddy Roosevelt famously said, if we are to fail, at least we fail while 'daring greatly', which is a more admirable fate than that of 'those cold and timid souls who neither know victory nor defeat'.

★ PRESSURE CAN SAVE YOUR LIFE

In preparation for this book, I interviewed more than ten health experts about the topic of stress, pressure and its impact on our health. One of the most surprising reoccurring concerns I had presented to me can be summarised in something said to me by Gary Brecka, founder of 10X Health:

'We are living in a comfort crisis. We are slowly suffocating ourselves to death with comfort by avoiding the hard things that are good for our health. Aging is our aggressive pursuit of comfort.'

He believes that humans physiologically thrive and are innately designed to live under the right types of pressure. He says we're supposed to experience extreme cold and hot temperatures – we're not meant to live in perfectly regulated room-temperature environments. And we're supposed to exert physical strain on our bodies; we're not meant to be this sedentary.

Other health experts I spoke to told me that the cost of avoiding these types of physiological pressure are seen in the obesity crisis, the rise in heart disease and many types of preventable illnesses.

Professional, psychological and physiological pressure is so often a privilege that we choose to ignore because it's … 'hard', and as stated previously we are discomfort-avoiding humans.

However, in all aspects of life, 'hard' is the price we pay today for an 'easy' tomorrow.

★ THE LAW: YOU MUST MAKE PRESSURE YOUR PRIVILEGE

Pressure doesn't have to be a negative thing, and – if framed correctly – it can be energising. Recognising, owning and using pressure can be a powerful tool when it comes to achieving our aims in business and life.

Comfortable and Easy are short-term friends but long-term enemies. If you're looking for growth, choose the challenge.

LAW 25

THE POWER OF NEGATIVE MANIFESTATION

This law teaches us the wonderful power of something I call negative manifestation and how it can help you see red flags, future risk and anything else that stands in the way of your success.

There exists a single question that, in my experience, has spared me more financial loss, squandered time and wasted resources than any other. This question, which I've grasped the significance of through a litany of failures, setbacks and blunders, often goes unasked due to the unease it stirs within us.

Avoiding this question places you in a perilous position, akin to the proverbial ostrich burying its head in the sand, as depicted in Law 23. Whether you ask this question or not, you will eventually find out the answer – either now, through an uncomfortable conversation, or in the future, in a much more painful way.

I was 18 years old in 2013, when I learned the value of this question through a painful lesson.

I had set out to build an online student platform called 'Wallpark', and after pouring three years of my time, investors' capital, and metaphorical blood, sweat and tears into the project, it ultimately culminated in failure.

As the saying goes, hindsight is 20/20. Looking back, the reason for my failure seems obvious – I was unknowingly competing with Facebook in a contest I stood no chance of winning.

But the thing is, this revelation needn't have required hindsight; I didn't need to experience failure to recognise it. If only I'd had the humility, experience and strength to sincerely ask myself one straightforward question, I believe I could have circumvented the loss of time, money and effort altogether.

That pivotal question is: 'Why will this idea fail?'

This question might appear straightforward and evident, yet when I surveyed more than 1,000 start-up founders, startlingly only 6 per cent claimed they were clear on why their idea could fail, while a tremendous 87 per cent were clear on why it would succeed.

The reality is that most start-ups eventually fail, and when they do, as mine did, the founders seem to suddenly see the obvious – with the majority of them attributing their downfall to overestimating their prospects and underestimating the risks.

For instance, according to the Small Business Administration in the United States, 52 per cent of failed founders acknowledged underestimating the resources needed for success, 42 per cent admitted to not realising the market didn't desire their product, and 19 per cent confessed to underestimating their competition.

I am convinced that the most crucial, revealing question these unsuccessful start-up founders ought to have asked themselves and their colleagues before pursuing their ventures was, 'Why will this idea fail?' Both doctors and ailing patients can attest to the notion that prevention is better than cure, and in business there's no chance of prevention without having a humble confrontation with the prospect of failure before starting out.

There are five main reasons why we shy away from engaging in this dialogue or even contemplating the possibility of failure. These five psychological biases, consistently identified across numerous studies, will likely prevent you and your team from asking this seemingly simple yet essential question:

1. **OPTIMISM BIAS:** Tali Sharot told me that about 80 per cent of us have this bias. Simply put, it makes us focus on good things and ignore bad things. It stopped me from asking 'Why will Wallpark fail?', because I innately believed and wanted things to end well. It's believed that this bias gave us an evolutionary advantage – optimism helped us take more survival risks, explore new environments and find new resources, but in our professional lives it prevents us from adequately considering risk.

2. **CONFIRMATION BIAS:** We all have this bias to some degree. It causes us to pay attention to information that supports our existing ideas and hypotheses – it caused me to pay attention to, and accept, information that proved Wallpark was a good idea and ignore all of the data, emails and feedback that suggested otherwise. Research shows that this human bias boosts our self-esteem and gives us emotional comfort by making our worldview feel consistent, coherent and correct.

3. **SELF-SERVING BIAS:** This bias impacts most of us to varying degrees and it leads us to believe that our success or failure is a result of our own skill and effort. It certainty stopped me from thinking about why Wallpark would fail, because it made me overestimate my own abilities while underestimating the impact of external factors - such as market conditions, competition or other unforeseen circumstances.

4. **SUNK-COST FALLACY BIAS:** This bias makes us stick with a decision - even when evidence suggests that it was a bad decision – because we've already spent time or money on it. It's the reason why Wallpark carried on for three years instead of one – subconsciously I didn't want to 'waste' or 'lose' the time and money that had been invested by quitting – but in doing so, I ended up wasting even more time and money.

5. **GROUPTHINK BIAS:** This bias prevents a group of people from asking 'Why will this idea fail?' because they don't want to disagree with the group. At Wallpark, at no point did any of the founding team question if the idea would fail; we had all likely conformed around the same blind hypothesis because of our desire for social cohesion, which created a strong conformity pressure for any new team members.

☆ THE QUESTION SAVED MY BUSINESS

In 2021, I had a bold idea. Riding the wave of success from my podcast, *The Diary Of A CEO*, I envisioned launching an entire podcasting network. This ambitious plan involved creating a multitude of fresh podcasts, each featuring renowned and talented hosts. My goal was to harness our team's commercial, production and marketing expertise to propel these podcasts to the same heights as *The Diary Of A CEO*.

We had a wealth of experience in scaling a number-one podcast, I had a phone book brimming with well-known personalities eager to collaborate with me on their own podcasts, I had a team of 30 people that worked on *The Diary Of A CEO* and I had the financial resources to invest in this new venture.

To bring my vision to life, I gathered a dedicated group of five people from the *Diary Of A CEO* team, and over the course of a year, we meticulously planned the network, meeting with potential hosts and scouting for partners. I invested hundreds of thousands of dollars into the planning and preparation process, along with countless hours of my own time and energy, as well as that of my team members. Six months into the project, I extended a formal offer to the head of one of the world's largest media companies to run the network as CEO. To my delight, he provisionally accepted and told me he would resign when I gave him the green light to join us.

Finally, after 12 months of planning, the day of reckoning arrived. I was faced with the critical decision of whether to ask the incoming CEO of this new podcast network to leave his well-paying job and join our ranks. I knew this choice marked the point of no return. If I took this decision, there would be no looking back – it would be full steam ahead with launching a large-scale podcasting network.

In that defining moment, the wisdom I had accumulated over a decade in business kicked in. I gathered my team and posed a simple yet profound question: 'Why is this a bad idea?' As I observed their uncomfortable expressions, it was evident that their minds were grappling with an entirely new challenge: one they had never contemplated before.

Within moments, the floodgates opened. One team member pointed out that our limited talent pool would be spread too thin, jeopardising our existing successful podcast business. Another chimed in, highlighting the potential unreliability of famous hosts and the risk of losing everything if a host decided to leave. Another pointed to serious concerns about the economy, and how this would cause dwindling sponsorship opportunities. Another explained that it would be more difficult than we thought to replicate our initial success because some of it was due to luck, circumstance and fortune.

Once the cascade of logical reasons had subsided, a team member turned the question back on me: 'Why do *you* think this is a bad idea?' In this moment, I realised that my subconscious had been harbouring a concern rooted in past experience, which I had been avoiding due to psychological bias. My response was simple and honest: 'focus.'

I explained that our collective focus was our most valuable resource. Failure tempts people to lose focus as motivation and belief decreases, but success tempts people to lose focus even more as opportunities, offers and capabilities increase. Maintaining focus on our existing project, which was still in a critical growth phase, was going to be both the most difficult and the most important thing for us to do. Our limited supply of focus, attention and thinking power could not be stretched across multiple projects without serious consequences. Those shower thoughts, that 1am epiphany, that passing conversation in the hallway – we needed all those precious moments to be focused on our existing podcast business, on finding marginal ways to improve and on reaching our potential.

I emphasised that by concentrating our efforts, we could achieve compounding returns far greater than those from any podcast network.

Just minutes later, we unanimously voted to shut down the project.

Remarkably, just an hour earlier, everyone in the room had been supportive of the idea and eager to launch the new venture. But one simple, uncomfortable question had shifted our collective mindset, invited important critical thinking and led us to see the project's flaws in high definition.

A year later, with the benefit of hindsight, I can confidently say that pursuing the network would have been a costly mistake. Our team would have been stretched to its limits, our existing business would have suffered, and the economic downturn of 2022 would have severely impacted our financial performance.

Our focus paid off, and in 2022 our existing podcast business grew by 900 per cent in terms of audience size, and revenues climbed by more than 300 per cent.

In the world of business, teams like ours often devote months to meticulously outlining how and why their ideas will succeed. Yet they seldom allocate the same level of time to examining the potential reasons why their ideas might not work. This is where the power of a simple question – 'Why is this a bad idea?' – comes into play.

By posing this question, we encourage an essential form of critical thinking that unveils risks and challenges often obscured by the aforementioned five innate human biases. Rather than merely seeking validation for our ideas, we challenge ourselves to confront their weaknesses head-on. Our intention is not simply to find reasons to abandon an idea, but rather to embrace the adage that prevention is better than cure. Identifying potential issues before embarking on a project enables us to address and circumvent them, paving the way for a smoother journey to success.

★ THE PRE-MORTEM METHOD: YOUR SECRET WEAPON FOR AVOIDING FAILURE

Regrettably, human nature often prevents us from thinking or acting pre-emptively to avoid worst-case scenarios. Many of us neglect to adopt healthy habits, such as proper exercise and nutrition, until our wellbeing is in jeopardy; we overlook the importance of keeping our car maintained until we face a breakdown; and we won't replace a damaged roof until water droplets pitter-patter on our heads.

The post-mortem examination, or autopsy, is a procedure undertaken by medical professionals to determine the cause of death by examining a body. A 'pre-mortem' is the hypothetical opposite of a post-mortem – you do it before the death has occurred. The 'pre-mortem method' is a decision-making technique developed by scientist Gary Klein, which encourages a group to think from a place of failure, before a project has begun. Instead of simply asking 'What could go wrong?', the pre-mortem relies on you imagining that the 'patient' has died and asks you to explain what *did* go wrong.

Now, imagine if we could harness this concept and apply it to our daily lives and professional endeavours. Scientific research shows that this simple thought experiment – performing a metaphorical 'autopsy' before a calamity occurs – can drastically reduce the chance of failure altogether.

In a groundbreaking 1989 study, researchers delved into the fascinating world of the pre-mortem method and its impact on predicting outcomes. Participants were split into two groups: one group harnessed the power of the pre-mortem method to envision various business, social and personal events as if they had already unfolded, and dissect the possible reasons that they hadn't succeeded. In contrast, the other group merely made predictions without any direction at all.

The group employing the pre-mortem method exhibited significantly higher accuracy in predicting how the given scenarios would play out and determining the causes of those outcomes. These findings show that by contemplating failure in advance, we can better comprehend its potential origins and take proactive measures to avoid it.

An additional study conducted in 1989 by researchers at two universities found the same stark results – this simple method of imagining that a failure has already occurred increased the ability to correctly identify the reasons for the future outcome by 30 per cent!

Since 2021, I've implemented the pre-mortem analysis across all my companies to great success. Here is the five-step process I use to deploy the pre-mortem method:

1. **SET THE STAGE**: Gather relevant team members and clearly explain the purpose of the pre-mortem analysis – to identify potential risks and weaknesses, not to criticise the project or individuals.

2. **FAST-FORWARD TO FAILURE**: Ask your team to imagine that the project has failed and encourage them to visualise the scenario in vivid detail.

3. **BRAINSTORM REASONS FOR FAILURE**: Instruct each team member to independently generate a list of reasons that could have led to the project's failure, considering both internal and external factors. It's important that this is done independently and on paper to avoid groupthink.

4. **SHARE AND DISCUSS**: Have each team member share their reasons for failure, fostering an open and non-judgemental discussion to uncover potential risks and challenges.

5. **DEVELOP CONTINGENCY PLANS**: Based on the identified risks and challenges, work together to create contingency plans and strategies to either mitigate or avoid these potential pitfalls altogether.

★ THIS ISN'T JUST BUSINESS ADVICE, IT'S LIFE ADVICE

The truth is, humans make really shitty decisions – decisions clouded in emotion, induced by fear and influenced by insecurity. We're not very logical, we're riddled with biases, and in our decision-making, we're always searching for shortcuts.

The power of the pre-mortem method extends far beyond the realm of business; it's been a potent tool for making better decisions in various aspects of my personal life. Having robust decision-making frameworks has allowed me to make more effective and less regrettable decisions in the most important areas of my life at the most important moments in my life.

Here's how you can apply it in different scenarios:

1. **CHOOSING A CAREER PATH**: When deciding on a career, conduct a pre-mortem analysis by envisioning yourself years into the future, having experienced significant dissatisfaction or failure in that career. Work backwards to identify potential reasons for this dissatisfaction, such as lack of interest in the job, limited growth opportunities or work-life imbalance. By considering these factors, you can refine your career choice or devise strategies to mitigate potential issues.

2. **CHOOSING A PARTNER**: When contemplating a long-term relationship or marriage, imagine a scenario in which the relationship has failed or become unfulfilling. Identify factors that may have contributed to the decline, such as misaligned values, poor communication, intimacy problems or differing expectations. By addressing these concerns proactively and proactively searching for red flags, you can make a more informed decision about the partnership or work on strengthening the relationship from the outset.

3. **MAKING A CONSIDERABLE INVESTMENT:** When contemplating a significant investment, such as purchasing a home or investing in the stock market, envision a scenario in which the investment leads to financial loss. Identify potential causes for this outcome, such as market fluctuations, inadequate research, or overestimating your financial capacity ahead of time. By understanding these risks, you can make more informed decisions, perform thorough due diligence, and take steps to minimise potential losses.

In the present age, it appears that every social media quote I encounter demands that I 'visualise success', extolling the virtues of 'manifestation' and 'positive thinking'. While optimism undoubtedly holds immense value and positive thinking has genuine merit, there lies an equally profound potency in embracing negative contemplation – visualising failure and planning accordingly.

★ THE LAW: THE POWER OF NEGATIVE MANIFESTATION

Our cognitive wiring instinctively steers us away from thoughts that induce psychological unease. However, much like the proverbial ostrich with its head buried in the sand, this avoidance often leads us towards even greater psychological distress.

Paradoxically, in all facets of life, engaging in an uncomfortable conversation today paves the way for a more comfortable life in the future – prevention is easier than cure.

Embracing this duality of thought – balancing positivity with negativity – equips us with the wisdom, fortitude and foresight to forge a more successful path forward.

You can predict someone's success in any area of their life by observing how willing and capable they are at dealing with uncomfortable conversations. Your personal progression is trapped behind an uncomfortable conversation.

The Diary Of A CEO

LAW 26

YOUR SKILLS ARE WORTHLESS, BUT YOUR CONTEXT IS VALUABLE

This law explains how you can get paid multiples more for the skills you already have, and how all the value comes from the context, not the skill itself.

★ 'WE'LL GIVE YOU $8 MILLION, IF YOU HELP US!'

In 2020, after a rollercoaster decade of building a social media marketing company that worked with some of the world's most renowned brands, I waved goodbye to my CEO role and embarked on a journey of self-discovery.

Shortly after my resignation, I declared that I would never work in marketing again. The allure of exploring uncharted territories in different industries was too strong to resist. The idea of slipping back into the familiar shoes of a social media marketing CEO didn't spark the same fire within me as it had a decade ago. More importantly, I yearned to break free from the limiting professional labels society assigns us – generic job titles like lawyer, accountant, dentist, social media manager or graphic designer. I believed that such labels constrict our potential, ultimately leading to a sense of unfulfillment.

I get it – labels act as shortcuts, they make us feel understood, they tell us that we belong somewhere, and they subtly reassure us that we have a purpose in this world. However, these labels also become professional shackles, stifling our creativity and narrowing the scope of our experiences.

At 27, I was far too young to be confined by any label. The only one I was willing to give myself was 'curious guy with a diverse set of skills'. I aspired to work on broader societal challenges, rather than solely aiding companies in boosting sales for sneakers, carbonated beverages or electronic gadgets.

And so, my exciting new chapter began.

Well, not really …

I have always been fascinated, concerned by and deeply curious about the global mental health crisis, its causes and potential solutions.

In 2020, the year I resigned, the Covid-19 pandemic forced the world into lockdown, depriving us of many psychological stabilisers and pushing mental health into the spotlight of public conversation. With time on my hands, I began a digital expedition through various intriguing subjects relating to mental health, the most captivating of which was the world of psychedelics.

I devoured countless research papers, clinical studies and online articles about the efficacy of certain psychedelic compounds in treating mental health disorders in humans. The science and untapped potential of these compounds left me completely awestruck.

Life sometimes presents us with inexplicable moments of serendipity, chance encounters and seemingly aligned stars, and what I'm about to say next is certainly one of them.

Just days after completing my deep dive into the world of psychedelics, I received a text from a business acquaintance asking, 'Hey Steven, could you retweet this for me?' To my astonishment, the link led to a news story about the IPO (Initial Public Offering – a stock launch) of a psychedelic company I had just been researching! I responded, 'I've spent weeks reading about this company – I'm fascinated by it. Are you involved?' He replied, 'I'm the largest shareholder, and I'm working on a similar project right now. I'd love for you to help us with the marketing!'

'Let's discuss this further,' I replied, and we arranged a lunch meeting later that week. After spending just a few hours learning about the company's mission, meeting the executive team and examining their work, I knew I wanted to be part of their journey.

The company operated within the 'biotech' sector, an industry teeming with brilliant minds – intelligent individuals donning white coats in laboratories – yet devoid of cutting-edge marketing talent adept at crafting compelling stories on the modern digital platforms that drive public conversation.

To succeed in their impending IPO, the company knew it needed to effectively communicate their incredibly timely cultural mission, not only to large institutional investors but also to the general public, using all the available social media platforms.

The company had its sights set on a multi-billion-dollar IPO, and the distinction between effective and ineffective storytelling and marketing could make or break their valuation.

I possessed the expertise they required.

With experience across every digital platform and having worked with leading brands in nearly every industry, I was the perfect candidate to help them tackle this challenge. A week after our meeting, I offered to join the company for the nine months leading up to the IPO.

My responsibilities would include crafting the marketing strategy, defining the brand, assembling the long-term marketing team, setting the team's philosophy and laying the foundation for all marketing efforts before my departure. They accepted my proposal and promised to send me an offer the next day.

To be honest, my motivation for joining their company wasn't monetary. If anything, I was eager to invest in the company because of my growing belief in the power of psychedelics. I wanted to immerse myself in the science – surround myself with pioneers at the forefront of the sector, fill my knowledge bucket and quench my curiosity while I decided what to do next in my career.

The following day, I awoke to an email from the company with the subject line 'remuneration package'. As I read the contents of the email, my eyes narrowed in disbelief. They were offering me a potential $6–8 million in stock options on top of a monthly salary to lead their marketing efforts for nine months, up until the stock market listing. This was more than ten times my expectation.

In this moment, I learned four enduring lessons about the value of any skill.

1. Our skills hold no intrinsic value.

Our skills are worth nothing. As the phrase goes, value is what someone is willing to pay.

2. The value of any skill is determined by the context in which it is required.

Every skill holds a different value in a different sector.

3. The perception of a skill's rarity influences how much people value it.

In the biotech sector, my high-level social media and marketing skills were akin to a diamond in the rough – so rare that companies were more than willing to pay a premium for them. However, when I had sold these same skills in other industries – such as e-commerce, consumer goods and technology – in my previous role, their perceived value was significantly diminished. In these contexts, my skills were more common, which meant that the fees I could charge were a tenth of what a client was willing to pay me in the biotech industry.

4. People will assess the worth of your skill based on how much value they believe it can generate for them.

The biotech company was teetering on the edge of a potential multi-billion-dollar IPO, and in this high-stakes environment, my skills possessed the potential to substantially influence the company's valuation. Naturally, they were prepared to pay accordingly for such an impact.

Reflecting on my prior career, I realise that when I had used the same skills to market consumer products like dresses, T-shirts and accessories, the financial returns I generated for clients paled in comparison to the potential returns for this biotech company. Consequently, the fees I received were proportionally tiny.

★ ★ ★

The truth is, the market you decide to sell your skills in will determine how much you get paid far more than the skills themselves. Technical or medical writers in the engineering or biotech sectors earn higher salaries than writers in the media and publishing industries, even though the core skill of writing is the same.

Data analysts working in finance or consulting earn more than those in academia or government roles, even when performing the same data analysis tasks.

Software developers and programmers in high-demand industries such as artificial intelligence, cybersecurity or fintech command higher salaries than those working in traditional IT roles or web development, even when utilising the same programming languages.

Project managers in the technology sectors receive higher pay than those managing projects in the arts, education or social services sectors, though the fundamental skill of project management is the same.

Sales professionals in high-value industries like pharmaceuticals, medical devices or real estate can earn significantly more through commissions and bonuses than those in retail or consumer goods, despite both roles requiring the same fundamental sales skill.

PR professionals working in entertainment, sports or luxury brands have higher earning potential than those in non-profit organisations, healthcare or education, even when using the same skills to manage PR campaigns.

Photographers working in fashion, advertising or commercial photography can charge higher rates than those in photojournalism or wedding photography, even though the fundamental skill is very similar.

HR professionals in industries with higher revenue and growth, such as technology or finance, earn more than their counterparts in non-profit or public sectors, despite performing the same HR functions, like recruitment, training and benefits administration.

Financial analysts working in investment banking, private equity or hedge funds are likely to earn more than those in corporate finance or government roles, even when applying the same financial analysis skills and knowledge.

A common misconception is that the only avenues for securing a pay increase are to either vie for a promotion in one's current position or to seek a similar role within the same industry. However, a more effective and potentially rewarding approach may lie in **transplanting one's skill set to an entirely new context** – a different industry – where it can deliver greater value for the employer. By doing so, your current abilities may be seen as a rarer commodity, increasing their worth and, in turn, enhancing your value.

Maybe the starkest example of how context creates the perception of value can be seen in a social experiment conducted by the *Washington Post* in 2007. The experiment was designed to explore how people perceive and value talent and art in an everyday, unexpected setting.

On a bustling January morning, Joshua Bell, a world-renowned violinist, dressed in ordinary attire, disguised himself as a street performer and positioned himself at a Washington DC subway station. He played for about 45 minutes, performing six classical pieces on his Stradivarius violin, which was worth $3.5 million at the time.

Despite Bell's immense talent, skill and the beautiful music he played, very few of the thousands of commuters passing by that day stopped to listen or appreciate his performance. Over the course of his performance, only seven people paused to listen for at least a minute and Bell collected a mere $52.17 – a stark contrast to the thousands of dollars he typically earns per minute when performing in the world's most prestigious concert halls.

The story highlighted how people often overlook value in certain contexts, raising questions about how good we truly are at appreciating and rewarding talent in our daily lives.

This also serves as an apt metaphor for my own professional life; I had previously been selling my skills in a subway station – and just by moving the same skills to a prestigious concert hall, I earned ten times more.

In 2021 I shared this story and what it taught me with one of my best friends, who was at an impasse in his career – sick of not having enough money for a mortgage, but seemingly working every available hour in the day. At the time he was a graphic designer designing nightclub flyers and local company logos in Manchester for £100–£200 a piece – he was averaging about £35,000 a year in income. A few weeks after our conversation, he made a bold decision to sell his skill set in a new context – he moved to Dubai and repositioned his design service to focus on luxury brands and blockchain technology companies.

In his first year in Dubai he generated £450,000 in revenue and in 2023 – alongside his new business partner – he's forecasting more than £1.2 million in revenue.

The same skill of graphic design, sold in a different context, earning thirty times more.

★ THE LAW: YOUR SKILLS ARE WORTHLESS, BUT YOUR CONTEXT IS VALUABLE

Different markets will place different values on your skills. If an employer or client sees your expertise as rare or unique, they will be willing to pay more for it than those in an industry in which your skill set is more common. Context is key – you can significantly boost your earning potential by offering the same skills to a different industry.

To be considered the best in your industry, you don't need to be the best at any one thing. You need to be good at a variety of complementary and rare skills that your industry values and that your competitors lack.

LAW 27

THE DISCIPLINE EQUATION: DEATH, TIME AND DISCIPLINE!

This law teaches you how to be disciplined in anything that you set your mind to through a simple 'discipline equation', and why discipline is the ultimate secret to being successful in any ambition we have.

These might be the most uncomfortable pages you read in this book.

I'm 30 years old. Which means if I'm fortunate enough to live to the current (US) life expectancy of roughly 77 years old, I have just 17,228 days left. It also means I've already spent 10,950 days, which I have no way of getting back.

Here's a breakdown of how many days you have left if you live to the average (US) life expectancy, and how many you've already spent.

Age (Years)	Days Spent	Days Left
5	1,825	26,315
10	3,650	24,455
15	5,475	22,630
20	7,300	20,805
25	9,125	18,980

Age (Years)	Days Spent	Days Left
30	10,950	17,228
35	12,775	15,403
40	14,600	13,650
45	16,425	11,825
50	18,250	10,073
55	20,075	8,248
60	21,900	6,570
65	23,725	4,745
70	25,550	3,131
75	27,375	1,306

For most of you, confronting this reality will be unsettling. As I detailed in my first book, *Happy Sexy Millionaire,* as humans we seem hard-wired to avoid the topic of death, treating it as a taboo subject, much like sex in the Victorian era. We seem to view death as an event that occurs only to others and we seemingly lack the emotional strength to accept our own mortality until a tragic diagnosis forces us to.

It's my sincere belief that there are many things the human mind is incapable of truly grasping: one of them is how insignificant we are – life at every touchpoint will seduce us into overestimating the importance of day-to-day things, and another is that we are actually going to die someday. Yes, logically we know death is a thing – we've seen it happen to animals, relatives and other people, but if you look closely at the things we preoccupy ourselves with, how we treat others, how we hoard possessions, how we worry, you'll see that we have both overestimated our own importance and, at some deeper level, seem to believe we're going to live for ever.

Scientists have long said that as humans we struggle to comprehend infinity, but perhaps we are also blind to the concept of finality and the inescapable truth that our journey will one day come to an end.

Our innate assumption that life will continue for ever likely evolved as a psychological mechanism to alleviate anxiety, encourage forward-thinking and ultimately enhance our chances of survival. In essence, if humans were persistently conscious of their own mortality, they might be more susceptible to paralysing anxiety, making it difficult to concentrate on other crucial tasks such as securing life-sustaining resources like food and shelter.

However, in today's fast-paced digital world, we are constantly bombarded with a myriad of stimuli – news, social media, emails and countless notifications – that often cause us to worry, project ourselves into the future, fall into meaningless distraction, become disconnected and perpetually float in a state of unease.

Perhaps the antidote to this modern ailment lies in embracing our mortality. By acknowledging our finite nature, we can **prioritise what truly matters**, shed what doesn't and foster the calm sense of urgency that helps us focus on living more fully, authentically and in line with our most important values.

I need to borrow your imagination for just a second. Imagine waking up in the middle of the night in a friend's apartment on the 20th floor of an old high-rise building to the sounds of screams and the smell of smoke. Imagine stumbling to the door to try and escape to find it locked, realising the windows are locked too and that there is no way out. Imagine eventually giving in to the fire, losing consciousness and dying.

When researchers asked groups of people to imagine this exact scenario in a 2004 study, and then to answer some questions about it, they discovered that participants' gratitude levels skyrocketed. People who undergo these 'death reflection' exercises report greater life satisfaction, a stronger desire to spend time with loved ones, an increase in motivation to achieve meaningful goals, increased kindness, increased generosity and a greater willingness to cooperate with others. They also reported lower levels of anxiety and stress compared to a control group.

You're going to die, and in a distracted, noisy, complex modern world this truth is therapeutic, liberating and a wonderful way to stay focused on another important truth, which is that your time – and how you choose to spend it – is the only influence you have on the world.

> The allocation of your time will determine if you succeed or fail in your life's work, if you'll be healthy and happy, if you'll be a successful partner, husband, wife or parent. Our time – and how we allocate it – is the centre point of our influence.

Earlier, I said that humans struggle to comprehend abstract concepts like finality, infinity and our own insignificance, but we also cannot comprehend time itself. It slowly creeps, intangibly and invisibly, somewhere out of sight. In order to make it perceptible enough for us to appreciate it, I created a mental model that I'm prompted to reflect on every day by a small roulette-wheel clock that sits on my office desk. I call this mental model 'time betting'.

★ TIME BETTING

We are all gamblers, stood over the roulette table of life.

In this gamble that is life, the number of betting chips we hold is equal to the number of hours we have left to live. As a 30-year-old, I'm likely holding about 400,000 chips, but I don't know for certain – nobody does. I could have just one left, I could have 500,000.

The one rule of the game is that we have to place one chip every hour, and once a chip is placed, we will never get it back. The wheel is always spinning, and how we place our bets determines the type of rewards we win from life.

We can place these chips on whatever we like; you might place them on watching Netflix, going to the gym, cooking, dancing, spending quality time with your partner, building a business, learning a skill, raising a child or walking a dog.

How you place these chips is the one thing in life we can control, and it's the one factor that will have the greatest impact on shaping our success, happiness, relationships, intellectual development, mental wellbeing and legacy.

Although you can never get your chips back once they've been placed, if you allocate some of your chips to activities that improve your health, the croupier will hand you a few more chips.

The game ends when you run out of chips, and once the game is over, you don't get to keep any of the things you've won anyway.

With this in mind you should be conscious of what prizes you bet your chips trying to win – you should prioritise the things that bring you joy and deprioritise trying to attain hard-fought prizes that deliver nothing more than negativity, anxiety and illusion.

If I do have 400,000 chips left, I'll likely bet 133,333 of those chips on sleep; if I meet the average I'll place 50,554 chips on mindlessly scrolling through social media, 30,000 of them eating and drinking, and 8,333 chips in the bathroom. Which leaves me with about 200,000 chips – 200,000 hours or about 8,000 days left to achieve my goals, build my relationships, raise my family, pursue my hobbies, travel, dance, learn, exercise, walk my dog and live the rest of my life.

I say this not to scare you.

I say this to help you realise how unbelievably important, precious and valuable each chip – each hour of your day – is. It's this crystal-clear realisation of the importance of your time, caused by the crystal-clear realisation of our impending death, that serves to motivate us to place every chip we have with clear intention – not to allow them to be snatched from your hands unconsciously by digital, social and psychological distraction – but to be placed considerately, chip by chip, on the things that truly matter the most.

At 50 years of age, Steve Jobs delivered one of the most widely viewed college commencement speeches of all time. At the end of his speech, he said, 'Remembering I'll be dead soon is the most important tool I've ever encountered to help me make the big choices in life.'

Having overcome a life-threatening bout with cancer (although he ultimately succumbed to the disease in 2011), he went on to argue that 'death is very likely the single best invention of life'. Jobs believed that the inevitability of death could inspire individuals to pursue their passions, to take risks and to chart their own course in life. He implored his audience of students to avoid wasting their time living up to someone else's expectations, reminding them that their time was limited.

Of all the things Steve Jobs could have said to those young, impressionable college graduates, having just confronted his own mortality, he felt that reminding them of their own impermanence was the most important thing to say.

★ THE DISCIPLINE EQUATION

When writing this law, I had considered sharing some time-management tactics, tricks and hacks with you – there are more than I can name; the pomodoro technique, time blocking, the two-minute rule, the Eisenhower Matrix, the ABCDE method, the Ivy Lee method, task batching, the Kanban method, the one-minute to-do list, the 1-3-5 rule, the timeboxing method, the Seinfeld Strategy, the four Ds of time management, the two-hour solution, the action method, and the list goes on.

Here's the truth: the reason why there are so many time-management 'methods', 'techniques' and 'strategies' is the same reason why there are so many fad diets – because frankly and fundamentally, none of them actually solve the problem – there is no time-management system, procrastination-ending method or productivity hack that's going to give you the underlying thing you need in order to stay the course, make the right decisions and focus on what matters over the long term – discipline.

If you have discipline, any of the hundreds of available methods, hacks and tricks will work. If you have no discipline, none of them will work.

So instead of giving you productivity 'methods', which you won't be able to stick to in the absence of discipline, let's just talk about discipline.

To me, discipline is the ongoing commitment to pursuing a goal, independent of fluctuating motivation levels, by consistently exercising self-control, delayed gratification and perseverance.

The psychological reasons for long-term discipline can be multifaceted and influenced by a combination of personal traits, mindset, emotional regulation and environmental factors.

However, when I reflect on the key areas of my life where discipline has remained consistent across years and decades – with my health and fitness regime, with building my companies, with my romantic relationship and even with my family relationships – it's clear that there are three central factors to discipline, which form what I call the discipline equation:

1. *Your perceived value of achieving the goal.*

2. *How psychologically rewarding and engaging the process of pursuing the goal is.*

3. *How psychologically costly and disengaging the process of pursuing the goal is.*

★ DISCIPLINE = THE VALUE OF THE GOAL + THE REWARD OF THE PURSUIT – THE COST OF THE PURSUIT

Let me use DJ'ing as an example, I've been learning to DJ for the last 12 months. I show up, practise for an hour, five times a week, and I have done so with good consistency for the last 12 months.

Value of the goal: I really want to become a DJ and produce my own songs because I'm obsessed with music, I love the art of DJ'ing and after doing my first show to six colleagues in my kitchen and then to 3,000 people at a rave, I'm hooked on how live music can make me and a room of people feel amazing.

The reward of the pursuit: downloading new music every week, engaging in the challenge of mixing it in new ways and falling into the therapeutic flow state of practice has been incredibly psychologically rewarding, and because of the power of progress (discussed in Law 29) – which highlights how the feeling of progress creates motivation – I'm extremely engaged in the process.

The cost of the pursuit: the time it takes to practise, the energy it requires to focus and the mild anxiety I have to endure in order to perform in front of people.

Because the value of the goal and the reward of the pursuit outweigh the cost of the pursuit, my discipline – regardless of fluctuations in my motivation – has remained robust.

HOW TO INFLUENCE YOUR DISCIPLINE EQUATION

Through ignorance, insecurity and immaturity, I spent my late teens and early adulthood doggedly pursuing monetary goals, social status and romantic relationships. As adults we tend to seek validation from the things that made us feel invalid when we were younger, and for me it was all of the above.

Was I aware that my actions were fuelled by insecurity? Far from it. In truth, I wasn't 'driven' – I was dragged. Did I understand the actual goal I was striving for? Certainly not.

I believed that wealth, success and external validation were my goal, when in reality, the underlying goal was to quench my deep-seated insecurities and childhood shame. I had no idea what was dragging me, and I didn't know where I was being dragged to.

I suspect this is the case for most people reading this book. I suspect most of you aren't truly, authentically and fundamentally clear on what your goals are and why those goals truly matter to you.

To determine factor one in the discipline equation, your perceived value of achieving the goal, you need to get crystal clear on what your goal is, and establish exactly why accomplishing that goal intrinsically and authentically matters to you. Doing this helps to set up systems and cues that remind you of your goal's value on an ongoing basis.

This is where visualisation has been scientifically proven to hold tremendous weight. Once we can see ourselves there, and we visualise it as a great place to be, the perceived value (factor one) of getting there increases.

The average person spends 3.15 hours a day on their mobile phone; for me it's more than 5 hours a day, so I've converted the wallpaper of my phone into a visualisation mood board. If you're staring at a phone screen for 3 hours a day, having wallpaper that reinforces the perceived value of the goals in your life can have a tremendous subconscious influence.

For factor two in the discipline equation, how rewarding the pursuit of the goal is, you must do everything you can to enjoy the process and deploy psychological tactics to keep your engagement high.

I've managed to stay disciplined with going to the gym for three consecutive years, six days a week. Not only does my physiology reward me with a natural dopamine boost every time I train, but I've intentionally created accountability and gamification systems to maximise my engagement with the process.

I've created something called 'the fitness blockchain', which is essentially a WhatsApp group containing ten of my friends and colleagues, where every day we submit a screenshot of our workout taken from a wearable fitness tracker. At the end of the month the least consistent gym-goer is evicted, and a new person is added by raffle; the top three most consistent gym-goers are awarded gold, silver and bronze medals, and each medal gives points that are added to our league table.

The daily conversations, the end-of-month medal ceremony, the jokes, the connection, the jeopardy and the competition all create what is known as a social pact – a mutual agreement among individuals to support and hold each other accountable for achieving their goals. This gamification – incorporating game-like elements, such as rewards, points and challenges – has been scientifically proven to increase accountability and enjoyment and therefore engagement with the process.

Not only has this made the process more enjoyable and engaging (factor two), but it's also made the goal itself – becoming fitter and healthier – more valuable (factor one), because now I can win an imaginary title and take great pleasure in rubbing it in my best friends' faces for several months.

If your long-term discipline is to be sustainable, you must do everything you can to limit the psychological friction and material hurdles that are associated with the pursuit of your goal, and this is where factor three in the discipline equation – the psychological cost of pursuing the goal – comes into play.

Anything that makes the process feel less intrinsically enjoyable – making it seem too difficult, too complicated, full of too much negative feedback, too much unfairness, too time consuming, too financially draining, too fear-inducing, too autonomy-removing, too isolating or too hard to see progress – will increase the perceived cost of pursuing the goal, and therefore lower your chances of sustaining your discipline.

When I embarked on learning to DJ, I was aware that my discipline to practise would be significantly improved if the barrier and cost of practising was as low as possible. With that – and the habit framework from Law 8 that highlights the power of cues – in mind I set up my DJ'ing equipment on the kitchen table, in plain view for the whole year, and ensured that I only had to press one button to turn the entire system on and begin to practise.

Had it been packed away and required 20 minutes to set up each session, or even set up in a spare room where I wouldn't see it as often, I'm absolutely convinced that my discipline would have faltered. The perceived friction of the process is a burden on your chances of reaching your goal – you must work to remove any factor that will add a psychological cost and/or disengage you from the process.

Remember: **discipline = the value of the goal + the reward of the pursuit – the cost of the pursuit.**

'We don't have to be smarter than the rest. We have to be more disciplined than the rest.'

Warren Buffett

★ THE LAW: THE DISCIPLINE EQUATION: DEATH, TIME AND DISCIPLINE

Success is not complicated, it's not magic and it's not a mystery. Luck, chance and fortune may give you a wonderful tailwind, but the rest will be a by-product of how you choose to use your time. Most of it hinges on finding something that captivates us enough to persevere daily and a goal that resonates profoundly enough to remain steadfast in our pursuit. Success is the embodiment of discipline – though it may not be easy, its core principles are beautifully simple.

Being selective about how you spend your time, and who you spend your time with, is the greatest sign of self-respect.

PILLAR IV
THE TEAM

LAW 28
ASK WHO NOT HOW

This law shows how to create incredible companies, projects or organisations the easy way – without having to learn more or do more yourself.

At the other side of the table sat Richard Branson, one of the most famous entrepreneurs in the world, adventurer, space traveller and founder of Virgin Group. I had attended a private screening of a new life-story documentary in the heart of Manhattan, and the next day I had asked him for two hours of his time to interview him for *The Diary Of A CEO*. He explained:

> I was dyslexic and pretty hopeless at school; I just assumed that I must be a little bit thick. I could just about add up and subtract. But when it got to more complicated stuff I couldn't.
>
> I was in a board meeting at about 50 years old, and I said to the director, is that good news or bad news? And one of the directors said, 'Come outside, Richard.' I came outside and he said, 'You don't know the difference between net profit and gross profit, do you?'
>
> I said, 'No.'
>
> He said, 'I thought not,' and brought out a sheet of paper and some colouring pens and he colours it in blue

and then he puts a fishing net in it and then he puts a little fish in the fishing net. And he says, 'So, the fish that are in the net, that's your profit at the end of the year, and the rest of the ocean, that's your gross turn-over.' And I went, 'I got it.'

It really doesn't matter. For somebody who's running a company, what matters is can you create the best company in its sector? Somebody else can add up the figures. It helps to add up and subtract, but if you can't do those things, I wouldn't worry too much. You can find somebody else that can.

I'm just good with people. I can trust people. I surround myself with really good people. That's the thing with being dyslexic; I had no choice but to delegate.

I sat there, stunned into silence. There was something incredibly liberating, inspiring and empowering to hear a multi-billionaire, rock star entrepreneur, whose group consists of 40 companies, employing 71,000 people and generating $24 billion in annual sales, tell you that he can't read well or do maths well, and that it 'doesn't really matter'.

This admission was music to my ears, not only because it was humanising and honest, but also because it made me feel less like a fraud myself! By my 27th birthday, the company I'd founded was generating hundreds of millions in sales, we employed hundreds of people around the world, and I spent most of my time flying between our offices in Continental Europe, the UK and America. But, somewhere deep inside me, I had a nagging feeling that I wasn't a real CEO because I'm not brilliant at maths, spelling or most of the operational aspects of running a business. For the last ten years,

I've focused my energy on creating the best products I can, and I've delegated anything I don't like doing and can't do (usually the same thing) to someone who is much more capable, experienced and confident.

This has always worked for me – I've long given up hope of becoming an expert in the things I'm not good at and don't enjoy – but this perspective is inconsistent with the advice I hear from business schools, entrepreneurship books and success blogs, which typically assert that you need to be good at a variety of things to become successful.

I interviewed Jimmy Carr, the stand-up comedian, at my home in London, and he backed this point up with wisdom and hilarity:

> I think school teaches us maybe the wrong lesson. School teaches us a lesson about mediocrity and being all-rounders. And yet we live in a world that does not reward all-rounders. Who gives a fuck about all-rounders? If you get a D in physics and you get an A in English, just go to English lessons … 'We'll get you to a C grade in physics' … I tell you what the world doesn't need – someone who's shit at physics! So, find out what you've got a natural ability for, what's the thing that you do best and just lean in to that!

This statement by Jimmy seems to perfectly encapsulate the strategy I've followed over the last ten years. The truth is, as evidenced from my 31 per cent school attendance and subsequent expulsion, I'm really bad at doing things I don't enjoy, and that has proven to be a superpower because it's allowed me to double and triple down on the few things I'm both good at and enjoy.

In business – especially if you have dreams of creating a really big business – it's not about learning how to do something, it's about knowing who can do it for you. Business is all about people. Every company, whether they realise it or not, is simply a recruitment company. Every CEO and founder will be judged simply on their ability to 1. hire the best individuals, and 2. bind them with a culture that gets the best out of them – where they become more than the sum of their parts, where 1 + 1 = 3. Had I hired a 16-year-old Richard Branson and created a culture that got the best out of him, I would have had a $20 billion company on my hands.

Founders, especially inexperienced founders, have a tendency to horrifically overstate their own importance – they fall into the trap of believing their outcomes will be decided by their own brilliance, ideas and skills.

The truth is, your destination will be defined by the sum total of the ingenuity, ideas and execution of the group of people that you assemble. Every great idea, everything you create, your marketing, your products, your strategy – all of it will come from the minds of the people you hire.

You are a recruitment company – that's your priority, and founders that realise this, build world-changing companies.

'I consider the most important job of someone like myself as recruiting ... I've built a lot of my success off finding these truly gifted people and not settling for B and C players, but really going for the A players. It doesn't make sense to hire smart people and tell them what to do; we hire smart people so they can tell us what to do.'

Steve Jobs

✭ THE LAW: ASK WHO NOT HOW

When we need something done, we've been trained to ask ourselves: 'How can I do this?' The better question, which the world's greatest founders default to asking, is 'Who is the best person that can do this for me?'

Your ego will insist that you do.

Your potential will insist that you delegate.

LAW 29
CREATE A CULT MENTALITY

This law explains the secrets to creating a truly great culture within any team, company or organisation.

'You should run your start-up like a cult.'

Peter Thiel, PayPal co-founder

Have you ever wondered where the phrase 'drinking the Kool-Aid' comes from?

It comes from a mass suicide pact: the ultimate expression of groupthink.

Jim Jones was the leader of the Peoples Temple cult. In 1978 he brainwashed his followers into believing that the world was about to end. One day, following his instructions, more than 900 of his disciples – among them women and children – ended their lives by drinking a cocktail of cyanide and the drink Kool-Aid.

★ IT'S PRETTY MUCH IMPOSSIBLE FOR A BUSINESS TO BECOME A FULL-BLOWN CULT

Cults are venal, sinister, manipulative and use psychological brainwashing to control their members. They require the type of leader who prevents followers from thinking for themselves. By contrast, modern businesses operating in a fast-changing, unpredictable, turbulent world require employees at all levels to be able to think independently. The last thing you want, as a leader today, is employees who are incapable of independent thought.

As Jim Collins has argued, though, in his landmark book *Built to Last*, there is nothing wrong with a cult-like *commitment* from employees to specific *values*. Collins found that architects of visionary companies intentionally encourage this, rather than relying purely on their employees' work ethic, ideals or ability to execute their brief.

Cults are gruesome, evil and horrendous institutions. They prey on people's vulnerabilities, insecurities and faithfulness. I am by no means encouraging you to replicate their immorality, wickedness or delusion. I am, however, fascinated and perplexed by how a group of people can become so committed, devoted and dedicated to a cause, a brand or a mission that they would make the fateful decision to give their life to it.

I've sat with CEO after CEO of some of the world's most adored brands, a few of which that have – in their own words – a 'cult following'. Some of them also have a 'cult-like' company culture, and others have referred to a 'cult mentality' when the company was founded.

Peter Thiel, the German-American billionaire entrepreneur and co-founder of PayPal. said:

Every company culture can be plotted on a linear spectrum: the best start-ups might be considered slightly less extreme kinds of cults. The biggest difference is that cults tend to be fanatically wrong about something important. People at a successful start-up are fanatically right about something those outside it have missed.

Why work with a group of people who don't even like each other? Taking a merely professional view of the workplace, in which free agents check in and out on a transactional basis, is worse than cold: it's not even rational. Since time is your most valuable asset, it's odd to spend it working with people who don't envision any long-term future together.

If you look closely at the T-shirts people in San Francisco wear to work, you'll see the logos of their companies – and tech workers care about those very much. The start-up uniform encapsulates a simple but essential principle: everyone at your company should be different in the same way – a tribe of like-minded people fiercely devoted to the company's mission.

Above all, don't fight the perk war. Anybody who would be powerfully swayed by free laundry pickup or pet day care would be a bad addition to your team. Just cover the basics and then promise what no others can: the opportunity to do irreplaceable work on a unique problem alongside great people.

We've all seen the throwback imagery of a small group of people huddled around computers in a shed, basement or apartment, building what would go on to be the next big, billion-dollar company. They always seem to look really tired and a little malnourished but incredibly focused.

Facebook, Amazon, Microsoft, Google, Apple started this way, to name a few. All these companies had cult-like attributes in their earliest years, and their founders often attribute that religious dedication, conviction and obsession to their eventual success.

'The energy at a start-up is like being part of a movement or a cult.'

Kevin Systrom, co-founder of Instagram

'When I was starting the company, I thought, "Who wants to be in a cult? That sounds horrible." But when you're a start-up, that's exactly what you want to create. You want to create a company that people are really passionate about.'

Tony Hsieh, former CEO of Zappos

'It's kind of a cult, you
know? The energy, the
camaraderie, the sense of
mission and purpose.'

Evan Williams, co-founder of Twitter

★ THE FOUR STAGES OF BUILDING A COMPANY

It's my belief – derived from my own experience launching more than ten successful start-ups and my conversations with hundreds of successful founders – that the best companies go through an evolutionary process, which does – although it may sound uninviting to some – initially resemble a cult.

The four stages of a company's life are the cult, growth, enterprise and decline phases. In the cult or 'zero to one' phase, the founding team members are typically so consumed by their delusional belief, enthusiasm and urgency, that they go 'all-in', sacrificing their social life, relationships and, unfortunately, their wellbeing, to try and get their baby off the ground.

In the growth phase, the company is a mess behind the scenes. Employees are overworked, under-resourced and often inexperienced. They don't have the systems, processes or people they need to handle the growth, but they feel like they're on a rocket ship to somewhere great, so they hold on to the ship with great excitement, terror and hope regardless.

In the enterprise phase, people are stable. Their lives tend to have greater balance, employee retention improves, and expectations, processes and systems are defined.

The final phase, decline, comes to all companies eventually – usually because of the risk-aversion, complacency and ostrich effect that I described in Law 23.

★ ★ ★

The most important decision you will make when you launch a company is picking the first ten people. Each of them represents 10 per cent of your company culture, your values and your philosophy, so getting those ten people right and binding them together with the right culture, will irreversibly define your company. When a culture is strong, new people become like the culture. When a culture is weak, the culture becomes like the new people. Your 11th person will curiously resemble the other ten in values and philosophy.

'I found that when you get enough A players together, when you go through the incredible work to find five of these A players, they really like working with each other because they've never had a chance to do that before and they don't want to work with B and C players. And so it becomes self-policing, and they only want to hire more A players. And so you build up these pockets of A players and it propagates. And that's what the Mac team was like. They were all A players.'

Steve Jobs

That initial team of ten is a window into the culture that you will have when there's a hundred of you. This is why companies that become great start out feeling like cults – they were clear on their values, devoted to the cause and obsessed with solving a problem.

Although that unsustainable mentality dilutes as it moves through its inevitable life cycle, its essence remains as a set of clear values that continue to permeate through everything the company does.

So the question becomes, what are the ingredients of a cult?

1. A SENSE OF COMMUNITY AND BELONGING
Joshua Hart, a professor of psychology at Union College who has studied cults, said, 'They provide meaning,

purpose and belonging. They offer a clear, confident vision and assert the superiority of the group. And followers who are craving peace, belonging and security might gain a sense of those things as well as confidence through participation in the group.'

2. A SHARED MISSION

'A cult is a group or movement with a shared commitment to a usually extreme ideology,' says Janja Lalich, an expert in cultic studies. They also have a clear shared identity, sometimes a uniform – in business, sometimes a company logo.

3. AN INSPIRATIONAL LEADER

'As to the leaders themselves, they typically present themselves as infallible, confident and grandiose. Their charisma draws people in,' Joshua Hart says.

4. AN 'US VS. THEM' MENTALITY

Cults tend to have a clear adversary. In the case of the Heaven's Gate cult, civilisation as a whole and non-believers were their adversary. In business, it tends to be the industry competitors – other teams with competing missions.

'When you're at a start-up, the first thing you have to believe is that you're going to change the world.'

Marc Andreessen, co-founder of Netscape and Andreessen Horowitz

★ THE TEN STEPS TO BUILDING A COMPANY CULTURE

1. Define the company's core values and align them with aspects such as mission, vision, principles or purpose to create a solid foundation for the organisation.

2. Integrate the desired culture into every aspect of the company, including hiring policies, processes and procedures across all departments and functions.

3. Agree upon expected behaviours and standards for all team members, promoting a positive work environment.

4. Establish a purpose that goes beyond the company's commercial goals, fostering a deeper connection for employees.

5. Use myths, stories, company-specific vocabulary and legends, along with symbols and habits, to reinforce the company culture and embed it in the collective consciousness.

6. Develop a unique identity as a group and cultivate a sense of exclusivity and pride within the team.

7. Create an atmosphere that celebrates achievements, progress, and living the company culture, boosting motivation and pride.

8. Encourage camaraderie, community and a sense of belonging among team members, encourage mutual dependence and a collective sense of obligation, reinforcing the interconnected nature of the team.

9. Remove barriers and enable employees to express themselves authentically and embrace their individuality within the organisation.

10. Emphasise the unique qualities and contributions of both employees and the collective, positioning them as distinct and exceptional.

✱ WHY YOU SHOULD NOT MAINTAIN A CULT-LIKE CULTURE IN THE LONG RUN

If you're building something to last, for the long term, cultish obsession won't be enough. Cults in any context – and especially in business – are fundamentally unsustainable, emotionally gruelling and therefore ineffective at achieving long-term objectives in business and life. The most important overarching principle for anyone hoping to achieve a long-term business goal is to create a culture that is sustainable; where people are authentically engaged with a mission they care about; trusted with a high degree of autonomy; sufficiently challenged in their work; given a sense of forward motion and progress; and surrounded by a caring, supportive group of people that they love to work with and that provide them with 'psychological safety'.

If you can achieve this, you're setting yourself up for long-term success.

★ THE LAW: CREATE A CULT MENTALITY

A cult-like mentality, and cult-like commitment from staff, can be incredibly useful in the beginning stages of a start-up; it can determine the culture and generate the passion required to launch a new business. But as a company grows, it needs to develop in order to achieve longer-term objectives – cults are not sustainable.

If the culture is strong, new people will become like the culture.

If the culture is weak, the culture will become like the new people.

THE THREE BARS FOR BUILDING GREAT TEAMS

This law shows you how the greatest leaders in the world decide who to hire, fire and promote in their organisations and why you need to put culture before everything when building a team.

Sir Alex Ferguson is widely considered to be the greatest football manager of all time. During his 26 years at the head of Manchester United he won 38 trophies, and in the summer of 2013, after winning the Premier League one last time, he announced he was retiring at the age of 71.

When he first joined the struggling side in 1986, he said 'The most important thing at Manchester United is the culture of the club. The culture of the club comes from the manager.' He emphasised that culture and values – not just players and tactics – determine a team's success. He said that these values must be instilled in players from the moment they join the team, and must be upheld by everyone at the club, from the players and coaches to the staff and executives.

A few years ago, Patrice Evra, a player who joined Ferguson's winning Manchester United side in 2006, told me that the manager met him in the backroom of an airport in France ahead of potentially signing him to join the team.

'Sir Alex wanted to look in my eyes and ask me one question. He looked at me with a steely stare and said, "Are you willing to die for this club?" I replied "Yes", and he immediately reached across the table and said, "Welcome to Manchester United, son!"'

Ferguson believed that creating a strong, united culture within the club would result in a winning team on the pitch and build a sustainable success over the long term. He was right. No football manager, before or after, has ever managed to dominate with such stability, consistency and success as Ferguson did.

A hallmark of his philosophy was to never let individual players get in the way of his team ethos, culture or values. He became known for saying the phrase 'nobody is bigger than the club' in press conferences, and unexpectedly transferring any player that no longer embodied the 'United way', regardless of how well they were playing, how famous they were or how much he needed them.

I've interviewed five former Manchester United players over the last few years, and all of them said that one of Ferguson's greatest strengths was his ability to move star-players on – even when they were at the peak of their powers.

Rio Ferdinand told me:

> Jaap Stam was the best defender in the world at the time, and Sir Alex said, 'See you later'. David Beckham was in the form of his career and he let him go! Ruud van Nistelrooy was the top goal scorer at United and he shipped him out the team! The man just saw something early.

Under Ferguson's leadership, Beckham became widely considered as the best right-sided midfielder in Europe. But Ferguson grew weary of the constant paparazzi that hounded Beckham following his marriage to pop star Victoria. When his popularity skyrocketed in Manchester, and Beckham became a growing distraction, it was against everything Sir Alex wanted for his team's culture and – the next summer – Beckham was sold to Real Madrid.

Another example was Keane, who was United's captain of a golden era, winning seven titles with the club and steering them to win the treble (FA Premier League, FA Cup and UEFA Champions League) in 1999. But after training-ground arguments and outbursts in interviews in which he criticised teammates, the outspoken midfielder ended up falling out with Ferguson and was sold to Celtic in 2005.

Ruud van Nistelrooy was one of the most prolific goal scorers in United's history. But when he stormed out of the stadium after being benched on the last game of the season, he was never seen at Manchester United ever again.

Your average manager, in sport or in business, wouldn't have the guts, foresight and conviction to make such bold pivotal decisions – sacking your most valuable employee because they're challenging your culture is a problematic thing to do. But every truly great sport or business manager that I've interviewed instinctively knows that the even more problematic thing is letting one 'bad apple' spoil the rest, regardless of their talent.

'The hardest thing I had to learn was to fire people.
You must do it to protect the integrity of the company and the culture of the team.'

Richard Branson

Barbara Corcoran is the 73-year-old American business-woman, *Shark Tank* investor, and founder of a billion-dollar New York real estate empire. In my interview with her, she stressed how critically important it is to remove 'toxic influences' from your team, before they infect your other 'children' (employees):

> I couldn't wait to fire individuals who were negative and didn't fit. They were ruining my good kids. People who are negative always need somebody to be negative with them. You've got to get rid of them. I never carried a negative person that didn't fit the culture for more than a couple of months. These people are thieves in the night, they take your energy away, and your most valuable asset is your energy.

Hesitating to fire someone that I knew was a net negative for my companies culture is my single biggest regret in business. As Corcoran highlights, these people are contagious – they have the toxic power to turn younger, high-potential, great team members into negative, average worriers.

'The cost of one bad apple can be the loss of many good ones.'

CEO of General Electric

Harvard Business Review undertook a study into the effects of bad employees on a business. The study aimed to understand how new ideas and behaviours can spread among co-workers.

Using regulatory filings and employee complaints, the study found that employees were 37 per cent more likely to commit misconduct at work when they encountered a new co-worker who had a history of misconduct themselves. Incredibly, this study shows that toxic employees really are contagious. Results show that misconduct in the workplace has a social multiplier of 1.59, which means that each case of misconduct in a company – like a virus – spreads and results in an additional 0.59 cases of misconduct when a misbehaving employee is allowed to remain.

Will Felps, a former researcher at the University of Washington Business School, was asking his wife if things at her work were still bothering her. 'They're not in the office this week, and the atmosphere is so much better,' she said.

Felp's wife was referring to a single co-worker who was particularly toxic, regularly picking on and humiliating individuals in her team, which made an already hostile working environment even worse. But when this employee was off sick for a few days, a funny thing happened, recalls Felps.

People started helping each other, playing classical music on their radios and going out for drinks after work. But when he returned to the office, things returned to the unpleasant way they were. She hadn't noticed this employee as being a very important person in the office before he came down with this illness but, upon observing the social atmosphere when he was gone, she came to believe that he had a profound and negative impact. He truly was the 'bad apple' that spoiled the barrel.

Intrigued by the impact of this single individual on a wider team, Felps and his colleague Terence Mitchell, a professor of business and psychology, combed through 24 published studies about how teams and groups of employees interact, and followed up with their own research to show just how much a single 'negative' team member – someone who avoids taking their fair share of the work, bullies their teammates or is emotionally unstable – can derail an otherwise well-functioning team. And they're more common than you might think: most people, it turns out, can think of at least one 'bad apple' they've worked with in the course of their career.

Their study also indicated that most organisations do not have effective ways of dealing with negative employees, particularly when the negative employee has longevity, experience or power within the company.

> They found that negative behaviour completely outweighed positive behaviour, meaning that a single 'bad apple' can spoil the team's culture, while one, two or three good workers cannot un-spoil it.

They concluded that when a 'bad apple' isn't fired, it can lead to employee disengagement, other employees copying the behaviour, social withdrawal, anxiety and fear. This culminates in a deterioration of trust within the team and further disengagement of team members.

The researchers discovered something I've learned time and time again throughout my business career: no one person leaving a good company kills it, but sometimes one person staying can.

'A bad apple can ruin the barrel but it's important to remember that the barrel can be cleaned. It's important to take action and remove toxic individuals to maintain a positive culture.'

Oprah Winfrey

★ THE THREE BARS: FIRE, HIRE, TRAIN

Firing someone is never easy. All of the aforementioned great leaders, who understand the importance of protecting a company culture at all costs, also speak of the difficulty, agony and emotional turmoil of the experience when they have to let someone go. It's this psychological friction, and the ostrich effect it creates (see Law 23), that causes us to procrastinate, second-guess ourselves and avoid doing what we know we should do.

With this in mind, I created a simple framework, which I've consistently and successfully used within my management teams over the last decade to help us see through this friction, and to clarify which team members should be hired, promoted and fired. I call this my 'three bars' framework.

It starts with asking yourself (or your management team) a very simple question in relation to a specific team member:

'If everyone in the organisation had the same cultural values, attitude and level of talent as this employee, would the bar (the average) be raised, maintained, or lowered?'

This question doesn't seek similarity in perspectives, experience or interests. We know that diversity of thought, lived experience, or worldview is beneficial. But it does seek similarity in company cultural values, standards and attitude.

Think of any team you're in – a sports team, a creative team or the team you're in at work – and now think of one person at random in that team and ask yourself, 'If everyone in the team embodied their cultural values, would the bar be raised, maintained or lowered?'

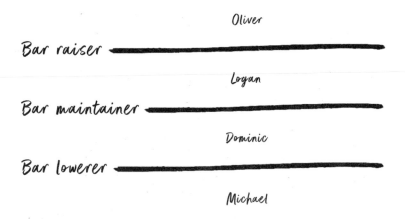

On this image I've plotted four hypothetical people using this question. It's simple: Michael – the bar lowerer – needs to be fired, and Oliver – the bar raiser – needs to be promoted into a management position. As the research demonstrated, Michael will be a disproportionately toxic influence on team culture, and Oliver can become a disproportionally positive influence on team culture if he's given the chance to sit higher in the organisation.

This framework has also been incredibly useful when assessing new recruits against current team standards.

★ THE LAW: THE THREE BARS FOR BUILDING GREAT TEAMS

With every hire, you should be looking to raise the bar, and just like Sir Alex Ferguson did, if any current hire – regardless of how many trophies they've won you in the past – becomes a bar lowerer, you must quickly and decisively act to stop their influence destroying the sacred collective culture.

The
definition
of the word
'company'
is just
'group of
people'.

LAW 31

LEVERAGE THE POWER OF PROGRESS

This law shows the most important force for team engagement, motivation and fulfilment in any organisation. If you can make people feel this, they'll love being part of your team.

'Winning medals seemed so far away, it seemed like such a mountain, in the distance, untouchable. People were thinking, wow, how on earth are we going to get from where we are now to up there? What can we believe in? How do we get some momentum? How do we get some contagious enthusiasm?'

Sir David Brailsford, former performance director of British Cycling, on *The Diary Of A CEO*

A few years ago I interviewed Sir David Brailsford, who is known as the mastermind behind a theory called '**marginal gains**'. His theory was popularised by the story of the 2008 British Cycling team and their continued success across multiple Olympic Games.

Prior to 2008, British Cycling was widely regarded as the laughing stock of the sport. In an effort to fix things, the governing body hired performance director David Brailsford to transform the philosophy, strategy and culture of the team.

Brailsford believed that 1 per cent improvements across all aspects of cycling would aggregate into a significant performance gain. Under his guidance, British Cycling stopped thinking about major steps forward and started obsessing over the smallest, easiest details: using antibacterial hand gel to cut down on infections, rubbing alcohol on bicycle tyres for better grip, redesigning bike seats for greater comfort, changing the pillows in the athletes' bedrooms to improve their sleep, extensive wind tunnel testing of bikes and racing suits, etc.

Brailsford took over and within five years, British Cycling won 57 per cent of all road and track cycling gold medals at the 2008 Beijing Olympics, and at the 2012 London Olympics set seven world records and nine Olympic records! From 2007 to 2017, British cyclists won 178 world championships, 66 Olympic or Paralympic gold medals and captured five Tour de France victories. This made this ten-year span the most successful era for any cycling team in history!

In my interview with Brailsford, I asked him how focusing on small marginal progress caused such tremendous motivation, success and consistency, and he told me:

People want a feeling of progression, and if we aim for perfection, we'll fail, because perfection is so far away.

So instead of perfection, let's have a little progression, just a little, and that will make us feel good. So, let's identify the basics, get them right and then next week ask ourselves, what other little things could we do?

There are a million things that could impact a cycling performance. Could we, I don't know, change our diet to be slightly more optimal than it is this week, and do that by next week? And everybody goes, yep, we could do that! OK. What else could we do? Could we do more in the gym this week? Could we alter our attitude slightly? Could you do that? Yeah, we could do that. OK. So off we go. And then you get to next week and ask, did we do all that stuff? Yeah, we did. We haven't moved a long way, but I tell you what, it felt pretty good.

And suddenly you kind of start to get this idea that you're on the move. And when you feel like you're on the move, you feel good about yourself. Tiny progress means a lot to people, and when they feel it, they realise they can do it again tomorrow.

Whereas when you're trying to do something big, it's less sustainable. We all go full gas in the gym in January and then of course by February, we've all stopped again. And why is that? It's quite rare that you can make major change and make it sustainable, but it's quite easy to make small incremental changes and make them stick. And it's the stickability over time, I think, which makes the big difference. We never ever thought about the podiums, or the finish line, or trophies – we didn't talk about that – we thought about the smallest things we could do today to make progress.

When you create this culture, people feel the progress, and they're energised. Even more ideas start coming to the surface from the team and they get adopted too. And a narrative emerges in the team that we're on the move, we're changing, we're doing all the little things because we can be arsed to do the little things that other people can't be arsed to do. And that makes a difference.

And I say that quite often in our team, we'll be working late, and I say, right, guys, let's just all get together for a minute. The reason we've been good, is because we can be arsed to do all these little things that all these other teams who are now locked up and gone to bed in their hotel, can't be bothered to do. And it works, you know, it works, 100 per cent it works, been at it 20 years. And it's as much about that kind of enthusiasm and a positivity about embracing and not viewing small change as a chore. Progress is a powerful force.

★ THE SUPERPOWER OF SMALL WINS

The concept of progress is often perceived as a tangible outcome, yet research continues to show that the true motivational power of progress is more feelings and emotions than facts and stats.

As researcher Teresa Amabile notes in the *Harvard Business Review*, 'On days when workers have the sense they're making headway in their jobs, or when they receive support that helps them overcome obstacles, their emotions are most positive and their drive to succeed is at its peak.'

The key phrase here is 'when workers have the sense they're making headway'.

How much you're actually achieving is pretty much irrelevant to your motivation: but if you feel like you're getting somewhere, you'll be driven to keep going.

When joining a poorly motivated, struggling team, the collective psychology resembles that of a double-decker bus broken down on the side of the road with four flat tyres. Inspiration and collective belief is the energy that all teams run on – it's the cause of their drive, the air in their tyres and the fuel in their engine.

Sir David Brailsford understood this when he joined the failing British Cycling team – he knew that making large tangible accomplishments mattered less at that point than giving the team the feeling that they were accomplishing something, and that's why he focused on the small wins first – because that's the easiest way to unlock the motivational power of progress, to jump-start the bus, put petrol in the engine and get the wheels in motion.

'These small wins matter more because they are so much more likely to occur compared to the big breakthroughs in the world. If we only waited for the big wins, we would be waiting a long time. And we

would probably quit long before we see anything tangible come to fruition. What you need instead of the big wins is simply the forward momentum that small wins bring.'

Teresa Amabile

Through her incredible research, which involved the analysis of nearly 12,000 diary entries and daily rankings of motivation and emotions, Amabile found that 'making progress in one's work – even incremental progress – is more frequently associated with positive emotions and high motivation than any other workday event'.

When I interviewed Nir Eyal, the author of the landmark book *Indistractible*, which uncovers why humans procrastinate, he asserted that the sole reason why people procrastinate is because they're trying to avoid some form of 'psychological discomfort' in their life. The bigger the task and the less competent we feel about accomplishing it, the greater the procrastination. That essay you have to write on a topic you don't fully understand, that sensitive issue you have to confront in your relationship that will likely result in a major argument, that business you want to launch without clarity on where you need to start – these challenges feel like mountains to climb; they cause tremendous psychological discomfort, so they inspire tremendous procrastination.

The key to overcoming that discomfort and preventing procrastination is to 'smallify' the task into easy, achievable micro-goals.

Making goals sound and feel achievable is something the great organisational theorist Karl E. Weick has explored at length over his decades of researching organisational life.

In 1984, Weick published a seminal paper that blamed society's failure to solve big social issues on how we *present* the challenges to the world. 'The massive scale on which social problems are conceived often stops innovation and action,' he complained. 'People often define social problems in ways that overwhelm their ability to do anything about them.' He went as far as to say that 'people can't solve problems unless they think they aren't "problems"':

> When the magnitude of problems is scaled upward, the quality of thought and action declines, because processes such as frustration, arousal, and helplessness are activated.

Therefore, the key to action, confidence and movement is scaling your challenge *down*.

Small wins 'may seem unimportant', he concedes. But 'a series of wins' begins to reveal 'a pattern that may attract allies, deter opponents, and lower resistance to subsequent proposals'. Small wins 'are compact, tangible, upbeat, and noncontroversial.'

Too few leaders understand this.

In a seminal article published in the *Harvard Business Review* in 1968, American psychologist Frederick Herzberg theorised that individuals are most motivated in their jobs when they are provided with 'opportunities for achievement'.

However, when *Harvard Business Review* surveyed almost 700 managers across various companies and industries worldwide, they discovered that most managers, leaders and CEOs simply didn't believe or understand this.

When asked to rank the tools most effective in impacting employee motivation and emotions, a mere 5 per cent of respondents placed 'making progress in work' as the primary motivator, with 95 per cent placing it last or third.

Instead, the majority ranked 'recognition for good work' as the most crucial factor in motivating workers and promoting happiness. While recognition undoubtedly enhances an employee's inner work life, it is ultimately dependent upon achievements.

As a leader, it is crucial to understand the transformative power of progress and the ways in which it can be nurtured and catalysed. This knowledge can provide significant influence over employee wellbeing, innovation, motivation, and creative output.

HOW TO CREATE THE PERSPECTIVE OF PROGRESS IN TEAMS

Professor Amabile's five methods can help you facilitate your team's progress and reap the benefits of low-hanging fruit:

1. CREATING MEANING

Humans have a deep-seated desire to do meaningful work. Steve Jobs used this to his advantage in 1983, when trying to convince John Sculley that he should leave his extremely successful job at PepsiCo to become Apple's new CEO, by asking him, 'Do you want to spend the rest of your life selling sugared water or do you want a chance to change the world?' His strategy was successful – Sculley joined Apple shortly after – because it focused on the meaningfulness of the work that Apple does. Making progress boosts your professional motivation, but only if the work matters to you.

In all my companies over the last ten years, one of the most valuable things we've done is put systems in place that make sure that every team member, in every department, feels the meaningful impact the work is having on the world. In one company we have an internal workplace channel called 'Impact', which is dedicated to sharing powerful stories, testimonials and feedback about how each team member's efforts has impacted the lives of real people, all over the world.

Managers cannot leave this to chance; in an increasingly digital world, where we're dealing more in numbers, stats and screens, it's easier than ever to lose sight of the meaning behind the metrics.

> **When work feels meaningless, motivation evaporates.**

According to 238 diary entries by workers in a variety of industries, the factor that kills meaning the fastest is a leadership team that dismisses an employee's work or ideas, removes their sense of ownership and autonomy and asks them to spend time on work that is cancelled, changed or disregarded before it's been completed.

2. SETTING CLEAR AND ACTIONABLE GOALS

It's important for leaders to lay out objectives clearly, so team members know exactly what they need to accomplish. The goal should be broken down into smaller, interim milestones, with a focus on early wins to build momentum. Progress should be tracked to ensure small wins don't go unnoticed.

In my companies we use OKRs (objectives and key results) – a periodic goal-setting framework – across all teams to ensure that this happens.

3. PROVIDING AUTONOMY

Once the desired outcome is clear, leaders should give their team members space to take charge. Encourage them to map their own path by utilising their skills and expertise.

One of the most important characteristics in all of my teams has been allowing people the space to both fail and succeed. My job as CEO is to play the role of a supportive enabler, not a critical micromanager.

4. REMOVING FRICTION

Leaders should proactively remove any obstacles, bureaucracy and sign-off processes that prevent the team from achieving daily progress. This includes identifying and providing resources they need to do their job.

As mentioned in Law 20, frequent check-ins with all of my directors has allowed me to do this quickly and decisively. Team members tend to know exactly what's getting in their way – but leaders rarely bother to ask them, and when they do, they rarely act quickly enough to resolve it. This causes a decay in trust, and team members become increasingly reluctant to speak up about friction causing issues in the future.

5. BROADCASTING THE PROGRESS

Leaders need to point out, publicise and praise progress as loud, far and wide as they possibly can. Recognition reinforces behaviour, but it also acts as evidence to adjacent teams that progress is possible for them too.

In every company and team I run, the head of the team is asked to broadcast a weekly update to the entire company detailing all the progress their team has made that week. This ritual has been incredibly powerful in creating a collective sense that we're 'going somewhere' as Sir David Brailsford would say, and when people feel like they're going somewhere, they're more motivated, feel happier and are more engaged with leadership.

★ THE LAW: LEVERAGE THE POWER OF PROGRESS

To solve problems, encourage and celebrate small wins. This provides continuous forward momentum, which creates an atmosphere of success and a positive sense that a team is moving towards their bigger goals. Employees are most motivated when they are engaged with the work that they're doing, and feel like they are making a difference.

The most
professionally
rewarding
feeling in
the world
is a sense
of forward
motion.

YOU MUST BE AN INCONSISTENT LEADER

This law will teach you how to become a truly great manager and leader – by being inconsistent.

I sat down with Manchester United legend Patrice Evra, who played left-back under Sir Alex Ferguson for almost ten years, to find out what, in his own words, made Ferguson the greatest sporting manager of all time. Patrice instantly referred to one day in 2007 that perfectly highlighted the manager's brilliance.

It was the afternoon of 4 February 2007, a cold, dreary Sunday in London. The sky was overcast, and a light drizzle was falling as Manchester United arrived at White Hart Lane stadium, then the home of Tottenham Hotspurs.

The Red Devils had started the season on formidable form, sitting at the top of the league, three points clear, and were today facing an on-form home team who were determined to take down the league leaders.

The first half of the match was a tense and tight affair, with neither team able to gain a clear advantage. Both teams battled fiercely for possession, with the midfield a blur of flying boots and sliding tackles. However, a fortuitous penalty awarded to Manchester United in the last minute of the first half gave them a lucky 1–0 lead as they headed into the dressing room at half-time.

As the team entered the dressing room, Ferguson walked in, sat down and said nothing for three minutes. The room was eerily quiet as the players sat nervously, avoiding eye contact with the silent manager. They knew that when Ferguson sat in silence, it wasn't a good sign.

Evra was playing what he would later describe as the 'best game of his life'. He had been a constant thorn in the side of the Tottenham defence, making surging runs up the left flank and delivering pinpoint crosses.

Patrice was smiling, drinking water and being congratulated by his teammates as he caught the gaze of Ferguson, who was looking straight at him. He recalls:

I'm playing the best game of my life. I promise you, I was on fire. I came back to the dressing room, I was relaxed, happy, drinking some water. My teammates were congratulating me, saying 'Wow, Patrice, you're on fire!' Then Ferguson walked in, sat down for three minutes and locked his eyes on me. He asked me, 'Patrice, are you OK?' I said, 'Yes, I'm OK, boss.' He then asked me 'Are you tired?'

Seriously, I looked around, thinking his question must be a prank. Maybe there was some hidden camera and he was winding me up. The players around me were equally confused.

'No, I'm fine', I replied.

'Why did you pass the ball back to the keeper,' he continued.

'Because I didn't have any options in front of me, that was the only option I had', I explained.

'If you do that again, you will come and watch the rest of the fucking game sat next to me. This is the worst game you've played since you've played for Manchester United.' He shouted, 'If you pass it back again I promise you, you will never play for Manchester United again'.

I kept my mouth shut. I was biting my lips. But I never wanted to answer him back in front of my team-mates. People were in shock. Everyone was thinking, *What's going on?*

Manchester United came out of the dressing room for the second half with renewed energy, a fire in their bellies and an increased focus. They dominated the second half, scoring three more goals and securing a 4–0 victory over the home team. It was a performance that would go down in the history books as one of Manchester United's greatest away victories. The *Independent* called it a 'divine demolition from a team at the height of their powers'.

Patrice was still perplexed by the berating he'd received from Ferguson at half time:

I took my shower, got my clothes on and I couldn't wait to sleep and come back to the training ground the next day to speak to him about what had happened. The next day I knocked on his office door and he invited me in.

'Ohhh Patrice, how are you my son? Come and sit down!' Ferguson said.

I replied: 'Boss what happened yesterday? Why did you say that to me?'

'Patrice, you were the best player on the pitch. But you know, Cristiano Ronaldo started doing too many skills, some of your teammates were wasting their chances on the ball, and when you play for Manchester United, you need to score one goal, and then a second, and then a third. You can't just score one goal. You were the best player, my son, get out of my office!'

He was whistling and singing and laughing.

He knew I could take the fire; he shouted at me because he wanted to send a message to the other players, to Cristiano, to make sure they kept focused and respected Tottenham. So, he picked the best player on the pitch, a player he knew could take it, so that every other player on our team thought, *If he's killing the best player on the pitch, I better improve my game.* That's what I mean by managing, that's Fergie.

To my surprise, every Manchester United player I've spoken to and interviewed said Sir Alex Ferguson didn't care about tactics, strategies and formations. He cared primarily about getting the best out of each individual, the team's culture and their attitude; he didn't want them ever to become complacent.

Gary Neville, who spent his entire playing career at Ferguson's Manchester United, told me:

He knew how to tap into your heart, no matter who you were, he knew how to tap into you. He would talk about my grandparents when he wanted to motivate me. My grandad was injured in the war, he still has shrapnel in his shoulder from the battle. So, Sir Alex would say, 'What about your grandparents, getting up every single day, putting their tie on, working hard, going off to war?'

When Sir Alex would say that to me, I would keep going. When he spoke to someone else, he would say something completely different. He would tap into every individual, in a different way, to make sure they would never give in.

Rio Ferdinand, who played as centre-back and captain for Manchester United for 12 years, told me that Ferguson's greatest attribute was his ability to know every individual and to be a different shape jigsaw piece to all of them:

> He understood people. He wouldn't treat two players the same. Blanket treatment isn't the best way to treat a team. Everyone's different, everyone takes advice differently. Everyone takes criticism differently. And that's why the leader or manager needs to know the individuals. This was one of Sir Alex Ferguson's greatest traits. He knew everything, about everyone. When my grandad was in hospital once, even though he'd only met him twice, he knew my grandad's favourite drink, and flowers turned up at my mum's house. He knew that mattered to me. It's little things like that, that made me fight harder for him.

The following quotes from other past players of Ferguson sum up what made him such an exceptional manager.

'He had different ways of dealing with different players. He knew how to get the best out of everyone.'

Peter Schmeichel

'He was very hard on me, but he had to be. He saw something in me that he didn't see in other players, and he pushed me to be the best I could be.'

David Beckham

'He always knew when to give me a kick up the backside and when to put an arm around me. He knew how to treat different players differently.'

Ryan Giggs

'He treated me differently than the other players, but in a good way. He pushed me to be better, and I think that's why I became the player I am today.'

Wayne Rooney

'He treated me differently
from the other players.
He would always talk to
me and give me advice.
He helped me to become
a better player.'

Cristiano Ronaldo

★ THE ART OF BEING AN INCONSISTENT LEADER

Every book dedicated to leadership and management espouses the virtues of consistency, predictability and fairness as hallmarks of great leaders. However, my decade-long study of truly exceptional managers has revealed the opposite to be true. My own experience leading more than 1,000 individuals across four companies has taught me that my ability to adapt to each individual, to be inconsistent in my approach and to skilfully shift my emotions like a chameleon in order to elicit the best from every member of my team, positively correlates with my ability to motivate.

As we have explored in previous laws in this book, humans are not the rational, logical and analytical creatures we presume ourselves to be. We are emotional, illogical and driven by a multitude of emotional impulses, fears, desires, insecurities, and childhood experiences. In light of this, a one-size-fits-all, reason-, information- and facts-centric approach to leadership is deeply inadequate for inspiring passion, motivation and action among any group of people.

> *For us as leaders, to become the complementary puzzle piece for each member of our team, we must be as <u>inconsistent</u>, <u>emotionally variable</u> and <u>fluctuating</u> as the people in our teams are.*

Rio Ferdinand recounts how Ferguson was a masterful actor, able to feign any emotion, from anger to elation, in order to evoke the emotions he believed would best serve the team's success:

> He was so calculated. We talked about it all the time amongst the players. The way he spoke – he would go on TV after a defeat and intentionally, furiously, hammer the referee to deflect attention away from the players. He did that to remove the focus from the team, to make sure we weren't feeling down about ourselves, so that we would be motivated for the next game. He was so calculated. The best man-manager.

★ THE LAW: YOU MUST BE AN INCONSISTENT LEADER

It is impossible to seamlessly blend into a team as a jigsaw piece unless you comprehend the unique shape of each of your team members. Sir Alex Ferguson's acumen in this regard was legendary, as attested to by his former players and staff, and even rival managers. He possessed an encyclopedic knowledge of everything from the hobbies of his players' wives to the names of their pets, and as Rio

Ferdinand told me, even their grandfathers' preferred brand of whisky. More significantly, he knew that every member of his team was propelled by vastly different motivators. While one player may have thrived under Ferguson's infamous 'hairdryer' treatment (where he would shout angrily at them in the dressing room or on the training ground), another may have required a more compassionate approach, and still another may have been motivated by a more hands-off approach. This is why Ferguson didn't have to be the tactical mastermind that many assume he must have been, but rather an emotional savant. When you're in the business of motivating people, emotional management is everything.

Great leaders are fluid, flexible, and full of fluctuation.

They are whatever shape they need to be, to complete your motivation.

LAW 33

LEARNING NEVER ENDS

SCAN HERE:

www.the33rdlaw.com

REFERENCES

THE FOUR PILLARS OF GREATNESS
Pillar I: The Self
Covey, S. R. (2004). *The 7 Habits of Highly Effective People: Powerful Lessons in Personal Change.* Simon & Schuster.
Duckworth, A. (2016). *Grit: The Power of Passion and Perseverance.* Scribner.
Langer, E. J. (1989). *Mindfulness.* Addison-Wesley.

Pillar II: The Story
Brown, B. (2010). 'The Power of Vulnerability' [Video file]. TED Conferences. https://www.ted.com/talks/brene_brown_the_power_of_vulnerability
Godin, S. (2018). *This is Marketing: You Can't Be Seen Until You Learn to See.* Portfolio. Penguin
Pink, D. H. (2005). *A Whole New Mind: Why Right-Brainers Will Rule the Future.* Riverhead Books.

Pillar III: The Philosophy
Covey, S. R. (2004). *The 7 Habits of Highly Effective People: Powerful Lessons in Personal Change.* Simon & Schuster.
Haidt, J. (2006). *The Happiness Hypothesis: Finding Modern Truth in Ancient Wisdom.* Basic Books.
Keller, T. (2012). *Every Good Endeavor: Connecting Your Work to God's Work.* Viking.

Pillar IV: The Team
Collins, J. (2001). *Good to Great: Why Some Companies Make the Leap and Others Don't.* Random House Business.
Duhigg, C. (2016). *Smarter Faster Better: The Secrets of Being Productive in Life and Business.* Random House.
Lencioni, P. (2002). *The Five Dysfunctions of a Team: A Leadership Fable.* John Wiley & Sons.

Law 1
Abbate, B. (2021, January 29). 'Why a Good Reputation is Important to Your Life and Career'. Medium. https://medium.com/illumination/why-a-good-reputation-important-to-your-life-and-career-80c1da06430e

Bolles, R. N. (2014, September 2). '4 Ways To Change Careers In Midlife'. *Forbes*. https://www.forbes.com/sites/nextavenue/2014/09/02/4-ways-to-change-careers-in-midlife/?sh=38da133419df

Forbes Coaches Council. (2017, October 10). '15 Simple Ways To Improve Your Reputation In The Workplace'. *Forbes*. https://www.forbes.com/sites/forbescoachescouncil/2017/10/10/15-simple-ways-to-improve-your-reputation-in-the-workplace/?sh=d88cf7f53607

Schoeller, M. (2022, November 15). 'Behind The Billions: Elon Musk'. *Forbes*. https://www.forbes.com/sites/forbeswealthteam/article/elon-musk/

SpaceX. (n.d.). SpaceX. https://www.spacex.com/mission/

Umoh, R. (2018, January 16). 'Billionaire Richard Branson reveals the simple trick he uses to live a positive life'. CNBC. https://www.cnbc.com/2018/01/16/richard-branson-uses-this-simple-trick-to-live-a-positive-life.html

WatchDoku – The documentary film channel. (2021, December 8). 'ELON MUSK: THE REAL LIFE IRON MAN' Full Exclusive Biography Documentary English HD 2021 [Video file]. YouTube. https://www.youtube.com/watch?v=TUQgMs8Fkto

Western Governors University. (2020, July 29). 'The 5 P's of Career Management'. Western Governors University. https://www.wgu.edu/blog/career-services/5-p-career-management2007.html#close

Williams-Nickelson, C. 'Building a professional reputation'. (2003, March). *gradPSYCH* magazine. https://www.apa.org/gradpsych/2007/03/matters

Law 2

The Decision Lab. (n.d.). 'Why do we buy insurance?' The Decision Lab. https://thedecisionlab.com/biases/loss-aversion

Education Endowment Foundation. (2021, September). 'Mastery learning'. | Education Endowment Foundation. https://educationendowmentfoundation.org.uk/education-evidence/teaching-learning-toolkit/mastery-learning

Feynman, R. P. and Leighton, R. (1992). *Surely You're joking, Mr Feynman!: Adventures of a Curious Character*. Vintage.

Harari, Y. N. (2018). *21 Lessons for the 21st Century*. Random House.

Hibbert, S. A. (2019). *Skin in the game: How to create a learning curve that sticks*. John Wiley & Sons.

Kahneman, D. and Tversky, A. (1979). 'Prospect theory: An analysis of decision under risk'. *Econometrica*, 47(2), 263-292. https://doi.org/10.2307/1914185

Manson, M. (2016). *The Subtle Art of Not Giving a F*ck: A Counterintuitive Approach to Living a Good Life*. Harper.

Sinek, S. (2011). *Start with Why: How Great Leaders Inspire Everyone to Take Action*. Portfolio Penguin.

Taleb, N. N. (2018). *Skin in the Game: Hidden Asymmetries in Daily Life*. Allen Lane.

Thaler, R. H. and Sunstein, C. R. (2008). *Nudge: Improving Decisions About Health, Wealth, and Happiness.* Yale University Press.

Thompson, C. (2013). *Smarter Than You Think: How Technology is Changing Our Minds for the Better.* William Collins.

Law 3

Bazerman, M. H. and Moore, D. A. (2013). *Judgment in Managerial Decision Making* (8th ed.). John Wiley & Sons.

Fisher, R. and Ury, W. L. (2011). *Getting to Yes: Negotiating Agreement Without Giving In.* Penguin Books.

Gladwell, M. (2000). *The Tipping Point: How Little Things Can Make a Big Difference.* Little, Brown and Company.

Heath, C. and Heath, D. (2007). *Made to stick: Why some ideas survive and others die.* Random House.

Sharot, T. (2017). *The Influential Mind: What the Brain Reveals About Our Power to Change Others.* Henry Holt & Company.

Sharot, T., Korn, C. W. and Dolan, R. J. (2011). 'How unrealistic optimism is maintained in the face of reality'. *Nature Neuroscience,* 14(11), 1475–1479. https://doi.org/10.1038/nn.2949

Thompson, L. (2014). *The Mind and Heart of the Negotiator* (6th ed.). Pearson.

Law 4

Carter-Scott, C. (1998). *If Life is a Game, These are the Rules.* Broadway Books.

Cialdini, R. B. (2008). *Influence: Science and Practice.* Pearson.

Dawkins, R. (2006). *The God Delusion.* Mariner Books.

Festinger, L. (1957). *A Theory of Cognitive Dissonance.* Stanford University Press.

Gladwell, M. (2006). *Blink: The Power of Thinking Without Thinking.* Penguin.

Haidt, J. (2013). *The Righteous Mind: Why Good People are Divided by Politics and Religion.* Penguin.

Harris, S. (2010). *The Moral Landscape: How Science Can Determine Human Values.* Free Press.

Kahneman, D. (2011). *Thinking, Fast and Slow.* Farrar, Straus and Giroux.

Lipton, B. H. (2005). *The Biology of Belief: Unleashing the Power of Consciousness, Matter and Miracles.* Hay House.

McTaggart, L. (2007). *The Intention Experiment: Use Your Thoughts to Change Your Life and the World.* Harper Element.

Pinker, S. (2018). *Enlightenment Now: The Case for Reason, Science, Humanism, and Progress.* Viking.

Prochaska, J. O., Norcross, J. C. and DiClemente, C. C. (1994). *Changing for Good: The Revolutionary Program that Explains the Six Stages of Changes and Teaches You How to Free Yourself from Bad Habits.* William Morrow.

Sharot, T. (2012). *The Optimism Bias: Why We're Wired to Look on the Bright Side.* Robinson.

Sharot, T., Korn, C. W. and Dolan, R. J. (2011). 'How unrealistic optimism is maintained in the face of reality'. *Nature neuroscience*, 14(11), 1475-1479. https://doi.org/10.1038/nn.2949

Sharot, T. (2017). *The Influential Mind: What the Brain Reveals About Our Power to Change Others*. Henry Holt & Company.

Shermer, M. (2002). *Why People Believe Weird Things: Pseudoscience, Superstition, and Other Confusions of Our Time*. Holt Paperbacks.

Shermer, M. (2017). *Skeptic: Viewing the World with a Rational Eye*. Henry Holt & Company.

Stokstad, E. (2018). 'Seeing climate change: Science, empathy, and the visual culture of climate change'. *Environmental Humanities*, 10(1), 108-124.

Tavris, C. and Aronson, E. (2007). *Mistakes Were Made (But Not by Me): Why We Justify Foolish Beliefs, Bad Decisions, and Hurtful Acts*. Houghton Mifflin Harcourt.

Zajonc, R. B. (1980). 'Feeling and Thinking: Preferences Need No Inferences'. *American Psychologist*, 35(2), 151-175. https://doi.org/10.1037/0003-066X.35.2.151

Law 5

Anderson, C. P. and Slade, S. (2017). 'How to turn criticism into a competitive advantage'. *Harvard Business Review*, 95(5), 94-101.

Aronson, E. (1969). 'The theory of cognitive dissonance: A current perspective'. In L. Berkowitz (Ed.), *Advances in Experimental Social Psychology*, 4, 1-34. Academic Press.

Chansky, T. E. (2020). 'Transitions: How to Lean In and Adjust to Change'. Tamar E. Chansky. https://tamarchansky.com/transitions-how-to-lean-in-and-adjust-to-change/

Festinger, L. (1957). *A Theory of Cognitive Dissonance*. Stanford University Press.

Ford, H. (1922). *My Life and Work*. Currency.

Grover, A. S. (1999). *Only the Paranoid Survive: How to Exploit the Crisis Points That Challenge Every Company*. Doubleday.

MacDailyNews. (2010, March 13). 'Microsoft CEO Steve Ballmer laughs at Apple iPhone' [Video file]. YouTube. https://www.youtube.com/watch?v=nXq9NTjEdTo

Mulligan, M. (2022, May 11). 'How iPod changed everything'. *Music Industry Blog*. https://musicindustryblog.wordpress.com/2022/05/11/how-ipod-changed-everything/

Orr, M. (2019). *Lean Out: The Truth About Women, Power, and the Workplace*. HarperCollins Leadership.

Ross, L. (1977). 'The intuitive psychologist and his shortcomings: Distortions in the attribution process'. In Berkowitz, L. (ed.), *Advances in Experimental Social Psychology*), 10, 173-220. Academic Press.

Ross, L. (2014). *The psychology of intractable conflict: A handbook for political leaders*. Oxford University Press.

Stoll, C. (1995, February 26). 'Why the Web Won't Be Nirvana'. Newsweek. https://www.newsweek.com/clifford-stoll-why-web-wont-be-nirvana-185306

Law 6

Cialdini, R. B. (1984). *Influence: The Psychology of Persuasion*. HarperCollins.

Cooper, J. (2007). *Cognitive dissonance: Fifty Years of a Classic Theory*. Sage Publications.

Festinger, L. (1957). *A Theory of Cognitive Dissonance*. Stanford University Press.

Kamarck, E. (2012, September 11) 'Are You Better Off Than You Were 4 Years Ago?' *WBUR*. https://www.wbur.org/cognoscenti/2012/09/11/better-off-2012-elaine-kamarck.

McArdle, M. (2014). *The Up Side of Down: Why Failing Well is the Key to Success*. Viking.

Maddux, J. E. and Rogers, R. W. (1983). 'Protection motivation and self-efficacy: A revised theory of fear appeals and attitude change'. *Journal of Experimental Social Psychology*, 19(5), 469-479. https://doi.org/10.1016/0022-1031(83)90023-9

O'Keefe, D. J. (2002). *Persuasion: Theory and Research* (2nd ed.). Sage Publications.

O'Mara, M. (2020, September 10). 'Are You Better Off than You Were Four Years Ago?: The Economy in Presidential Politics'. *Perspectives on History*. https://www.historians.org/research-and-publications/perspectives-on-history/october-2020/are-you-better-off-than-you-were-four-years-ago-the-economy-in-presidential-politics

Reagan Library. (2016, May 6). 'Presidential Debate with Ronald Reagan and President Carter, October 28, 1980' [Video file]. YouTube. https://www.youtube.com/watch?v=tWEm6g0iQNI

Schwarz, N. (1999). 'Self-reports: How the questions shape the answers'. *American Psychologist*, 54(2), 93-105. https://doi.org/10.1037/0003-066X.54.2.93

Sherman, D. K. and Cohen, G. L. (2006). 'The psychology of self-defense: Self-affirmation theory'. *Advances in Experimental Social Psychology*, 38, 183–242. Elsevier Academic Press. https://doi.org/10.1016/S0065-2601(06)38004-5

Sprott, D. E., Spangenberg, E. R., Block, L. G., Fitzsimons, G. J., Morwitz, V. G. and Williams, P. (2006). 'The question–behavior effect: What we know and where we go from here'. *Social Influence*, 1(2), 128–137. https://doi.org/10.1080/15534510600685409

Tavris, C. and Aronson, E. (2007). *Mistakes Were Made (But Not by Me): Why We Justify Foolish Beliefs, Bad Decisions, and Hurtful Acts*. Houghton Mifflin Harcourt.

Wood, W., Tam, L. and Witt, M. G. (2005). 'Changing circumstances, disrupting habits'. *Journal of Personality and Social Psychology*, 88(6), 918-933. https://doi.org/10.1037/0022-3514.88.6.918

Law 7

Aryani, E. (2016). 'The role of self-story in mental toughness of students in Yogyakarta'. *Journal of Educational Psychology and Counseling*, 2(1), 25-31.

Duckworth, A. L., Peterson, C., Matthews, M. D. and Kelly, D. R. (2007). 'Grit: perseverance and passion for long-term goals'. *Journal of Personality and Social Psychology*, 92(6), 1087–1101. https://doi.org/10.1037/0022-3514.92.6.1087

Eubank Jr, C. (2023, May 1). Personal communication.

Gladwell, M. (2008). *Outliers: The Story of Success*. Allen Lane.

Macnamara, B. N., Hambrick, D. Z., & Oswald, F. L. (2014). 'Deliberate Practice and Performance in Music, Games, Sports, Education, and Professions: A Meta-Analysis'. *Psychological Science*, 25(8), 1608–1618. https://doi.org/10.1177/0956797614535810

Polk, L. (2018). 'Self-concept and resilience: A correlation'. *International Journal of Social Science and Economic Research*, 3(2), 1280-1291.

Singh, P. (2023). *Your self-story: The secret strategy for achieving big ambitions*. HarperCollins.

Steele, C. M. and Aronson, J. (1995). 'Stereotype threat and the intellectual test performance of African Americans'. *Journal of Personality and Social Psychology*, 69(5), 797–811. https://doi.org/10.1037/0022-3514.69.5.797

Tentama, F. (2020). 'Self-story, resilience, and mental toughness'. *Journal of Applied Psychology*, 4(1), 13-21.

Wooden, J. (1997). *Wooden: A lifetime of observations and reflections on and off the court*. McGraw Hill.

Woolfolk Hoy, A., & Murphy, P. K. (2008). 'Identity development, motivation, and achievement in adolescence'. In Meece, J. L. and Eccles, J. S. (eds.), *Handbook of Research on Schools, Schooling, and Human Development*, 391–414. Routledge.

Zhang, S., Tompson, S., White-Spenik, D., & Blair, C. B. (2013). 'Stereotype threat and self-affirmation: The moderating role of race/ethnicity and self-esteem'. *Cultural Diversity and Ethnic Minority Psychology*, 19(4), 395–405.

Law 8

American Psychological Association. (2023, March 21) 'What you need to know about willpower: The psychological science of self-control'. https://www.apa.org. https://www.apa.org/topics/personality/willpower

Baumeister, R. F., Bratslavsky, E., Muraven, M. and Tice, D. M. (1998). 'Ego depletion: Is the active self a limited resource?'. *Journal of Personality and Social Psychology*, 74(5), 1252–1265. https://doi.org/10.1037/0022-3514.74.5.1252

Clear, J. (2020, February 4). 'How to Break a Bad Habit (and Replace It With a Good One)'. James Clear. https://jamesclear.com/how-to-break-a-bad-habit

Duhigg, C. (2014). *The Power of Habit: Why We Do What We Do, and How to Change*. Random House.

Eyal, N. (2013). *Hooked: How to Build Habit-Forming Products*. Portfolio Penguin.

Ferrario, C. R., Gorny, G. and Crombag, H. S. (2005). 'On the neural and psychological mechanisms underlying compulsive drug seeking in addiction'. *Progress in Neuro-Psychopharmacology and Biological Psychiatry*, 29(4), 613-627.

Friedman, R. S., Fishbach, A. and Förster, J. (2003). 'The effects of promotion and prevention cues on creativity'. *Journal of Personality and Social Psychology*, 85(2), 312-326.

Gollwitzer, P. M. and Sheeran, P. (2006). 'Implementation intentions and goal achievement: A meta-analysis of effects and processes'. *Advances in Experimental Social Psychology*, 38, 69-119. https://doi.org/10.1016/S0065-2601(06)38002-1

Hofmann, W., Adriaanse, M., Vohs, K. D. and Baumeister, R. F. (2014). 'Dieting and the self-control of eating in everyday environments: An experience sampling study'. *British Journal of Health Psychology*, 19(3), 523-539. https://doi: 10.1111/bjhp.12053.

Muraven, M., Tice, D. M. and Baumeister, R. F. (1998). 'Self-control as a limited resource: Regulatory depletion patterns'. *Journal of Personality and Social Psychology*, 74(3), 774–789. https://doi.org/10.1037/0022-3514.74.3.774

Segerstrom, S. C., Stanton, A. L., Alden, L. E., & Shortridge, B. E. (2003). 'A Multidimensional Structure for Repetitive Thought: What's On Your Mind, And How, And How Much?' *Journal of Personality and Social Psychology*, 85(5), 909-921. https://doi.org/10.1037/0022-3514.85.5.909

Sharot, T. (2019). *The Influential Mind: What the Brain Reveals About Our Power to Change Others*. Abacus.

Wegner, D. M., Schneider, D. J., Carter, S. R. and White, T. L. (1987). 'Paradoxical effects of thought suppression'. *Journal of Personality and Social Psychology*, 53(1), 5–13. https://doi.org/10.1037/0022-3514.53.1.5

Wood, W. and Neal, D. T. (2007). 'A new look at habits and the habit-goal interface'. *Psychological Review*, 114(4), 843–863. https://doi.org/10.1037/0033-295X.114.4.843

Law 9

Buffett, W. E. (1998). 'Owner's Manual'. *Fortune*, 137(3), 33.

Caci, G., Albini, A., Malerba, M., Noonan, D. M., Pochetti, P. and Polosa,

R. (2020). 'COVID-19 and Obesity: Dangerous Liaisons'. *Journal of Clinical Medicine*, 9(8), 2511. https://doi.org/10.3390/jcm9082511

Centers for Disease Control and Prevention. (2022, September 27) 'Obesity, Race/Ethnicity, and COVID-19'. Centers for Disease Control and Prevention. https://www.cdc.gov/obesity/data/obesity-and-covid-19.html

Obama, President. (2013, September 26) 'Remarks by the President on the Affordable Care Act'. whitehouse.gov. https://obama whitehouse.archives.gov/the-press-office/2013/09/26/remarks-president-affordable-care-act

Law 10

Allan, R. P. et al. (2021). 'Climate Change 2021: The Physical Science Basis. Contribution of Working Group I to the Sixth Assessment Report of the Intergovernmental Panel on Climate Change'. Cambridge University Press.

Brennan, S. (2018, May 14). 'Is this the best workplace in Britain?' *Mail Online*. https://www.dailymail.co.uk/femail/article-5718875/Is-best-workplace-Britain.html

Coldwell, W. (2018, February 20). 'Drink in the view: BrewDog to open its first UK "beer hotel".' *Guardian*. https://www.theguardian.com/travel/2018/feb/20/drink-in-the-view-brewdog-to-open-its-first-uk-beer-hotel

International Energy Agency. (2021, May). 'Net Zero by 2050: A Roadmap for the Global Energy Sector'.

McCarthy, N. (2019, February 8). 'The Tesla Model 3 Was The Best-Selling Luxury Car In America Last Year' [Infographic]. *Forbes*. https://www.forbes.com/sites/niallmccarthy/2019/02/08/the-tesla-model-3-was-the-best-selling-luxury-car-in-america-last-year-infographic/

Morris, J. (2020, June 14). 'How Did Tesla Become The Most Valuable Car Company In The World?' *Forbes*. https://www.forbes.com/sites/jamesmorris/2020/06/14/how-did-tesla-become-the-most-valuable-car-company-in-the-world/

NASA Global Climate Change. (n.d.). 'The Causes of Climate Change'. Retrieved April 30, 2023, from https://climate.nasa.gov/causes/

National Oceanic and Atmospheric Administration. (n.d.). 'Climate'. Retrieved 30 April 2023. from https://www.climate.gov/

Shastri, A. (2023, February 13). 'Complete Analysis on Tesla Marketing Strategy - 360 Degree Analysis'. IIDE. https://iide.co/case-studies/tesla-marketing-strategy/

Sutherland, R. (2019). *Alchemy: The Surprising Power of Ideas that Don't Make Sense*. WH Allen.

Union of Concerned Scientists. (2022). 'The Climate Deception Dossiers'.

United Nations Environment Programme. (2021, October 26). 'The

Emissions Gap Report 2021'. https://www.unep.org/resources/emissions-gap-report-2021

United Nations Framework Convention on Climate Change. (2015). 'Paris Agreement'. Retrieved 30 April 2023. https://unfccc.int/process-and-meetings/the-paris-agreement/the-paris-agreement

United States Environmental Protection Agency. 2023, May 2. 'Climate Change Indicators in the United States'. https://www.epa.gov/climate-indicators

World Wildlife Fund. (n.d.). 'Effects of Climate Change'. Retrieved 30 April, 2023. https://www.worldwildlife.org/threats/climate-change

Law 11

127 Hours. (2010). [Motion Picture]. Fox Searchlight Pictures.

Avery, S. N. and Blackford, J. U. (2016, July 21). 'Slow to warm up: the role of habituation in social fear', *Social Cognitive and Affective Neuroscience*, 11(11), 1832-1840. https://doi: 10.1093/scan/nsw095

BBC NEWS. (2002, October 23) 'I cut off my arm to survive'. http://news.bbc.co.uk/1/hi/health/2346951.stm

Davies, S. J. (2017). *The Art of Mindfulness in Sport Psychology: Mindfulness in Motion*. Routledge.

Diamond, D. M., Park, C. R., Campbell, A. M., Woodson, J. C. and Conrad, C. D. (2005). 'Influence of predator stress on the consolidation versus retrieval of long-term spatial memory and hippocampal spinogenesis'. *Hippocampus*, 16(7), 571-576. https://doi: 10.1002/hipo.20188.

Frederick, P. (2011, March). 'Persuasive Writing: How to Harness the Power of Words'. *ResearchGate*. https://www.researchgate.net/publication/275207550_Persuasive_Writing_How_to_Harness_the_Power_of_Words

Groves, P. M. and Thompson, R. F. (1970). 'Habituation: A dual-process theory'. *Psychological Review*, 77(5), 419–450. https://doi.org/10.1037/h0029810

James, L. R. (1952). 'A review of habituation'. *Psychological Bulletin*, 49(4), 345–356.

James, W. (1890). *The Principles of Psychology*. vol. 1. Henry Holt.

Keegan, S.M. (2015). *The Psychology of Fear in Organizations: How to Transform Anxiety into Well-being, Productivity and Innovation*. Kogan Page.

LeDoux, J. (2015). *Anxious: Using the Brain to Understand and Treat Fear and Anxiety*. Viking.

McGonigal, K. (2015). *The Upside of Stress: Why Stress Is Good for You, and How to Get Good at It*. Avery.

McGuire, W. J. (1968). 'Personality and susceptibility to social influence'. In Borgatta, E.F. and Lambert, W.W. (eds.), *Handbook of Personality Theory and Research* (pp. 1130-1187). Rand McNally.

Mitchell, A. A. and Olson, J. C. (1981). 'Are product attribute beliefs the only mediator of advertising effects on brand attitude?'. *Journal of Marketing Research*, 18(3), 318-332. https://doi.org/10.2307/3150973

Petty, R. E., & Cacioppo, J. T. (1986). *Communication and Persuasion: Central and Peripheral Routes to Attitude Change.* Springer.

Ralston, A. (2005). *Between a Rock and a Hard Place.* Simon & Schuster.

Sapolsky, R. M. (2017). *Behave: The Biology of Humans at Our Best and Worst.* Penguin Press.

Selye, H. (1976). *The Stress of Life.* McGraw-Hill.

Smith, C. A. (1965). 'The effects of stimulus variation on the semantic satiation phenomenon'. *Journal of Verbal Learning and Verbal Behavior,* 4(5), 447–453.

Sokolov, E. N. (1963). 'Higher Nervous Functions: The Orienting Reflex'. *Annual Review of Physiology,* 25, 545–580. https://doi.org/10.1146/annurev.ph.25.030163.002553

Wilson, F. A. W. and Rolls, E. T. (1993). 'The effects of stimulus novelty and familiarity on neuronal activity in the amygdala of monkeys performing recognition memory tasks'. *Experimental Brain Research,* 93(3), 367–82. https://doi:10.1007/BF00229353

Wilson, T. D. and Brekke, N. (1994). 'Mental contamination and mental correction: Unwanted influences on judgments and evaluations'. *Psychological Bulletin,* 116(1), 117-142. https://doi.org/10.1037/0033-2909.116.1.117

Winkielman, P., Halberstadt, J., Fazendeiro, T. and Catty, S. (2006). 'Prototypes are attractive because they are easy on the mind'. *Psychological Science,* 17(9), 799–806. https://doi: 10.1111/j.1467-9280.2006.01785.x

Law 12

Manson, M. (2016). *The Subtle Art of Not Giving a F*ck: A Counterintuitive Approach to Living a Good Life.* Harper.

Midson-Short, D. (2019, March 9). 'The Rise of Cursing in Marketing'. Shorthand Content Marketing'. https://shorthandcontent.com/marketing/curse-words-in-marketing/

Knight, S. (2018). *Calm the F**k Down: How to Control What You Can and Accept What You Can't So You Can Stop Freaking Out and Get on With Your Life.* Quercus.

Kludt, A. (2018, November 2). 'Dermalogica's Founder Thinks People-Pleasing Leads to Mediocrity'. *Eater.* https://www.eater.com/2018/11/2/18047774/dermalogicas-ceo-jane-wurwand-start-to-sale

The Diary Of A CEO. (2022, June 13). 'Dermalogica Founder: Building A Billion Dollar Business While Looking After Your Mental Health' [Video file]. YouTube. https://www.youtube.com/watch?v=0KDESUdPRXs

Law 13

Battye, L. (2018, January 10). 'Why We're Loving It: The Psychology Behind the McDonald's Restaurant of the Future'. behavioral economics.com. https://www.behavioraleconomics.com/loving-psychology-behind-mcdonalds-restaurant-future

Dmitracova, O. (2019, December 2). 'What companies can learn from behavioural psychology'. *Independent.* https://www.independent.co.uk/voices/customer-service-behavioural-psychology-uber-fred-reichheld-mckinsey-company-a9229931.html

Duhigg, C. (2013). *The Power of Habit: Why We Do What We Do, and How to Change.* Random House.

Fowler, G. (2014, July 22). 'The Secret to Uber's Success? It Isn't Technology'. *Wired.*

Hogan, Candice. (2019, January 28). 'How Uber Leverages Applied Behavioral Science at Scale'. Uber Blog. https://www.uber.com/en-GB/blog/applied-behavioral-science-at-scale/

Kim, W. C. and Mauborgne, R. (2004, October). 'Blue Ocean Strategy', *Harvard Business Review.*

Sutherland, R. (2019). *Alchemy: The Surprising Power of Ideas that Don't Make Sense.* WH Allen.

The Secret Developer. (2023, January 6). 'Uber's Psychological Moonshot. *Medium.* https://medium.com/@tsecretdeveloper/ubers-psychological-moonshot-8e75078722ae

Uber. (2023). 'About Uber'. https://www.uber.com/us/en/about/

Law 14

Ranganathan, C. (2019). *Friction is Fiction: The Future of Marketing.* HarperCollins Publishers.

Sutherland, R. (2009). 'Life lessons from an ad man'. TED Conferences. [Video file] https://www.ted.com/talks/rory_sutherland_life_lessons_from_an_ad_man

Tversky, A. and Kahneman, D. (1974). 'Judgment under uncertainty: Heuristics and Biases'. *Science*, 185(4157), 1124-1131. https://doi:10.1126/science.185.4157.1124

Wertenbroch, K. and Skiera, B. (2002). 'Measuring Consumers' Willingness to Pay at the Point of Purchase'. *Journal of Marketing Research*, 39(2), 228-241. https://doi.org/10.1509/jmkr.39.2.228.19086

West, P. M., Brown, C. L. and Hoch, S. J. (1996). 'Consumption vocabulary and preference formation'. *Journal of Consumer Research*, 23(2), 120-135.

Law 15

Babin, B. J., Hardesty, D. M. and Suter, T. A. (2003). 'Color and shopping intentions: The intervening effect of price fairness and perceived affect'. *Journal of Business Research*, 56(7), 541-551. https://doi.org/10.1016/S0148-2963(01)00246-6

Khan, U. and Dhar, R. (2006). 'Licensing Effect in Consumer Choice'. *Journal of Marketing Research*, 43(2), 259-266.

Kivetz, R. and Simonson, I. (2002). 'Earning the Right to Indulge: Effort as a Determinant of Customer Preferences Toward Frequency Program Rewards'. *Journal of Marketing Research*, 39(2), 155-170.

Koelbel, C. and Helgeson, J. G. (2008). 'Scarcity appeals in advertising: Theoretical and empirical considerations'. *Journal of Advertising*, 37(1), 19-33.

Kotler, P., Kartajaya, H. and Setiawan, I. (2017). *Marketing 4.0: Moving from traditional to digital.* John Wiley & Sons.

Levy, S.J. (1959). 'Symbols for sale'. *Harvard Business Review*, 37(4), 117-124.

Müller-Lyer, FC (1889). 'Optische Urteilstäuschungen'. *Archiv für Physiologie Suppl.* 1889: 263–270

Thaler, R. H. (1985). 'Mental accounting and consumer choice'. *Marketing Science*, 4(3), 199-214.

WHOOP. (2023). WHOOP Homepage. Retrieved 1 May, 2023. https://www.whoop.com/

Law 16

Alagappan, Sathesh. (2014, December 15). 'The Goldilocks Effect: Simple but clever marketing'. *Medium.* https://medium.com/@WinstonWolfDigi/the-goldilocks-effect-simple-but-clever-marketing-dfb87f4fa58c

Ariely, D. (2009, May 19). 'Are we in control of our decisions?' [Video file]. TED Conferences. https://www.youtube.com/watch?v=9X68dm92HVI

Clear, J. (2020, February 4). 'The Goldilocks Rule: How to Stay Motivated in Life and Business'. https://jamesclear.com/goldilocks-rule

Cunff, A. L. (2020). 'The Goldilocks Principle of Stress and Anxiety'. Ness Labs. https://nesslabs.com/goldilocks-principle

Kemp, S. (2019). 'The Goldilocks Effect: Using Anchoring to Boost Your Conversion Rates'. Neil Patel. https://neilpatel.com/blog/goldilocks-effect/

Kinnu. (2023, January 11). 'What is the Anchoring Bias and How Does it Impact Our Decision-Making?'. https://kinnu.xyz/kinnuverse/science/cognitive-biases/how-mental-shortcuts-filter-information/

Tversky, A. and Kahneman, D. (1991). 'Loss Aversion in Riskless Choice: A Reference-Dependent Model'. *The Quarterly Journal of Economics*, 106(4), 1039–1061. https://doi.org/10.2307/2937956

Law 17

Bratton, J. and Gold, J. (2012). *Human Resource Management: Theory and Practice* (5th ed.). Palgrave Macmillan.

Build-A-Bear. (n.d.). About Build-A-Bear Workshop®. Retrieved 1 May, 2023. https://www.buildabear.com/about-us.html

Buric, R. (2022). 'The Endowment Effect – Everything You Need to Know'. InsideBE. https://insidebe.com/articles/the-endowment-effect-2/

Kahneman, D. and Tversky, A. (1979). 'Prospect theory: An Analysis of Decision Under Risk', *Econometrica*, 47(2), 263-292. https://doi.org/10.2307/1914185

Kivetz, R., Urminsky, O. and Zheng, Y. (2006). 'The Goal-Gradient Hypothesis Resurrected: Purchase Acceleration, Illusionary Goal Progress, and Customer Retention'. *Journal of Marketing Research* 43(1), 39-58. https://doi.org/10.1509/jmkr.43.1.39

Thaler, R. (1985). 'Mental Accounting and Consumer Choice'. *Marketing Science*, 4(3), 199-214. https://doi.org/10.1287/mksc.4.3.199

Vohs, K. D., Mead, N. L. and Goode, M. R. (2008). 'Merely Activating the Concept of Money Changes Personal and Interpersonal Behavior', *Current Directions in Psychological Science* 17(3), 208-212. https://doi.org/10.1111/j.1467-8721.2008.00576.x

Law 18

Becker, H. S. (2007). *Writing for Social Scientists: How to Start and Finish Your Thesis, Book, or Article* (2nd ed.). University of Chicago Press.

Duistermaat, H. (2013). *How to Write Seductive Web Copy: An Easy Guide to Picking Up More Customers*. Henneke Duistermaat.

Ferriss, T. (2016). *Tools of Titans: The Tactics, Routines, and Habits of Billionaires, Icons, and World-Class Performers*. Vermilion.

Godin, S. (2012). *All Marketers Are Liars: The Power of Telling Authentic Stories in a Low-Trust World*. Portfolio Penguin.

Godin, S. (2012). *The Icarus Deception: How High Will You Fly?* Portfolio Penguin.

Guberman, R. (2016). *The Ultimate Guide to Video Marketing*. Entrepreneur Press.

Johnson, M. (n.d.). 'The Power of Pause'. Ethos3 – a presentation training and design agency. https://ethos3.com/the-power-of-pause/

Kawasaki, G. (2004). *The Art of the Start: The Time-Tested, Battle-Hardened Guide for Anyone Starting Anything*. Portfolio Penguin.

Pink, D. H. (2005). *A Whole New Mind: Why Right-Brainers Will Rule the Future*. Riverhead Books.

Ries, E. (2011). *The Lean Startup: How Today's Entrepreneurs Use Continuous Innovation to Create Radically Successful Businesses*. Crown Business.

Robbins, T. (2017). *Unshakeable: Your Financial Freedom Playbook*. Simon & Schuster.

Sinek, S. (2011). *Start with Why: How Great Leaders Inspire Everyone to Take Action*. Portfolio Penguin.

Thiel, P. with Masters, B. (2014). *Zero to One: Notes on Startups, or How to Build the Future*. Currency.

Vaynerchuk, G. (2013). *Jab, Jab, Jab, Right Hook: How to Tell Your Story in a Noisy Social World*. HarperBusiness.

Vorster, Andrew. (2021). '7 seconds'. https://www.andrewvorster.com/7-seconds/

Law 19

Altman, D. (2023, January 12). 'Go Big by Thinking Small: The Power of Incrementalism'. Project Management Institute. https://

community.pmi.org/blog-post/73777/go-big-by-thinking-small-the-power-of-incrementalism-theory#_=_

Amabile, T. M. and Kramer, S. J. (2011, May). 'The Power of Small Wins'. *Harvard Business Review*. https://hbr.org/2011/05/the-power-of-small-wins

Clifford, J. (2014, February 10) 'Power to the People – Toyota's Suggestion System'. Toyota UK Magazine. https://mag.toyota.co.uk/toyota-and-the-power-of-suggestion

Cunff, A. L. (2020). 'Constructive criticism: how to give and receive feedback'. Ness Labs. https://nesslabs.com/constructive-criticism-give-receive-feedback

Laloux, F. (2014). *Reinventing Organizations: A Guide to Creating Organizations Inspired By the Next Stage in Human Consciousness*. Nelson Parker.

Liker, J. K. (2004). *The Toyota Way: 14 Management Principles From the World's Greatest Manufacturer*. McGraw-Hill.

Senge, P. M. (1980). *The Fifth Discipline: The Art and Practice of the Learning Organization*. Doubleday.

Spear, S. J., & Bowen, H. K. (1999). 'Decoding the DNA of the Toyota production system'. *Harvard Business Review*, 77(5), 96-106.

Kos, B. (2023, April 12) 'Kaizen - Constant improvement as the winning strategy' Spica. https://www.spica.com/blog/kaizen-method

Toyota Blog. (2013, May 31). 'What is kaizen and how does Toyota use it?'. Toyota UK Magazine. https://mag.toyota.co.uk/kaizen-toyota-production-system/#:~:text=Kaizen%20(English%3A%20Continuous%20improvement)%3A,maximise%20productivity%20at%20every%20worksite.

Womack, J. P. and Jones, D. T. (2003). *Lean Thinking: Banish Waste and Create Wealth in Your Corporation*. Simon and Schuster.

Wye, Alistair. (2020, November 20). 'Never ignore marginal gains. The secret of how a 1% gain each day adds up to massive results for legal organisations'. Lawtomated. https://lawtomated.com/never-ignore-marginal-gains-the-secret-of-how-a-1-gain-each-day-adds-up-to-massive-results-for-legal-organisations

Law 20

Barbie, D. J. (ed.) (2012). *Tiger Woods Phenomenon: Essays on the Cultural Impact of Golf's Fallible Superman*. McFarland & Co.

Barabási, A.-L. (2018). *The Formula: The Universal Laws of Success*. Simon & Schuster.

Darwin, C. (1859). *On the Origin of Species by Means of Natural Selection, or the Preservation of Favoured Races in the Struggle for Life.* John Murray.

Gottman, J. M. and Silver, N. (2018). *Seven Principles for Making Marriage Work: A Practical Guide from the Country's Foremost Relationship Expert*. Harmony.

Hammer, M. and Champy, J. (1993). *Reengineering the Corporation: A Manifesto for Business Revolution*. Harper Business.

Harmon, B. and Andrisani, J. (1998). *Butch Harmon's Playing Lessons.* Simon & Schuster.

Kaizen Institute. (n.d.). 'What is kaizen?'. https://www.kaizen.com/about-us/what-is-kaizen.html

Kanigel, R. (2005). *The One Best way: Frederick Winslow Taylor and the Enigma of Efficiency.* MIT Press.

Liker, J. K. (2004). *The Toyota Way: 14 Management Principles From the World's Greatest Manufacturer.* McGraw-Hill.

McGrath, R. G. (2013). *The End of Competitive Advantage: How to Keep Your Strategy Moving as Fast as Your Business.* Harvard Business Review Press.

Nakao, Y. (2014). *The Toyota way: Continuous improvement as a business strategy.* Business Expert Press.

Law 21

Batten Institute University of Virginia Darden School of Business. (2012, June 20). 'Creating An Innovation Culture: Accepting Failure is Necessary'. *Forbes.* https://www.forbes.com/sites/darden/2012/06/20/creating-an-innovation-culture-accepting-failure-is-necessary/?sh=11dc9e21754e

Bezos, J. (2017, April 17). '2016 Letter to Shareholders'. Amazon. Retrieved from https://www.amazon.com/p/feature/z6o9g6sysxur57t

Cold Call. (2022, August 31). 'At Booking.com, Innovation Means Constant Failure'. [Podcast] *Harvard Business Review.* https://hbr.org/podcast/2019/09/at-booking-com-innovation-means-constant-failure

Donovan, N. (2019, August 6). 'The role of experimentation at Booking.com'. Booking.com Partner Hub. https://partner.booking.com/en-gb/click-magazine/industry-perspectives/role-experimentation-bookingcom

Hamel, G. and Zanini, M. (2016, September 5). 'Excess Management Is Costing the U.S. $3 Trillion Per Year'. *Harvard Business Review.* https://hbr.org/2016/09/excess-management-is-costing-the-us-3-trillion-per-year

Hamel, G. (2018, October 29). 'Yes, You Can Eliminate Bureaucracy'. *Harvard Business Review.*

Harris, S. (2014). *10% Happier: How I Tamed the Voice in My Head, Reduced Stress Without Losing My Edge, and Found Self-Help That Actually Works – A True Story.* Yellow Kite.

IBM. (2021). 'IBM History'. Retrieved from https://www.ibm.com/ibm/history/history/

Kahneman, D. (2011). *Thinking, Fast and Slow.* Farrar, Straus and Giroux.

Kaizen Institute. (n.d.). 'What is kaizen?'. Retrieved from https://kaizen.com/what-is-kaizen.shtml

Kim, E. (2016, May 28). 'How Amazon CEO Jeff Bezos has inspired people to change the way they think about failure'. *Business Insider India.* https://www.businessinsider.in/tech/how-amazon-ceo-jeff-bezos-has-inspired-people-to-change-the-way-they-think-about-failure/articleshow/52481780.cms

Kotter, J. P. (1996). *Leading Change*. Harvard Business Review Press.

Lencioni, P. (2012). *The Advantage: Why Organizational Health Trumps Everything Else in Business*. Jossey-Bass.

Lindzon, J. (2022). 'Do we still need managers? Most workers say "no".' *Fast Company*. https://www.fastcompany.com/90716503/do-we-still-need-managers-most-workers-say-no

Mackenzie, K. (2019). *What Is Empowerment, and How Does It Support Employee Motivation?* SHRM.

Obama, B. (2020). *A Promised Land*. Viking.

Peter, L. J. and Hull, R. (1969). *The Peter Principle: Why Things Always Go Wrong*. William Morrow.

Ruimin, Z. (2007, February). 'Raising Haier'. *Harvard Business Review*. https://hbr.org/2007/02/raising-haier

Sinek, S. (2011). *Start with Why: How Great Leaders Inspire Everyone to Take Action*. Portfolio Penguin.

Stone, M. (2020, September 24). 'The pandemic became personal when Booking Holdings' CEO caught COVID-19. Now, he's taking on Airbnb and calling on the government to save a battered travel industry'. *Business Insider*. https://www.businessinsider.com/booking-holdings-ceo-airbnb-pandemic-travel-future-2020-9?r=US&IR=T

Westrum, R. (2004). 'A typology of resilience situations'. *Journal of Contingencies and Crisis Management*, 12(3), 98-107.

Law 22

Atkinson, E. (2022, October 20). 'Andes plane crash survivors have "no regrets" over resorting to cannibalism'. *Independent*. https://www.independent.co.uk/news/world/americas/andes-plane-crash-survivors-cannabalism-b2203833.html

Delgado, K. J. (2009). 'Social Psychology in Action: A Critical Analysis of *Alive*'. https://corescholar.libraries.wright.edu/psych_student/2

Mulvaney, K. (2021, October 13). 'Miracle of the Andes: How Survivors of the Flight Disaster Struggled to Stay Alive'. History. https://www.history.com/news/miracle-andes-disaster-survival

Parrado, N. (2007). *Miracle in the Andes: 72 Days on the Mountain and My Long Trek Home*. Orion.

Read, P. P. (1974). *Alive: The Story of the Andes Survivors*. J.B. Lippincott.

Sterling, T. (2010). 'Thirty-two years of the "Alive" story'. *Air & Space Smithsonian*, 25(3), 16-22.

Stroud, L. (2008). *Survive!: Essential Skills and Tactics to Get You Out of Anywhere – Alive*. William Morrow & Company.

Law 23

Bride, H. (1912, April 20). 'Women Who Escaped Death Tell of Thrilling Rescues: Stories of Courage and Fortitude Told by Those Who Lived Through Sinking of *Titanic*'. *New York Times*.

Carter, W. (1912). *How I Survived the* Titanic. New York: Century Co.

Eyal, N. (2023, April 25). Personal communication.

Gollwitzer, P. M. and Sheeran, P. (2006). 'Implementation Intentions and Goal Achievement: A Meta-analysis of Effects and Processes'. *Advances in Experimental Social Psychology*, 38, 69–119. https://doi.org/10.1016/S0065-2601(06)38002-1

Hopkinson, D. (2014). Titanic*: Voices from the disaster*. Scholastic Press.

Lynch, D. (1995). Titanic*: An Illustrated History*. Hyperion Books.

Mowbray, J. (2003). *The Sinking of the* Titanic*: Eyewitness Accounts*. Dover Publications.

Reed, J. (2019, August 2). 'Understanding The Psychology of Willful Blindness'. https://authorjoannereed.net/understanding-the-psychology-of-willful-blindness/#:~:text=%E2%80%9CThe%20psychology%20of%20willful%20blindness,to%20let%20out%20is%20crucial.

Rosenberg, J. (2022). *The Ostrich Effect: The Psychology of Avoiding What We Most Fear and Deserve*. Viking Press.

Sprott, D. E., Spangenberg, E. R. and Fischer, R. (2003). 'Reconceptualizing perceived value: The role of perceived risk'. *Journal of Consumer Research*, 30(3), 433–448.

Thaler, R. H. (1999). 'Mental accounting matters'. *Journal of Behavioral Decision Making*, 12(3), 183–206. https://doi.org/10.1002/(SICI)1099-0771(199909)12:3<183::AID-BDM318>3.0.CO;2-F

Vaillant G. E. (1994). 'Ego mechanisms of defense and personality psychopathology'. *Journal of Abnormal Psychology*. 103(1):44-50. https://doi: 10.1037//0021-843x.103.1.44. PMID: 8040479.

Law 24

King, B. J. (2008). *Pressure is a Privilege*. LifeTime Media.

Lazarus, R. S. and Folkman, S. (1984). *Stress, Appraisal, and Coping*. Springer Publishing Company.

McGonigal, K. (2013). 'How to make stress your friend' [Video file]. TED Conferences. https://www.ted.com/talks/kelly_mcgonigal_how_to_make_stress_your_friend

Park, C. L. and Folkman, S. (1997). 'Meaning in the Context of Stress and Coping'. *Review of General Psychology*, 1(2), 115-144.

Sapolsky, R. M. (2004). *Why Zebras Don't Get Ulcers: The Acclaimed Guide to Stress, Stress-related Diseases and Coping*. St. Martins Press.

Sheldon, K. M. and Elliot, A. J. (1999). 'Goal striving, need satisfaction, and longitudinal well-being: The self-concordance model'. *Journal of Personality and Social Psychology*, 76(3), 482-497. https://doi.org/10.1037/0022-3514.76.3.482

Smyth, J. and Hockemeyer, J. R. (1998). 'The beneficial effects of daily activity on mood: Evidence from a randomized, controlled study'. *Journal of Health Psychology*, 3(3), 357-373.

Spreitzer, G. M. and Sonenshein, S. (2004). 'Toward the Construct Definition of Positive Deviance'. *American Behavioral Scientist*, 47(6), 828-847. https://doi.org/10.1177/0002764203260212

Tedeschi, R. G. and Calhoun, L. G. (2004). 'Posttraumatic Growth: Conceptual Foundations and Empirical Evidence'. *Psychological Inquiry*, 15(1), 1-18. https://doi.org/10.1207/s15327965pli1501_01

Wood, A. M. and Joseph, S. (2010). 'The absence of positive psychological (eudemonic) well-being as a risk factor for depression: A ten-year cohort study'. *Journal of affective disorders*, 122(3), 213-217. https://doi: 10.1016/j.jad.2009.06.032.

Law 25

Custer, R. L. (2018). 'Why do startups fail?'. *US Small Business Administration*. https://www.sba.gov/sites/default/files/Business-Survival.pdf

Delisle, J. (2017, April 2). 'Pre-mortem: an effective tool to avoid failure'. *Beeye*. https://www.mybeeye.com/blog/pre-mortem-effective-tool-to-prevent-failure

Dweck, C. S. (2017). *Mindset – Updated Edition: Changing the Way You Think to Fulfil Your Potential*. Robinson.

Kahneman, D. (2011). *Thinking, Fast and Slow*. Farrar, Straus and Giroux.

Klein, G. (2007, September). 'Performing a Project Premortem'. *Harvard Business Review*. https://hbr.org/2007/09/performing-a-project-premortem

Klein, G., Koller, T. and Lovallo, D. (2019, April 3). 'Bias Busters: Premortems: Being smart at the start'. *McKinsey Quarterly*. https://www.mckinsey.com/capabilities/strategy-and-corporate-finance/our-insights/bias-busters-premortems-being-smart-at-the-start

Sharot, T. (2012). *The Optimism Bias: Why We're Wired to Look on the Bright Side*. Robinson.

Shermer, M. (2012). *Believing Brain: From Ghosts and Gods to Politics and Conspiracies – How We Construct Beliefs and Reinforce Them as Truths*. Macmillan.

Smith, K.G. and Hitt, M. A. (2005). *Great Minds in Management: The Process Of Theory Development*. Oxford University Press.

Tversky, A. and Kahneman, D. (1974). 'Judgment Under Uncertainty: Heuristics and Biases'. *Science*, 185(4157), 1124-1131. https://doi.org/10.1126/science.185.4157.1124

Wegner, D. M. (2003). *The Illusion of Conscious Will*. MIT Press.

Law 26

American Psychological Association. (2010). *Publication Manual of the American Psychological Association* (6th ed.) American Psychological Association.

Berman, M. G., Jonides, J., & Kaplan, S. (2008). 'The cognitive Benefits of Interacting with Nature'. *Psychological Science*, 19(12), 1207-1212. https://doi.org/10.1111/j.1467-9280.2008.02225.x

US Bureau of Labor Statistics. (2022, April 8). 'Occupational Employment and Wages, May 2021'. United States Department of Labor. https://www.bls.gov/oes/current/oes_nat.htm

Carhart-Harris, R. L., Bolstridge, M., Rucker, J., Day, C. M., Erritzoe, D., Kaelen, M., and Nutt, D. J. (2016). 'Psilocybin with psychological support for treatment-resistant depression: an open-label feasibility study'. *The Lancet Psychiatry*, 3(7), 619-627. https://doi.org/10.1016/S2215-0366(16)30065-7

Hamilton, I. (2023, April 4). 'What Are The Highest-Paying Jobs in the U.S.?'. *Forbes Advisor*. https://www.forbes.com/advisor/education/what-are-the-highest-paying-jobs-in-the-u-s/

Hankel, I. (2021, January 8). 'In a Crowded Job Market, Here Are the Right Skills for the Future'. *Forbes*. https://www.forbes.com/sites/forbesbusinesscouncil/2021/01/08/in-a-crowded-job-market-here-are-the-right-skills-for-the-future/

Jeung, D. Y., Kim, C., and Chang, S. J. (2018). 'Emotional Labor and Burnout: A Review of the Literature'. *Yonsei Medical Journal*, 59(2):187-193. https://doi:10.3349/ymj.2018.59.2.187. PMID: 29436185; PMCID: PMC5823819.

Markman, A. (2012). *Smart Thinking: How to Think Big, Innovate and Outperform Your Rivals*. Piatkus.

Markman, A. (2023). '3 signs you need to improve your emotional intelligence'. *Fast Company*. https://www.fastcompany.com/90839541/signs-need-work-emotional-intelligence

Martocchio, J.J. (2018). *Strategic Compensation: A Human Resource Management Approach* (9th ed.). Pearson.

Perlo-Freeman, S., & Sköns, E. (2021). 'The State of Peace and Security in Africa 2021'. Stockholm International Peace Research Institute (SIPRI).

Reffold, K. (2019, March 28). 'Command A Higher Salary With These Five Strategies'. *Forbes*. https://www.forbes.com/sites/forbeshumanresourcescouncil/2019/03/28/command-a-higher-salary-with-these-five-strategies/?sh=353bea346467

Rice, R. E. (2009). 'The internet and health communication: A framework of experiences'. In Dillard, J.P. and Pfau, M. (eds.), *The Persuasion Handbook: Developments in theory and practice* (pp. 325-344). Sage.

Sadun, R., Fuller, J., Hansen, S. and Neal, P. J. (2022, July-August) 'The C-Suite Skills That Matter Most'. *Harvard Business Review* 100(4) 42–50. https://hbr.org/2022/07/the-c-suite-skills-that-matter-most

Stewart, D. W. and Kamins, M. A. (1993). *Secondary Research: Information Sources and Methods* (2nd ed.). Sage Publications.

Van Hoof, H. (2013). 'Social Media in Tourism and Hospitality: A Literature Review'. *Journal of Travel and Tourism*. https://www.academia.edu/14370892/Social_Media_in_Tourism_and_Hospitality_A_Literature_Review

Law 27

Carver, C. S., Scheier, M. F. and Segerstrom, S. C. (2010). 'Optimism'. *Clinical Psychology Review*, 30(7), 879–889. https://doi.org/10.1016/j.cpr.2010.01.006

Cohn, M.A., Fredrickson, B.L., Bown, S.L., Mikels, J.A. and Conway, A.M. (2009). 'Happiness unpacked: Positive emotions increase life satisfaction by building resilience'. *Emotion*, 9(3), 361–368. https://doi.org/10.1037/a0018895

Davis, D. E., Choe, E., Meyers, J., Wade, N., Varjas, K., Gifford, A. and Worthington, E. L. (2016). 'Thankful for the little things: A meta-analysis of gratitude interventions'. *Journal of Counseling Psychology*, 63(1), 20–31. https://doi.org/10.1037/cou0000107

Harvey, M. (2019). *The Discipline of Entrepreneurship*. Bantam Press.

Huta, V. and Waterman, A. S. (2014). 'Eudaimonia and its Distinction from Hedonia: Developing a classification and Terminology for Understanding Conceptual and operational Definitions'. *Journal of Happiness Studies*, 15, 1425–1456. https://doi.org/10.1007/s10902-013-9485-0

Mastracci, S. H. (2018). *Work smart, not hard: Organizational tips and tools that will change your life*. Chronos Publications.

Patterson, K., Grenny, J., McMillan, R. and Switzler, A. (2002). *Crucial Conversations: Tools for Talking When Stakes are High*. McGraw-Hill Education.

Rudd, M., Vohs, K. D. and Aaker, J. (2012). 'Awe Expands People's Perception of Time, Alters Decision Making, and Enhances Well-being'. *Psychological Science*, 23(10), 1130–1136. https://doi.org/10.1177/0956797612438731

Scheier, M. F. and Carver, C. S. (1985). 'Optimism, coping, and health: Assessment and implications of generalized outcome expectancies'. *Health Psychology*, 4(3), 219–247. https://doi.org/10.1037/0278-6133.4.3.219

Sinek, S. (2011). *Start with Why: How Great Leaders Inspire Everyone to Take Action*. Portfolio Penguin.

Tracy, B. (2003). *Eat that Frog!: 21 Great Ways to Stop Procrastinating and Get More Done in Less Time*. Berrett-Koehler Publishers.

United Nations Department of Economic and Social Affairs, Population Division. (2021). 'World Population Prospects 2019: Data Booklet'. United Nations.

Vanderkam, L. (2018). *Off the Clock: Feel Less Busy While Getting More Done*. Portfolio Penguin.

World Health Organization. (2021). 'GHE: Life expectancy and healthy life expectancy'. WHO.

Law 28

Branson, R. (2015). *The Virgin Way: How to Listen, Learn, Laugh and Lead*. Virgin Books.

Etem, J. (2017, August 10). 'Steve Jobs on Hiring Truly Gifted People' [Video file]. YouTube. https://www.youtube.com/watch?v=a7mS9ZdU6k4

Friedman, T. L. (2005). *The world is flat: A brief history of the twenty-first century.* Farrar, Straus and Giroux.

The Diary Of A CEO. (2021, November 15). 'Jimmy Carr: The Easiest Way To Live A Happier Life' [Video file]. YouTube. https://www.youtube.com/watch?v=roROKlZhZyo

The Diary Of A CEO. (2022, December 12). 'Richard Branson: How A Dyslexic Drop-out Built A Billion Dollar Empire' [Video file]. YouTube. https://www.youtube.com/watch?v=-Fmiqik4jh0

Virgin Group. (n.d.). 'Our Story'. Virgin. https://www.virgin.com/about-virgin/our-story

Law 29

Collins, J., Portas, J. and Collins, J. (2005). *Built to Last: Successful Habits of Visionary Companies.* Random House Business.

Higgins, D. M. (2019). 'The psychology of cults: An organizational perspective'. *Frontiers in psychology*, 10, 1291.

Hogan, T. and Broadbent, C. (2017). *The Ultimate Start-up Guide: Marketing Lessons, War Stories, and Hard-Won Advice from Leading Venture Capitalists and Angel Investors.* New Page Books.

Levy, S. (2011). *In the Plex: How Google Thinks, Works, and Shapes Our Lives.* Simon & Schuster.

Pells, R. (2018). *Blue sky dreaming: How the Beatles became the architects of business success.* Bloomsbury Publishing.

Thiel, P. with Masters, B. (2014). *Zero to One: Notes on Startups, or How to Build the Future.* Currency.

Law 30

BBC Sport. (2013, May 8). 'Sir Alex Ferguson to retire as Manchester United manager'. https://www.bbc.co.uk/sport/football/22447018

Branson, R. (2015). *The Virgin Way: How to Listen, Learn, Laugh and Lead.* Virgin Books.

Elberse, A. (2013, October). 'Ferguson's Formula'. *Harvard Business Review*. https://hbr.org/2013/10/fergusons-formula

Housman, M., and Minor, D. (2015, November). 'Toxic Workers'. Harvard Business School Working Paper, No. 16-057. (Revised November 2015.) https://www.hbs.edu/ris/Publication%20Files/16-057_d45c0b4f-fa19-49de-8f1b-4b12fe054fea.pdf

Hytner, R. (2016, January 18). 'Sir Alex Ferguson on how to win'. London Business School. https://www.london.edu/think/sir-alex-ferguson-on-how-to-win

Robbins, S. P., Coulter, M. and DeCenzo, D. A. (2016). *Fundamentals of Management.* Pearson.

Law 31

BBC News. (2015, September 15). 'Viewpoint: Should we all be looking for marginal gains?' BBC News. https://www.bbc.co.uk/news/magazine-34247629

Clear, J. (2020, February 4). 'This Coach Improved Every Tiny Thing by 1 Percent and Here's What Happened'. https://jamesclear.com/marginal-gains

Gawande, A. (2011, September 26). 'Personal best'. *New Yorker*. https://www.newyorker.com/magazine/2011/10/03/personal-best

Medina, J. C. (2021, July 12). 'How To Make Small Changes For Big Impacts'. *Forbes*. https://www.forbes.com/sites/financialfinesse/2021/07/12/how-to-make-small-changes-for-big-impacts/?sh=54ead259401b

Mehta, K. (2021, February 23). 'The most mentally tough people apply the 1% "marginal gains" rule, says performance expert—here's how it works'. *CNBC*.

The Diary Of A CEO. (2022, January 17). 'The "Winning Expert": How To Become The Best You Can Be: Sir David Brailsford' [Video file]. YouTube. https://www.youtube.com/watch?v=nTiqySjdD6s

Tomlin, I. (2021, May 27). 'How A Marginal Gains Approach Can Transform Your Sales Conversations'. *Forbes*. https://www.forbes.com/sites/forbescommunicationscouncil/2021/05/27/how-a-marginal-gains-approach-can-transform-your-sales-conversations/?sh=2eb47c5a2bad

Law 32

Elberse, A. (2013, October). 'Ferguson's Formula'. *Harvard Business Review*. https://hbr.org/2013/10/fergusons-formula

Evanish, J. (2022). 'Master the Leadership Paradox: Be Consistently Inconsistent'. *Lighthouse – Blog About Leadership & Management Advice*. https://getlighthouse.com/blog/leadership-paradox-consistently-inconsistent/

The Diary Of A CEO. (2021, April 12). 'Rio Ferdinand Reveals The Training Ground & Dressing Room Secrets That Made United Unbeatable' [Video file]. YouTube. https://www.youtube.com/watch?v=CwpSViM8MaY

The Diary Of A CEO. (2021, November 8). 'Patrice Evra: Learning How To Cry Saved My Life' [Video file]. YouTube. https://www.youtube.com/watch?v=UbF4p4yTfIY

The Diary Of A CEO. (2022, August 18). 'Gary Neville: From Football Legend To Building A Business Empire' [Video file]. YouTube. https://www.youtube.com/watch?v=cMCucLELzd0

ACKNOWLEDGEMENTS

Melanie Lopes

Graham Bartlett

Esther Bartlett

Jason Bartlett

Mandi Bartlett

Kevin Bartlett

Julija Bartlett

Alessandra Bartlett

Amélie Bartlett

Jacob Bartlett

Thomas Frebel

Sophie Chapman

Michael James

Dom Murray

Grace Andrews

Jack Sylvester

Danny Gray

Emma Williams

Jemima Erith

Berta Lozano

Olivia Podmore

Josh Winter

Anthony Smith

Harry Balden

Ross Field

Holly Hayes

Grace Miller

Jemima Carr-Jones

Meghana Garlapati

Charles Rossy

Shereen Paul

William Lindsay-Perez

Smyly Acheampong

Stephanie Ledigo

Damon Elleston

Qudus Afolabi

Oliver Yonchev

Ash Jones

Dom McGregor

Michael Heaven

Anthony Logan

Marcus Heaven

Adrian Sington

Drummond Moir

Jessica Anderson

Jessica Patel

Laura Nicol

Lydia Yadi

Abby Watson

Joel Rickett

Vanessa Milton

Shasmin Mozomil

Vyki Hendy

Richard Lennon

Hannah Cawse

Carmen Byers

Heather Faulls

Amanda Lang

Mary Kate Rogers

Jessica Regione

Radhanath Swami

Tali Sharot

Julian Treasure

Hannah Anderson

Rory Sutherland

Chris Eubank Jr

Johann Hari

Daniel Pink

Nir Eyal

Gary Brecka

Sir Richard Branson

Jimmy Carr

Rio Ferdinand

Barbara Corcoran

Patrice Evra

Gary Neville